Sawmill

Log cutters stand aside and a shortleaf pine falls to earth in the Ouachitas. The cutting of this unusually large tree near Pine Valley, Oklahoma, in 1930 was probably saved for the camera.

Frank J. Gibbs photo, courtesy Forest Heritage Center

Sawmill

THE STORY OF CUTTING THE LAST GREAT
VIRGIN FOREST EAST OF THE ROCKIES

by Kenneth L. Smith

The University of Arkansas Press
Fayetteville   1986

DESIGN: Joanna V. Hill
TYPEFACE: Linotron Garamond #3
TYPESETTER: G & S Typesetters

This project was funded in part by a grant from the Special Publications Fund of the Arkansas Historical Association.

LIBRARY OF CONGRESS CATALOGING-IN-PUBLICATION DATA

Smith, Kenneth L., 1934–
   Sawmill: the story of cutting the last great virgin forest east of the Rockies.

   Bibliography: p.
   Includes index.
      1. Sawmills—Ouachita Mountains (Okla. and Ark.)—History.   2. Lumbering—Ouachita Mountains (Okla. and Ark.)—History.   I. Title.
   TS806.A8S66   1986   388.4'7674'2097666   86-1453
   ISBN 0-938626-68-X
   ISBN 0-938626-69-8 (pbk.)

The paper used in this publication meets the minimum requirements of the American National Standard for Permanence of Paper for Printed Library Materials Z39.48-1984.

The following organizations and individuals have made major contributions toward the production of this book and its related educational materials, as well as establishing the Special Publications Fund of the Arkansas Historical Association: The Winthrop Rockefeller Foundation, Mr. and Mrs. J. R. Bemis, The Ross Foundation, Jim and Lynne Walton, Forester Historical Society, Inc., and Don and Anne Dierks.

Other charter contributors who have also helped insure the successful establishment of the Special Publications Fund include: William R. Wilson, Jr., Joe F. and Lillian Maxey, Bella Vista Historical Society, Ouachita-Calhoun Counties Genealogical Society, Smackover Genealogical and Historical Society, White County Historical Society, Rachel Watkins Goforth, and Robert J. Sawyer.

A portion of the description of Mauldin in this book appeared earlier in an article in *Arkansas Times* Magazine, February 1981. Portions of the material on Mauldin and Forester appeared in *The Looking Glass*, July 1981 and September 1981

Thanks are due to Doubleday & Company, Inc., for permission to quote from the book *Forests and Men* by William B. Greeley.

To
James Rosborough Bemis
who carried his family's pioneering spirit
into a new era of lumbering.

BY THE SAME AUTHOR:

The Buffalo River Country

Illinois River

Contents

Coming to the railroad near Mauldin about 1930, a mule skinner with his four-up team of mules moves a loaded eight-wheel wagon along a haulway cleared through the woods. The driver is riding his left-hand wheeler mule, hidden behind the right-hand leader mule.

U.S. Forest Service photo, courtesy Ouachita National Forest

Acknowledgments

It was my father, who loved trees and lumbering, who first guided me into this work. He took me as a child on his tours of the pine woods and sawmills of the Ouachitas, and I learned to share his feelings.

Much later, in 1979, the Arkansas Endowment for the Humanities provided a grant for the first stage of research toward this book, which was sponsored by Garland County Community College at Hot Springs. In 1984 the Winthrop Rockefeller Foundation provided funding that enabled completion of the book under the sponsorship of the Arkansas Historical Association.

At early stages of the project, several persons offered scholarly direction: Waddy W. Moore of the Office of Oral History at the University of Central Arkansas; George H. Thompson of Hendrix College; Stephen Strausberg, Donald Voth, Elliott West, and Randall B. Woods at the University of Arkansas; Harold K. Steen and Ronald J. Fahl of the Forest History Society; and Joseph A. Miller at Yale University.

Historic records were made available by the Arkansas History Commission; Forest Heritage Center; Forest History Society; Riley Library at Ouachita Baptist University; Special Collections of the Mullins Library, University of Arkansas; and International Paper Company, Weyerhaeuser Company, and the U.S. Forest Service. Others who provided useful information were David W. Bizzell, Virgil W. Cothren, Mary Mitchell Couch, Armin T. Dressel, Richard A. Grigsby, Mack Guinn, John Dickey Guthrie, W. Ray Hanley, Holly Harshman, Fred O. Henker, John C. Heuston, Betty Hopson, Mary Howell, Mary D. Hudgens, Evelyn Gregory Inman, Doyle Jones, Ralph Jones, Richard Judd, Albro Martin, John M. Martin, Keith McCullough, Gary Meador, Erbie L. Meeks, Gene and Nancy Owen, Ray Paetzell, Bonnie Salyer, G. W. Sisk, Donald E. Smith, Orpha Lundry Smith, Martha Varner, Carl Webb, and Keenan Williams.

The largest part of this book comes from the men and women whose recollections of firsthand experience are woven into the *Sawmill* story:

Almeda Tarkington Abernathy
Willie Adams
Max Adams
Fannie Allen
U. A. (Jack) Allen
Hugh Altstatt
Sam Anderson
Billie Carter Angel
Ed Angel
Edna Blalock Angel
Gerald Angel
Jim Angel
Pearl Byers Angel
Joe J. Angel
Shirley Stone Angel
G. W. Argo
William G. (Guy) Baker
Hulet Baker
O. E. (Ed) Banks
Carney L. Bardwell
Vernon D. Bardwell
Winfred H. Bardwell
Irene Dollar Barker
Lynn Barker
Gertie Barnett
Jeff J. Barnett
Lee Preston Barnett
John Barrong
James Hervey Bemis
Jane S. Bemis (Mrs. James R.)
Flora Benson
Majel Pitts Billingsley
Ervin D. Black
Paul B. Blackman
Dee Climons Blackmon
Ken Blackmon
Hazel Black Borman
Vesta Meeks Boyd
Alva Bradley
J. D. Bradley
Vanita Kimble Britton
A. D. Brown
Bonnie Brown
Emma Lois Buckley Brown
I. D. Brown
Myrtle Buck
Clara Buckley
Cecil W. Burks

Ida Helen Vise Burns
Harold H. Cabe
Rufus W. Caldwell
Robert Canady
Pres Cantrell
Marie Zimmer Carnahan
Jeff Carpenter
Charlie Carter
Mrs. Charles Carter
Vernon H. Carter, Sr.
Vernon H. Carter, Jr.
Roy Cathcart
Herman Chance
Billie Jo Pettijohn Chisholm
J. C. Christenberry
Charles Clark
Inez Cline
S. L. Cleghorn
Charlie Cockburn
Lenard B. Cockburn
Paul B. Cole
Teden H. Cole
Dave Cooks, Sr.
Hubert T. (Red) Crawford
Dodd Cross
Conley Culpepper
Frances Rodgers Dalton
Charlye Forrester Davidson
James Davis
Jennie Cox Davis
Louise Davis
Marlin Davis
Bud Denson
Mrs. R. R. Defoor
Mrs. Carl Depriest
Jessie Williams Diamond
Mrs. John Dickey
Fred M. Dierks
Frank J. Diggs
Eva Corley Diggs
Vernon Orbria Dollar
Mrs. V. O. Dollar
Lee Roy Douglas
Mae Douglas
Dallas Duggan
Dan Durham
Glen R. Durrell
Gladys Hunt Easterling

Verlin Clark Edds
Ruben B. Edmonds
Roy Edwards
Mary Helen Edwards
Willa Buford Elliott
Henry Erwin
Louis P. Erwin
John E. Evans
T. C. (Red) Evans
Mrs. Jewell Fagan
Hursell Faulkner
Elmer Ferguson
Harley Ferguson, Jr.
Herbert Ferguson
Wilma Johnson Ferguson
Imodel Hawkins Franklin
Missie Franklin
Thurman Franklin
Sam W. Fried
Paul Frost
True Robertson Frost
Cordelia May Fry
Amie Defoor Galloway
Cecil L. Gammill
H. W. (Woody) Gann
Dixie Gaston
Lura Gaston
Grady D. Gaston
Macy Gaston
Ted Gaston
Bill Gibbons
Ocus Gibbs
Robert B. Gierow
James Goines
Felon Golden
Norman Goodner
Grace Bailey Pounds Gould
Geneva Grayson
Lillian Sorrells Gregory
John R. Gwathney
John R. Halkum
Hope Halpin
James G. Hamilton
Gladys Hamm
Maude Crosby Hartwick
Frederick Hauenstein, Sr.
Laverne Adams Hawkins
Sherman Hawkins

Vernon Hawkins
William A. Hensley, Sr.
Earl Herrin
Sam Hickey, Jr.
Glenn H. Hicks
Ruth Hicks
Clarence Hodge
Dean Holden
Opal Holden
Elois Hunt
Doris Hutchings
Gordon W. Ingham
Arnold Ingle
Carl H. (Jack) Inlow
Colvin Irons
Betty Jo Vise Isenman
Ella Lee Jackson
Ernest Jackson
Letha Jameson
Mack Johnson
Twila Humphries Johnson
Willa B. Raines Johnson
Jim Jolly
Victoria Black Byers Jolly
Creo A. Jones
Frank Jones
J. Fred Jones
Gertrude Keeley
Harry Keeley
J. O. Kelly
Floyd Kimble
Juanita Kimble
Gaylon Kitchens
Margaret Lay
Fred H. Lang
Ione Shaffer Leith
Marion Jordan Lewallen
Margaret Hutchings Linsley
Eva Mae Little
Thelma Lowther
Nellie Lyons
Robert B. Lyons
Chester Mahurin
Horace Marsh
Marie Brown Marsh
Melvin Martindale
Albert A. Maupin, Jr.
Hess Maxey

Joe F. Maxey
Leonard (Whit) Maxey
Lillian Humphries Maxey
Louise Cockburn Maxey
O. C. (Babe) McAdams
Bill McBride
Jessie Crosby Clark McBride
Effie McCauley
Lewis H. McCauley
Haskell H. McConnell
Melvin E. McConnell
Vollie McDaniel
Preston McElroy
Ruby McKay
Era Baxter McKeown
H. W. (Bill) McMillan
William H. (Henry) McMillan
Duncan L. McRae, Jr.
Aileen McWilliam
Nellie Melton
Robert Melton
John Merchant
Jeraldine Turner Meredith
Velma Oden Merritt
E. L. (Les) Miller
Morna Turner Miller
Jimmy Mitchell
Glen Adams Moncus
R. O. (Sticky) Monroe
Cecil Montgomery
Clinton (Barber) Moore
Jorsh Moore
Lucy Moore
Tom E. (Ernest) Moran
George F. Morris
Agnes Neimeyer
June McAdams Nelson
Helen Nelson
William New
Dorothy Sage Newkirk
Alex Nichols
Charley Nichols
Lester Nichols
Roy Nichols
Virgie Nichols
Manuel A. Norman
Beulah Norwood
Howard K. Nutt

Opal Orr
Bertie Hight Overby
Henry Overby
R. C. (Red) Parsons, Sr.
Janet Jackson Pearcy
Elizabeth Purtle Peek
Kenneth Dan Pettijohn
Wayne S. Pettijohn
Cecil Phillips
Hollis Phillips
James Milton Phillips
Juanita Walters Phillips
Naomi Powell Phillips
Al Pollard
Patty Stockemer Pope
William Fay Pounds
Kitty Miller Price
Mina Rabb
Mildred Rackley
Raymond Rackley
Lawrence Raines
Alma Ruth Douglas Raines
Estey Campbell Read
Matt Turner Read
Margaret Watts Rieder
Glen Roberts
C. B. Rodgers
Voisey Rodgers
Walter Rogers
Anna Watts Rosborough
Earl Rose
Wayne Rowan
Horace D. (Red) Russell
John Allen Sage
A. R. (Red) Salmon
Callie Salmon
Louis Salmon
Mamie Trotter Samson
Bertha Sanders
Loyd Sanders
Mattie Raines Sanders
Rosie Carr Sargent
Daisy Maxey Scoggins
Selma Lewey Scoggins
Shirley Sevier
Audie Shaw
Alphalee Whitted Short
Barbara Marsh Simpson

Roy Vergil Simpson
W. C. (Willie) Slater, Jr.
Evelyn Standerfer Smalling
Roxie Smalling
Virgil Smalling
W. G. Smalling
Avanelle Hutchings Smith
Elmer Smith
Kenneth Smith
Lamar Smith
LaNell H. Smith
Louie Smith
Tina Palmer Smith
Henry Soderling
O. O. Stafford
Harry Standerfer
Eugene E. Stevenson
Nina Stevenson
Dorothy Bemis Stewart
Eula Stinson
Lester Stinson
Luke Stinson
Walt Stinson
T. J. (Jack) Strauss
Erwin A. Sutton
Don Swiger
Boyd A. Tackett, Sr.
Norma Armstrong Tackett
Lillie Taft
Zelda Rapp Taft
Robert Tarvin
Jean A. (Toby) Bratton Tate
Archie Dennis Taylor
Nettie Mae Rowe Taylor
William E. Taylor
Richard Thomas
Buster Thompson
L. J. Thompson
Odell Thompson
Tellious Thompson
Clint Thornton
Inez Phillips Thornton
Kenneth Thornton
D. H. Thrasher
Frances Thrasher
Wallace Trotter
Cleo T. Tucker
Herman Tucker

Georgia McKinney Turner
Luther C. Turner
Norman Dean (Mutt) Turner
Erenstine L. Tyler
Raymond Vallery
Vina Short Van Pelt
Felbert Vaught
Lloyd Vines
Mattie Winnie Baker Waites
Joel A. Walker
R. L. Wallace
Scott Ward
Martha Jane Shaffer Warren
Marion Watkins
Mildred Manning Watson
Talmadge Watts
William Park Watts
Juanita Walls Wetzell
Alvin B. Wheat
John Hester Whisenhunt
Norman Whitaker, Jr.
Alva White
Marvin White
W. A. (Bill) Whitted
Dick Whittington
Vera Davis Whittington
Gerlene Angel Wiley
John L. Wiley
Arlean Williams
Bernice Williams
Cecil Williams
Charles E. Williams
Gertrude Williams
Lester Williams
Lora Finney Williams
Louise Williams
Mary Singleton Mahurin Williams
Max A. Williams
McKinley Williams
Vernon Williams
Delzie Fagan Williamson
Louise Angel Willsey
D. W. Wilson
Vada Bowen Wilson
William Roy Wilson, Jr.
W. E. (Bill) Wingfield
Erma Winner
Elbert Winton

Joe Woodall
Ethel Workman
James D. Workman

Kenneth Yandell
James Dwight Yeargan

In addition to lending moral support, the directors of the Arkansas Historical Association set up a Special Publications Committee to assist with this book. Tom Baskett, the first chairman, and his successor, Tom W. Dillard, have handled much of the committee's work, which has also frequently involved the Association's president, Michael B. Dougan; treasurer, Walter L. Brown; and administrative secretary, Denyse Killgore. Tom Dillard and committee members T. Harri Baker, Walter Brown, and Betsy Jacoway Watson also read an early draft of *Sawmill* and made helpful suggestions.

Shirley Abbott, a Ouachitas native and gifted writer, read the manuscript and provided valuable criticism. Doug Knapp and Sandy Pringle, friends and neighbors, read the manuscript and offered useful comments. Gordon Morgan and Nudie Williams of the University of Arkansas contributed helpful insights for the portions dealing with black history. Representatives of the Ouachita National Forest checked the portions relating its history. Lee Robinette, along with several veteran foresters from the Weyerhaeuser and Dierks companies, reviewed and commented on sections describing changes in the forest products industry. Don Dierks, Jr., corrected factual errors and provided other valuable help with the history of the Dierks companies.

At the University of Arkansas Press, Director Miller Williams, Senior Editor Kathie Villard, and other staff members have done much to insure that the book's quality surpasses that of my manuscript. Several initial contributors to the Arkansas Historical Association's Special Publications Fund have provided for timely publication of the book as well as substantial help for the fund and the Press.

So many persons have aided this undertaking with information, encouragement, and hospitality, that it is not possible to name everyone. To all who did provide assistance, whether named here or not, I acknowledge my indebtedness and offer my thanks.

KENNETH L. SMITH

Sawmill

Men in work clothes, women wearing corsages, and children gathered close, typical rural timber people stand in front of logs stockpiled for a sawmill near Mena, Arkansas, soon after 1900.

Bert Hiltebrand photo, courtesy Eloise Goodwin Plaster

Prologue

This book is about the cutting of the last great virgin forest east of the Rocky Mountains.

The story takes place in the Ouachita Mountains of Arkansas and Oklahoma. Most of it is about the lumber companies and their people who cut the shortleaf pine forest there between 1900 and the 1950s.

During the nineteenth century, preceding the arrival of large-scale lumbering in the Ouachitas, American lumbermen developed their basic technology and expanded operations across the continent. In 1800, laborers or slaves made lumber by hand-sawing it from logs. One man could produce a hundred board feet in a day. (A board foot is the equivalent of a board 12 x 12 x 1 inches.) By 1900, after the invention and development of water and steam power, the circular saw and the band saw, and equipment to move logs and boards through a sawmill and to season and finish the lumber, the crew of a large sawmill could produce one hundred *thousand* board feet in a day. The development of powerful steam locomotives also enabled lumbermen to bring trainloads of heavy logs to their mills, and the extension of trunk line railroads let them send finished lumber to markets almost anywhere. A sawmill owner could then put his mill wherever there were trees for the cutting.[1]

Before the Civil War, sawmillers largely "cut out" or exhausted the timber along the New England seaboard and resettled in western New York and Pennsylvania. After the war they moved into the Great Lakes states, Virginia, the Carolinas, and Georgia.[2] At that time, something very important took place. In his book *Forests and Men,* forester William B. Greeley describes what happened:

> In the vast pineries surrounding the Great Lakes, following the War between the States, lumber manufacture took the form which molded its destinies. It became the great nomad among American industries, driving from one virgin forest to another like a threshing machine from one ripe wheat field to the next. . . .
>
> Lumbering in the region of the Great Lakes became an industry of tremendous driving power. Its captains and kings were hardy and resourceful,

skilled in organizing men and machines and in overcoming physical obstacles. Many of them were highly successful. . . . Powerful economic forces were set in motion. Among them were speculation in timber, the amassing of huge properties, and a rapid increase in the capitalization of the industry.

The drive of large capital investments for speed and profit brought about the rapid skinning of enormous areas of timberland. Twenty years, or even less, became the common lifetime of a sawmill. Then—dismantle, junk, and move on. Not only did lumbering perforce become a nomadic industry, it became an industry with no permanent interest in the land. A logged-off section was in the same category as a junked sawmill—to be sold for what it might bring, or abandoned and forgotten.[3]

The sawmiller's habit of exhausting the timber at one location and then moving on was soon referred to as "cut out and get out." About 1880, scarcely after getting settled around the Great Lakes, lumbermen and timber speculators began to buy tracts of longleaf pine in Louisiana and Mississippi, and shortleaf pine in southeastern Missouri. As the white pine of the lakes region was cut out, lumber companies moved to the South and set up new mills to cut the southern yellow pine. By 1900 there were mills throughout the longleaf pine area and operators began to cut the loblolly and shortleaf pine of southern Arkansas. Most of the timberland in the South had been "blocked out" by then, purchased by lumber companies and committed to one sawmill or another. Tracts that remained available to buyers were in the hardwood regions of the southern Appalachians and the Ozarks. There was also one important pine forest remaining, a very large area of virgin shortleaf in the Ouachita Mountains.[4]

The Sawmill story begins with a description of the land and people of the Ouachitas as they appeared around 1900 when timber buyers and sawmillers came into the region. About 1908, the boom in lumbering began with the opening of six large sawmills. Eventually there were more than a dozen big mills and hundreds of smaller ones in the Ouachitas, so many sawmills that it is necessary to focus attention on one more or less typical lumber manufacturer, the Caddo River Lumber Company. Caddo River was run by T. W. Rosborough—"Old Man Rosborough," as he was called—who built sawmills that cut timber across the midsection of the Ouachitas from 1908 to 1952. In the Ouachitas region, Caddo River was exceeded in size by only one other firm, the Dierks Lumber and Coal Company, whose history is also described in some detail. The operations of the other mills, large and small, are interesting in themselves but there is room only to touch on them.

From the beginning of the sawmilling boom, succeeding chapters cover the expansion of Caddo River and Dierks into the 1920s when they became the region's two largest lumber companies. The history takes them through the periods of the Great Depression and World War II to the end of the available virgin timber after 1950, an event symbolized by the closing of the big sawmill at Forester, Arkansas, a mill that Caddo River built and Dierks later operated. Caddo River's logging operation in the 1920s and the company's mill town of Forester in the 1930s and

1940s are also described in detail. A central chapter focuses on how "cut out and get out" began to give way to sustained yield forestry in the Ouachitas during the 1920s.

While part of the story is about forestry and lumbering, a larger portion deals with people: the lives of the entrepreneurs who developed the lumber companies, and of the farm folk who went to work for them. Most of this book is based on the oral history accounts of some 350 individuals who were involved with the region's lumber industry—especially with Caddo River—between 1906 and the 1950s. The written record of those years in the Ouachitas is sparse, but personal recollections are detailed and vivid. Scenes and events have been reconstructed, based upon descriptions given by one or more of the people who were there, to make those things easier to visualize, but the oral history informants themselves are the ones who provide the essence of the past, and they do it well.

These recollections form a picture of how people worked and lived in a forested backwater at the edge of the South. They also suggest how people in the Ouachitas progressed from their agrarian backgrounds toward today's society, moving along in the broader flow of history that includes not only the Ouachitas and the South but also the United States as a whole.

1. New Century

Beyond every family's cleared ground was the virgin forest. In moist bottomlands and on shady north slopes the trees were hardwoods, but in drier places those always gave way to shortleaf pine. On the elevated flats and benches and along the south-facing hillsides and mountainsides were pure stands of pine, an open forest where the trees stood widely spaced, with clean straight trunks and little undergrowth. One could ride a horse, or even drive a team and wagon through these groves of virgin shortleaf pine thickly carpeted with grass. On a warm day, a traveler could inhale the aroma of pine needles and hear the trees softly singing in the breeze.[1]

Here in the Ouachitas at the turn of the century, everybody knew the outdoors. In wide spacious freedom, settlers hunted the forest and fished the creeks. Men gathered at night and listened to their dogs chasing the fox. Many families were content to let the seasons flow and simply enjoy life.

The Ouachita Mountains that provided a home to these rural people are the end result of slow geologic processes. Many millions of years ago, layers of sedimentary rock that comprised this portion of the earth's crust were subjected to enormous sidewise pressure, so that the rock was compressed and folded. Over an immense span of time, the standing folds of rock were cut into by erosion. Softer materials, including vast beds of shale, were worn down to gentler slopes and the debris was carried away and deposited in the valleys. The harder layers of rock—sandstones and flinty novaculite—did not erode as easily and remained in place to become the backbones of mountain ridges. In some areas these ridges lie far apart, bordering the broad valleys of sizeable streams such as the Ouachita, the Kiamichi, and the Fourche LaFave rivers. Seen from mid-valley, these long ridges of the Ouachitas may be miles distant, hazy blue on the horizon. Elsewhere the ridges lie close together, their narrow crests overlooking steep-sided canyons, exposed rock, and tumbling creeks. In many other areas, however, the hills are lower and less steep but are very

U.S. Forest Service photo, courtesy Virgil W. Cothren

Virgin shortleaf pines in the Ouachitas grew in an open forest of trees widely spaced, with little undergrowth and a thick carpet of grass. A person could ride a horse, or drive a team and wagon, through these woods.

numerous, forming an uneven terrain having many small watercourses.

The first geographers thought of this region as merely the southern end of the Ozarks. Later, scholars came to realize that these ridges and valleys with their tilted and folded rock strata were different from the deeply eroded Ozark plateaus that lay north of the Arkansas River, and different even from the isolated mountains that stood here and there along the Arkansas valley. They observed that although the narrow ridges varied in length and height, they most often ran east and west, in a belt of country extending westward for 250 miles from central Arkansas into southeastern Oklahoma. Geologists who established the age and structure of the rock formations were able to draw regional boundaries that separated the Ouachitas from the geologically younger Gulf Coastal Plain to the south and from the more gently folded Arkansas valley to the north. Geologists, then, formally labeled the region with the name already commonly used, the Ouachita Mountains. "WASH-i-taw" is the white man's pronunciation of an Indian word whose exact origin and meaning appear to have been lost in the passage of time.[2]

Early in the nineteenth century the region's native Indians were pushed farther west, and by the outbreak of the Civil War, settlers occupied the most fertile land in the major valleys. After the war—remembered in

8 SAWMILL

East-west ridges and val-
leys, a scattering of small
farms, and large areas of
shortleaf pine were charac-
teristic features of the
Ouachitas region.

the Ouachitas as a time of skirmishes, outlawry, and house-burnings—other settlers moved into secondary valleys, to ground at higher elevations, and eventually to any place where a small acreage could be cleared for crops. Like homesteaders everywhere, they followed the lure of free land, but by 1900, latecomers found very little that was both available and cultivable.

To the eastern Ouachitas that lay within Arkansas, most of the early settlers came from southeastern states; many emigrated from the hill country of Mississippi, Alabama, and Georgia. The western Ouachitas became part of the Choctaw Nation in the Indian Territory (now Oklahoma) and early settlers were either full-blooded or part Choctaw, removed from their homeland in Mississippi. In background and habits, those who settled in the Ouachitas were more "southern" than pioneers in the Ozarks who had come from farther north in the Appalachians of Kentucky, eastern Tennessee, and western North Carolina and Virginia. But in the Ouachitas, as in the Ozarks, nearly all of the white settlers were of English or Scotch-Irish stock, not from the lowland South of plantation owners, but rather from the hillbilly South of small farmers.

Some of the Ouachitas farmers did own slaves and after the Civil War blacks remained in a few isolated enclaves. Neither blacks nor the Choctaws were very numerous in the Ouachitas; the mountains were mainly white man's territory. Beginning in the late nineteenth century, other white settlers came from the malarial lowlands of Louisiana, southern Arkansas, and east Texas, seeking a more healthful place to live. During the 1890s there was a strong influx of whites, many of whom were squatters, emigrating into the northern Ouachitas of the Indian Territory.[3]

The average farm family by this time tended a garden and fruit trees, and some cows, hogs, and chickens. All able-bodied members of the family, from children to grandparents, helped to plant, cultivate, and harvest the corn and field peas that were grown to feed the livestock, and the cotton sold to raise cash for family needs. Farm work was hard, but not of year-round duration. Farmers could labor at their own pace, except for those times when nature dictated that everybody get out and take care of the crops.

No matter how big the family, very often the farmer's home was a one-pen log house having a main room downstairs, a sleeping loft upstairs under the roof, a kitchen in a lean-to at the back, and a gallery (porch) across the front. Eventually, however, people began to build "box" houses of lumber from the small sawmills then existing in many neighborhoods. Often the "box" with its board-and-batten siding was not as tight and solid as a log house. Whether log or "box," the house usually had a stone fireplace with a chimney of clay that had been plastered over a frame of split pine sticks. Windows were few and simple, with sashes purchased in town and hauled home in a wagon. Doors were homemade of boards and often had homemade hinges of wood, and a latchstring. Doors did not have locks.

People ate amply. Breakfast invariably included meat, ham or bacon or occasionally wild game such as venison or roast possum. There were always homemade biscuits with milk gravy, and coffee. The noon meal was called dinner, rural America's big meal of the day, again with meat. Cornbread was a staple, and the family usually had garden vegetables, either fresh or preserved. Supper, the evening meal, often consisted of leftovers from noon. Three times a day, meat was on the table. Sometimes it was beef, a yearling or a calf freshly killed, and sold to or shared among neighbors because there was no refrigeration to preserve it. More often it was ham or bacon from the family's smokehouse, or sausage or fresh pork. And, even after 1900, a few individuals in the Ouachitas killed bears and salted down the meat.

Outside the home, a rural family's world comprised the local community that lay within walking distance. Its central structure was a plain, box-like church, usually Baptist, though in some cases it was Methodist, and in a few, Presbyterian. (After 1900 in many communities, there were churches of one or another of the Pentecostal denominations.) Regardless of denomination, church services were marked by a simplicity in keeping with that place and time: hymn singing, often without any instrumental accompaniment; preaching, if a circuit riding preacher could be on hand; and testifying, by those in attendance whose souls had come in touch with the Lord.

After services, people stayed and talked a while, got the news, maybe went home with friends for dinner and an "evening" (afternoon) of visiting. On special days the local congregation and others from surrounding churches gathered for all-day singing and dinner on the grounds (with "dinner" being an outdoor noonday meal with great amounts of food that everyone brought). At Christmas the entire community gathered at church for a special program around the Christmas tree. In the summertime many neighborhoods had brush arbor revivals, preaching and singing for days on end to bring new lambs and strayed sheep into the fold of the church. Whether Baptist or Methodist, the revival climaxed with a mass baptizing by immersion at a nearby creek. Everybody attended church activities, even those who nowadays would not go to church, since they offered a social gathering and provided the only place where people could get together, except for maybe a few activities at the school.

Each neighborhood's one-room school "took up" in the summer after crops were laid by (hoed clean of weeds until the cotton and corn could grow on their own) and the hoe-wielders were free to be in the classroom. The summer term of three months ran from about July first until late September when the children were dismissed for the harvest. Then, if the school district had funds to hire a teacher and the school was provided with a stove, there was a three-month winter term from December until time to plow and plant in the spring.

The school had six or eight grades. Seldom did a rural child even finish eight grades, and of course there was no high school, but having an education wasn't considered important. People learned to farm by working the land, not by studying books; every community had successful farmers (and wives, too) who had never learned to read or write. Most agreed, though, that young folks should learn how to read a newspaper,

Bert Hiltebrand photo, courtesy Eloise Goodwin Plaster

write a letter, and do arithmetic well enough to cope with tax statements and the like. And maybe it was good to let them learn a little history and geography, too.

The rural people's lack of formal education showed most obviously in their speech. They used what linguists now call Nonstandard English, not really "bad" language, but certainly not the Standard English that educated people speak and write. Many forms of speech used by Ouachitas country folk, although acceptable in earlier times, had been discarded by educated town dwellers. In the hills, as in other isolated areas throughout the United States, old ways of expression were protected from change. People still said *holp* for "helped," used *ain't* and *he don't*, and said *you was* as a singular; all of these forms were holdovers from days gone by.

Many neighborhoods had a crossroads hamlet or village, with a country store that was often combined with an establishment where the owner ran a grist mill on Saturdays, a cotton gin in the fall, and a sawmill at other times, all powered by one steam boiler. In most communities a family operated a sorghum mill, pressing the sweet juice from their own cane and their neighbors' and boiling down the juice to make molasses. With community services, church and school activities, the ministrations of a country doctor, and entertainment provided by the community's amateur baseball team, most of the people's needs were cared for.

These country neighborhoods also developed a strong *sense* of community. Every able-bodied person was expected to help with the work, but aged parents, maiden aunts, and orphaned children were all taken in and cared for by next of kin. Outside the family, neighbors helped whenever anyone was in need; they assisted at births, buried the dead, and helped carry out all kinds of projects in between. For these acts of mutual assistance, no money changed hands. Everybody was cash poor but enjoyed a kind of social security from helping and being helped, from knowing everyone else in the community, and from having a sense of belonging.

Many of these people lived their entire lives in or near the communities where they were born. The only long journey they ever made was the once or twice yearly trip to town. Often they went in the fall, after harvest, and took two days, even if they were only going to the county seat. Travelers arrived in town late the first day and stayed at a wagon yard. (Every town had one, where transients bought feed for their mules and bedded down for the night in their wagons or in a bare, but heated room by the feed barn.) Next morning they would sell their wagon load of cotton and purchase coffee, cloth, and other supplies for the coming seasons. Then they commenced the long, slow ride back home.[4]

There were about fifteen towns and villages in and around the Ouachitas serving as trading centers for the rural people. Six lay within the region's boundaries, while the others were not far outside. Only two of the six boasted a population of more than a thousand souls: Mena, a newly established railroad town on the Kansas City Southern line, in 1900 had a population of 3,423; and Hot Springs, a health resort where people came to take the mineral waters, had 9,973 residents.

By the turn of the century, however, the rural population was nearing its upper limits. Already, families in the Ouachitas were trying to live on land described by one native as "flake rocks and red clay." Farmers struggled with poor soil and many other obstacles. Creo Jones, the son of a homesteader in Montgomery County, Arkansas, recalls that once in his boyhood the family planted ten acres of cotton, and the boll weevils and armyworms got it. "We picked eighteen pounds and had it ginned and had it made into a mattress," Jones says. "That was our year's work."

Another year the family tried growing wheat. Father and sons cut and gathered the ripe grain by hand and hauled it to a neighbor for threshing. "We got four bushels of wheat, off ten acres—and half of that was weed seed. My sister and I drove the wagon clear over to Black Springs to have that ground into flour. And it was black—real dark. All that debris, we didn't have any way of separating it. But we made bread out of it. Dark bread, but it was food."

———

By 1900, trunk line railroads had come to the Ouachitas, and timber lookers and timber buyers were trekking through the area seeking bargains in stumpage (standing timber). Many of these northern visitors

The Wooden Age C. O. Pike photo, courtesy Norman Goodner

Second only to food as a basic life-supporting commodity in the America of 1900 was a substance often overlooked: wood.[5] *The most versatile of materials, wood could be used for house and furniture and fuel for the stove; it could be made into buckets and barrels and birdhouses, rail fences and stair rails and railway cars. Iron and steel were essential too, of course. But wood, with its insulating, warmth-giving properties, was even more necessary. And lumber, once described as the "world's most useful product," was universally available, usually affordable, and surprisingly well made.*

This modest farmstead

ventured into the Ouachitas carrying popular impressions of the day: Arkansas was the Bear State, isolated and backward; the Indian Territory was the Wild West, full of savages and desperadoes. They found people who subsisted in a rural backwater as they had for several generations, but the people were friendly enough—though far from being as well off as farmers in the northern agricultural states.

As timber country, the Ouachitas looked much less inviting to lumbermen than the level pinelands farther south. The mountain grown pine was smaller, and the Ouachitas were a rough place to build a logging railroad. But when the lumbermen read their timber cruisers' estimates, they learned that much of the country had at least five thousand board feet to the acre. The board footage wasn't as good as on longleaf pine timberland, or even on the loblolly-shortleaf country south of the Ouachitas, but still there seemed a chance. According to a loggers' rule of thumb, anything over four thousand feet to the acre would let a man go in with a railroad, get the logs out and still make some money. Here in the Ouachitas, railroads could take the easy grades up the creek valleys and the logs could be skidded by mules or hauled on wagons down the hills to the tracks.[6]

It was also becoming known that this shortleaf pine from the Ouachitas produced lumber of exceptional quality. In 1896 Dr. Charles T. Mohr of the U.S. Division of Forestry wrote that: "the wood produced in these hills is of a lighter color, less resinous, and of a fine grain. Specimens of finished lumber from such timber resemble somewhat that of the white pine." It was the slow growth of this mountain pine that created a superior kind of lumber.[7]

Shortleaf pine grows on dry upland soils across a broad reach of the United States, from New Jersey to southern Missouri, and from north Florida to east Texas and eastern Oklahoma. Over much of its range it grows in scattered stands or mixed with other species of pine, but in the Ouachitas, shortleaf was virtually the only pine, and the most abundant tree of any species. Loblolly pine existed along the region's southern fringe and in small patches elsewhere, but those areas were negligible. Considering that the Ouachitas extend over eleven thousand square miles, the original area of pine and pine-hardwood forest must have covered at least five thousand square miles (by a rough but conservative estimate). Thus the region contained what was easily the largest shortleaf pine forest in the world.

Many people became interested in the pine of the Ouachitas, not only lumbermen and speculators who bought standing timber, but also local residents who could help survey land and estimate board footage, as well as lawyers, abstractors, and notaries who could do legal and title work, and perform as agents for out-of-state buyers. One who entered the game was an attorney and congressman from Prescott, Arkansas, named Thomas Chipman McRae. On March 7, 1902, McRae wrote a letter to a potential client, Samuel S. Barney of West Bend, Wisconsin:

> Referring to the several conversations that we have had, in relation to opportunities for bargains in timber lands in Arkansas, I will say that a great deal of money has been made by the purchase of such property . . . and there are still many opportunities for profitable investments. . . . The most of the large private holdings are now owned by persons who know that timber values are advancing, and it will not be as easy to make as much profit out of these as in the location of scrip on public lands. . . .[8]

McRae said he would show Barney where to find unappropriated public land and would obtain land warrants or scrip for Barney to purchase and turn in to the government's General Land Office to get title to the tracts that he wanted. Land warrants were certificates given by the government as bounties or bonuses to veterans of the country's various wars. With one of these certificates a veteran could select a tract of government land as a homestead, free of cost. Each certificate specified an area of 40, 80, 120, or 160 acres, depending on the government's generosity following a particular war.

Instead of using their warrants to secure homesteads, almost all veterans sold their certificates to raise cash; more than one land bounty changed hands in a bar for the cost of drinks. Certificates were transferable, like shares of stock, and a market developed for them. They could be bought for less than the value of land that they could secure, which made them attractive to anyone looking for timberland on the public domain. At times, warrants were called scrip, a name given also to other

near Waldron, Arkansas, appears to utilize only wood. The photograph was taken around 1910 when the consumption of wood in the United States was at an all-time high. Lumber was being manufactured not only for uses that we still know today, but also for farm implements, railroad cars, refrigerators, silos, ships, and wagons— and by 1910, in increasing quantities for automobile frames and bodies.

During that period large-scale lumbering was getting underway in the Ouachita Mountains. The region's farm population remained near its maximum, but in the hills were many small farms, much like this one, where families could not make their living from the land. People were beginning to leave their rural homes to work for the lumber companies.

kinds of government certificates entitling their holders to select public land, and which were also traded in the marketplace.[9]

Warrants or scrip, McRae told Barney, could be bought for an average of $5.00 an acre, and McRae then disclosed that he had "the best possible connections for getting it when there is any on the market." Scrip could be used to acquire land in Arkansas having an average of five thousand feet of timber per acre, McRae said, so the timber would cost $1.00 per thousand board feet, an attractive price for southern pine stumpage at that time.

McRae then advised that a railroad would probably be built soon into the Ouachitas north of Prescott, along the Caddo River. To his letter he attached maps showing vacant public lands near the projected track. Barney could come to Arkansas and look at the timber. Finally, McRae stated his fee: for helping to locate land and scrip that Barney could purchase, he would expect not less than fifty cents an acre.

Standing timber is what Samuel Barney and many others sought. The nation needed more building material, lumber prices were going up, and southern yellow pine had gained acceptance as a substitute for the diminishing supply of northern white pine. From the 1880s, when magnificent longleaf pine in Louisiana and Mississippi had been available for as little as eight cents a thousand board feet, the price of stumpage had moved steadily upward. Southern pine had become attractive as an investment, not only for lumbermen but also for anybody who had money to buy parcels of timberland and combine them into blocks large enough for a sawmiller to purchase as the basis for a mill. Such transactions practically guaranteed a big profit for the land speculator. Uncut timber was valuable. As for timberland that had been cut over, unless such land could be sold to farmers it was considered practically worthless.

The attitudes about timber and land were obvious in several transactions involving a timber trader from Michigan named Uriel Lee Clark who dealt with McRae for land scrip. In 1890 Clark had acquired a sawmill in the yellow pine district of southeastern Missouri, where he had also begun to buy and sell timber. He must have found his land deals more profitable than his sawmill, for by 1893 he was out of the mill and into timberland speculation in Arkansas. Three years later he organized the Detroit Timber and Lumber Company, not so much as a lumber manufacturer as a timber trading operation.

In 1901, Clark bought a sawmill with a railroad and ten thousand acres of timber on the southern edge of the Ouachitas at Pike City, Arkansas. Soon afterward he purchased another twenty thousand acres in the same area, and a few months later sold the entire thirty thousand acres with mill and railroad to investors from Wisconsin.[10]

Clark and the previous owners ran the Pike City mill long enough to cut a few square miles of timber, and by 1903 the cutover land was reverting to the state for nonpayment of taxes. In Arkansas, as in the Great Lakes region that William B. Greeley wrote about, logged-off land was either to be sold for what it might bring, or abandoned and forgotten.[11]

McRae declared to Samuel Barney that the Ouachitas had more unappropriated government timberland than was available in any other state having land that remained in the public domain. McRae well knew that, beginning in 1891, the government had withdrawn or reserved many millions of acres of public forest land in the West to protect watersheds and to help assure a future supply of timber for the nation as virgin forests elsewhere were cut out. These reserves were to become the first national forests. But in 1902, as McRae dealt with Barney, no forest reserve existed in the Ouachitas. There, another large body of public land, unfit for agriculture but having good pine timber, was still up for grabs.

This public land included almost the entire central core of the Ouachitas and many areas around the perimeter. Nearly all of the mountain ridges and narrow canyons were public, as were some wider valleys in less accessible territory. One such area that remained in federal ownership even after 1900 was located south of the Fourche LaFave River, north and northwest of Hot Springs. A series of creek drainages formed a broad "trough" of valleys and low hills set between higher ridges that lay to the north and south. Along these creeks was some of the finest timber in the Ouachitas, and it could all be logged from one main line railroad following the alignment of the drainages. In 1904, two northerners and the managers of the Santa Fe Railroad cooperated in acquiring this area.

Years before, the federal government had given the Santa Fe a grant of land to induce the railroad to build trackage across northern Arizona to open up that country. The railroad's holdings lay in a checkerboard of alternate one-mile squares for several miles on each side of the tracks. In the 1890s, however, the government withdrew public land in the region around Flagstaff for forest reserves, including many of the alternate square miles it still owned within the Santa Fe grant. Congress then told the Santa Fe (and other private owners within the exterior boundaries of the new forest reserves) that if they wanted, they could deed back to the government their land within the reserves and, in lieu thereof, select unappropriated lands elsewhere. Making use of this option, the Santa Fe proceeded in 1904 to become the owner of thousands of acres of timberland along the drainages south of the Fourche River in Arkansas.[12]

While there is no known record of an agreement, it appears that in selecting Arkansas timber, the Santa Fe people were helped by a pair of northern lumbermen (or timber speculators?) who, at about the same time, started buying land in that area on their own account. Paul D. Rust and Frank H. Drummond, from related families who owned and managed the Rust-Owen Lumber Company at Drummond, Wisconsin, bought the Santa Fe land south of the Fourche very soon after the railroad had acquired title.[13] The land had been chosen piece by piece from the public domain, to obtain the finest timber in an area that was compact enough to support a railroad logging operation.

On acquiring the Santa Fe's "lieu selection" land, Drummond and Rust began to "block up" the timber by purchasing timberland from adjoining small landowners. Along the drainages south of the Fourche, they bought any available tracts that lay within an area from two to five miles wide and extending for fifty miles across three counties. Rust purchased land along the western two-thirds of the chosen strip while Drummond—obviously by prior agreement—stayed at the eastern end.[14]

At times Rust used land bounty warrants. In 1906 he acquired 160 acres with a warrant originally given by the United States to one Joseph Short, a private with the Oregon Mounted Volunteers in the Oregon and Washington Indian War. Rust, however, obtained more land by direct purchase from owners in the area. His purchases in 1904 included tracts of forty-eight acres for $110, sixty acres for $150, and seventy acres for $125. At that time Rust picked up five small parcels totaling about 320 acres for a total cost of $735, to average about $2.30 an acre. It was far less than McRae's man Barney would have had to pay for warrants or scrip. Rust was dealing with isolated rural people, however, and they were probably unaware of the current market prices for stumpage.[15]

While some of these small landowners may have acquired land merely to sell the timber and reap a profit, many of them had owned their parcels for five years or longer before they sold to Rust, suggesting that they had tried to subsist on their land but failed. And, while many lumbermen and speculators were not averse to prying public domain timber away from the government by a variety of methods, including some that were illegal, the kind of timber grabbing that was common practice in the West appears not to have taken place to any great extent in the Ouachitas. After all, with many small landowners willing to sell acreage and timber at favorable prices, there was little need to resort to subterfuge.[16]

––––––––

Rust, Drummond, and agents who worked for them caused a long lasting change in ownership and management of their piece of the Ouachitas, but now there were others buying Ouachitas land and timber whose influence would far outstrip theirs. At the time that Drummond and Rust were making their deal with the Santa Fe Railroad, the Dierks brothers were building a timberland base for expanding the lumber business that they operated.

The brothers were sons of an immigrant from north Germany, Peter Henry Dierks, who had become a successful farmer and banker in eastern Iowa. Hans, the oldest son, became part owner of several small-town lumberyards in southwestern Iowa during the early 1880s, then sold out and opened a yard at Broken Bow, Nebraska. Soon after he moved to that state, Hans was joined by his brother Herman. Within a few years they acquired lumberyards in nearby towns and were joined by their brothers Peter and Henry. In 1895 the four partners incorporated as the Dierks Lumber and Coal Company, which sold heating fuel as well as lumber. In 1896 Hans moved with the company's headquarters to Kansas City, a major distribution point for southern yellow pine, to be better able to buy lumber for the yards. By 1900 the Dierks brothers had built up a string of twenty-four lumberyards, most of them on the plains of central Nebraska.[17]

Retailing was a quick money-maker that enabled the brothers to add yard after yard to multiply their earnings. Apparently they had no idea of manufacturing lumber, however, until one day in 1897 when a stranger walked into the Kansas City office, offering to sell them "a very good planing mill" on the Kansas City Southern Railroad in Indian Territory. They could buy rough lumber from small sawmills in the neighborhood, air dry it, finish it in the planing mill, and ship it north on the railroad. With the planer were a few cheap houses and a commissary store. The price was $15,000 for everything.

Hans conferred with his brothers. The man wanted too much money, and at first they turned him down. But after more investigation, they changed their minds and made a deal.[18]

The planing mill was located at a small place named Petros, at the north edge of the Ouachitas near the present-day town of Heavener, Oklahoma. Before long the brothers realized that Petros was at the northern limit of the pine belt and timber was not abundant. Apparently they had trouble buying enough rough lumber to supply the planer, for after three years they closed it down. But by then they had gotten a taste of lumber manufacturing and were able to buy some timberland and a large sawmill farther down the KCS Railroad at De Queen, Arkansas.

In 1902 Herman Dierks moved to De Queen to manage the sawmill and its logging operation. The brothers also wanted to buy more timber, for only a small acreage had been purchased with the mill and they needed to avoid the supply problem they had encountered at Petros. Herman soon learned there was not much timber available in the country close to De Queen; it had already been bought up or cut over. But by going farther to the northeast, he could buy plenty of timberland at acceptable prices. Herman Dierks began to purchase land in the southern Ouachitas thirty miles northeast of De Queen, presuming that it would be within reach of an extension of the sawmill's logging railroad.

He also looked west into Indian Territory. Perhaps at first he hoped to find more timber for the De Queen mill, but instead he discovered an exciting new prospect. In the Territory a vast area of untouched forest spread for forty miles along the southern flank of the Ouachitas, enough timber for a big mill—or even *two* big sawmills! A few miles south was a new railroad, the Arkansas and Choctaw, which had been completed in 1902. From the A. & C. (which later would become part of the Frisco system) a short line could be run north to the mill sites. From the mills the logging railroads could go farther north into the timber, following the creeks upstream into the Ouachitas.

The Dierks family now had a sawmill busily producing lumber for two dozen retail yards that were making lots of money, a liberally flowing "cash cow" that would pay for this southern expansion. And there was the timberland, waiting to be blocked out for two more mills. Herman Dierks, especially, must have thought all this was wonderful. He loved to get out and make deals.

Courtesy F. McD. (Don) Dierks, Jr.

And so, in the four or five years that Herman Dierks lived in De Queen before moving back to Kansas City, groundwork was laid for a timber empire.

One of the brothers, Henry, had died in 1895. Peter Dierks was in Nebraska managing the yards, removed from what was going on in the South. Hans's sons Herbert and Harry were already in the company, and before long the sons of Herman and Peter would join the firm. During these years just after 1900, however, Hans and Herman were the ones who guided the expansion of the Dierks Lumber and Coal Company, Hans in Kansas City as president and financial overseer and Herman in De Queen (and later Kansas City) looking after the sawmill and timberlands.

Both Hans and Herman knew the lumber trade. Herman was a man of new ideas and intense enthusiasm, aggressively going after timber. Herman was also volatile, apt to be carried away by his enthusiasm, and needed a stabilizing force. His brother Hans, thirteen years older, was quieter and more methodical, probably not as innovative as Herman but a good organizer and money manager. Together they formed a strong team. Herman accumulated timberland and, as Dierks family legend has

His younger, more aggressive brother Herman took the lead in accumulating the company's timberlands.

it, Hans watched the nickels and kept his wheeling, dealing brother from going broke.

———

In that period there was only one other man who looked at Ouachitas timber and triggered more widespread change than the Dierks brothers. This was a newcomer named William Logan Hall. Sometime around 1905, Hall traveled through the Ouachitas in a wagon, touring the still unappropriated federal lands which remained huge in area. He had been sent there by another wheeler and dealer, Gifford Pinchot, chief of the newly established U.S. Forest Service.[19]

———

The lumber industry by 1899 could gain access to the Ouachitas forest from five trunk line railroads:
- The Missouri-Kansas-Texas (M-K-T or Katy), completed in 1873, came through Indian Territory and touched the region's western end.
- The St. Louis, Iron Mountain & Southern (later part of the Missouri Pacific system), opened in 1874 from St. Louis to Texas, and skirted the Ouachitas on the southeast.
- The St. Louis-San Francisco (Frisco), completed in 1887, also from

St. Louis to Texas, crossed the western Ouachitas in Indian Territory.
- The Kansas City Southern (KCS), opened in 1896, crossed the Ouachitas along the border between Arkansas and Indian Territory.
- The Choctaw, Oklahoma & Gulf (later a part of the Rock Island system), completed in 1899, ran along the region's northern edge.

With these railroads came sawmills that produced lumber for outside markets rather than purely local needs. The first of these mills within the Ouachitas was installed in the 1870s at the region's extreme west end, at a stop on the M-K-T called Stringtown. For a few years a steam sawmill cut pine boards that were loaded on railroad cars and hauled south on the Katy to Texas. Stringtown, however, lay at the western limit of the pine belt and its trees were small and sparse, so in time the mill shut down and disappeared.[20]

During those years from the 1870s to 1900, most of the mills in the Ouachitas were small, temporary affairs. Usually a mill would cut timber in a local area and then move somewhere else. Only three operations were of any size or permanence, and they were not as large as several (including the Dierks mills in Oklahoma) that came soon after the turn of the century. Those, however, were headed up by three individuals typical of successful sawmill entrepreneurs of their day.

Andrew Johnson Neimeyer, who would later become one of the major lumbermen of the Ouachitas, was the son of an Ohio farmer. Neimeyer's career in lumbering was surprisingly like that of the Dierks brothers. He started out at seventeen in his brother's retail lumberyard in Iowa, at twenty-eight opened a yard of his own in Nebraska, and within seven years developed a string of six lumberyards in that state and acquired a sawmill in southwest Arkansas. By 1895 he was directing his lumber manufacturing and sales organization from headquarters in St. Louis, and in that year acquired controlling interest in the Saginaw Lumber Company, a medium-sized mill on the Ouachita River ten miles below Malvern, Arkansas.[21]

William Richard Abbott, born in Pennsylvania and reared in northern Missouri, also went to work at a retail lumberyard during his teens. After learning the trade in yards at Wichita, Kansas, and Ogden, Utah, he relocated to the Indian Territory and got into sawmilling, where he quickly learned about manufacturing and distribution. In 1892, when only twenty-four years old, Abbott persuaded a banker at Fort Smith, Arkansas, to back him in organizing the Fort Smith Lumber Company. Abbott's company expanded from sales into manufacturing, and did so well that in 1899 Abbott bought 76,400 acres of timberland on the north edge of the Ouachitas along the Rock Island tracks west of Little Rock. He promptly set up five small sawmills on this line to cut the timber, and organized a logging railroad, known as the Central Railway of Arkansas, to deliver logs from the woods to the mills.[22]

Both Abbott and Neimeyer became important enough in lumbering to have their portraits printed with those of other turn-of-the-century sawmill kings in a set of three heavy volumes entitled *American Lumbermen*. Neither, however, really looked like a man of power. Abbott,

The Saginaw Lumber Company built the first extensive railroad system into the Ouachitas. Wood-burning, gear-driven Shay locomotives, like this one near Saginaw about 1900, pulled trainloads of logs to the mill.

smooth skinned and youthful, looked as if he was right out of college. Neimeyer, scrawny of neck and a little weak of chin, resembled a worried dry goods clerk. The laudatory biographies that accompany the portraits suggest indirectly why both succeeded as lumbermen. Both came from Yankee-Midwestern backgrounds that undoubtedly stressed the work ethic and getting ahead. Both received a broad practical education in the lumber business when they were quite young. They were both willing to move around the country to better themselves, and found that lumbering was a way to make money fast, Neimeyer with his yards in Nebraska, and Abbott with his Fort Smith Lumber Company. Both profited in lucrative retail sales, but decided that sawmilling, or a combination of sawmilling and sales, would make even more money.

Adalbert Strauss, another member of this trio of pioneer lumbermen, grew to manhood in Germany, then came to America and settled in St. Louis. In 1880 he built a sawmill on the Iron Mountain Railroad at Perla, near Malvern, Arkansas, and began to log the flatlands of the Coastal Plain to the south and east of his mill. For two decades his Malvern Lumber Company continued to log that area by railroad, but in 1904 Strauss organized the Perla Northern Railroad and built track into the Ouachitas where he had purchased timberland from the Iron Mountain.[23]

Strauss was a small, frail man who wore a beard and suffered from asthma; he looked more the scholar than sawmiller. Why he chose lumbering as a career is not known, except that the industry seemed to attract men of German heritage: Neimeyer, the Dierks brothers, and many others including the leading lumberman of the time, Frederick Weyerhaeuser.

None of the three—Abbott, Neimeyer, or Strauss—had any experience with the white pine of the Great Lakes. By the time that Abbott's mills were cutting along the Rock Island, however, another mill was being built on the same railroad some miles to the east by the Bigelow Brothers & Walker Company, a Chicago based firm in the white pine trade since 1862. After cutting out a mill in Michigan and selling one in Wisconsin, Bigelow Brothers started up their Arkansas mill, the Fourche River Lumber Company, in 1904. The new mill was equipped with two band saws and could produce one hundred and twenty-five thousand board feet of lumber a day. It was the first sawmill of such magnitude to be built in the Ouachitas.

Three stories tall, this mill stood beside the Fourche LaFave River a few miles upstream from the junction of the Fourche with the Arkansas River. The company owned forty-two thousand acres of pine in the hills south of the Fourche and planned to log the area by railroad; from other areas they would float logs down the river to the mill. To local folk who had never seen a big sawmill, this one was a marvel. Its strong heavy framework was set on a base of concrete, so that even when all the machinery was running full speed there was almost no vibration (". . . as steady as a church," one man said). There was a fireproof brick powerhouse with six boilers and a massive steam engine to run the sawmill's machinery. And as the industry's leading trade journal, *American Lumberman,* reported soon after the mill was completed, the plant included five large brick dry kilns, nearly two acres of lumber storage sheds, a hundred-kilowatt electric light plant, a two-story office building, a network of cast iron water mains for fire protection, and a telephone exchange.

The *Lumberman* went on to say that the company had built "a new, modern and model saw mill town . . . fine cottages for the men . . . a three story hotel . . . [and] a remarkably fine store building. . . ." The mill town was located at a settlement named Esau, which in 1911 would be renamed Bigelow for the company's president, Nelson P. Bigelow. The logging railroad was named, in a flush of optimism, the Fourche River Valley & Indian Territory, which in everyday usage was shortened to F. R. V. & I. T.[24]

————

The Fourche River mill contained machinery and equipment that the lumber industry had developed during the previous fifty years, and that would remain in use in every big mill for most of the next half-century. The process of making lumber (sawing, seasoning, finishing) was settled; it would be an identical process in all the larger mills of the Ouachitas from that time on.

One by one, logs were pulled from a mill pond, which at Fourche

River was the river itself, with a barrier or boom stretched across the stream to keep logs from floating away. From the pond an endless chain carried the logs up a long incline to the second floor of the mill. There they were rolled off onto the deck, where they were next rolled onto a carriage (which traveled on tracks), and fastened there.

The sawyer then set the carriage in motion (it was pushed by a long piston rod called the shotgun feed) past a band saw (an endless steel belt toothed along one edge and running over pulleys) that sliced off one outside part of the log—a slab, with the bark on. Back came the carriage, the log was turned or set forward toward the saw, then back again past the saw that *zippp!* sliced off another slab, or a board. The outside parts of the log were removed first, leaving a squared piece of timber (called a cant) that was then sawed into boards. Back and forth, back and forth went the carriage; in a few seconds the log was reduced to slabs and boards. To move the log into the best position for each cut, the sawyer and the men riding the carriage had to do rapid mental calculations.

The saw that sliced up the log as it rode the carriage was known as the headsaw—the first saw that cut the log after it entered the mill. A mill with a circular headsaw could produce twenty-five thousand board feet of lumber in a day; a mill with a band saw, fifty thousand feet; a mill having two band saws and two carriages (one headsaw on each side of the mill),

An engraving of a band saw used as a headsaw shows the arrangement of its pulley wheels, and the carriage that moved logs back and forth past the saw. On the carriage are levers used by the two doggers who held the log in place, and by the blocksetter who moved the log into position for the next cut.

Henry Disston & Sons *Handbook for Lumbermen,* 1902 edition, page 104, courtesy Library of Congress

This gang saw, having six vertical blades that moved rapidly up and down, could slice a log into boards as it passed through the saw's supporting frame.

Courtesy Science and Technology Research Center, The New York Public Library, Astor, Lenox and Tilden Foundations

one hundred thousand feet or more. In the Ouachitas as elsewhere in the southern pine region, most of the mills large enough to log by railroad used either one or two band saws as headsaws. Such mills often were referred to as "single-band" or "double-band" mills.

In some mills the cants were not sawed into boards by the headsaw, but were pushed off the carriage beyond the headsaw and onto a conveyor that carried them through a "resaw" that sliced them into boards. The resaw was usually a gang saw, having a group of saw blades set at even intervals in a reciprocating frame, through which the cants were fed to reduce them to boards in a single pass. Fourche River did not have a gang saw, but some of the large mills that came in later years did have them.

Beyond the headsaw or resaw, the newly cut boards were conveyed lengthwise through a gang of small circular saws (the edger) that cut off the uneven edges having bark on them. Beyond the edger, boards moved sidewise through another gang of circular saws (the trimmer) that squared off the uneven ends. Then, along a conveyor known as the green

sorter or green chain, a line of men sorted and stacked the boards according to length, width, thickness, and grade of quality.

The rough sawn boards were called "green" lumber, not from color but
because of their high moisture content. From the green chain the lumber
was taken to dry kilns, which were enclosed buildings where stacks of
boards were steam heated to drive off excess moisture in the wood. Pine
lumber remained in the kilns for about seventy-two hours, or enough
time to evaporate about eighty-five percent of its water content. At
Fourche River, only the higher grades of lumber were kiln dried, while
lower grades were stacked outside on the yard and air dried for a month
or more. (Air drying, however, allowed fungi to attack and discolor the
boards. From about 1920 on, the big mills kiln dried all of the output to
obtain better quality lumber.)

The kiln dried boards usually were again sorted by grade and stored in
the rough lumber shed until needed for further processing in the remanufacturing plant or planing mill. "Remanufacturing" meant any
reshaping of the lumber beyond what had been done in the sawmill. A
two-inch-thick piece might be resawed into two one-inch-thick boards,
or one defective end of a piece might be trimmed off to raise the grade of
the remainder. Almost all of the rough dry lumber was run through
planers, machines with revolving knives that shaved boards to an exact
size and a smooth finish. Some of it was shaped into moldings of various
patterns, tongue-and-groove flooring, or patterned siding. After re-

*Before the advent of kiln
drying, lumber was air
dried before being finished
in the planing mill or
shipped out in rough form.
At this drying yard of the
Walker-Hopkins Lumber
Company at Moyers,
Oklahoma, about 1912,
teamsters with their mules
and wagons brought green
lumber from the sawmill,
and took dry lumber to the
planer.*

manufacturing, the lumber was stored in the finished lumber shed until it was shipped to fill customers' orders.[25]

At Fourche River and everywhere else, the most dramatic action in a sawmill took place at the headsaw. The log carriage flew back and forth; the wide band saw ripped through the log. On the carriage, two men dogged the log (held it in place) while a third set blocks (positioned the log for sawing). The swift-riding doggers and blocksetter always attracted the attention of visitors to the mill, but it was the sawyer, standing unobtrusively near the headsaw, who ran the whole show. He pulled the lever that operated the steam piston devices that kicked the log onto the carriage and then turned it as needed between cuts. He controlled the speed and direction of the carriage in its back-and-forth travel past the saw. He signalled the blocksetter how to move the log for the next cut (using hand signals, for no one could be heard above the noise of the machinery).

The sawyer was told what size boards were most needed to fill current orders. He concentrated on cutting those dimensions, at the same time trying to cut the highest grade of lumber of all sizes. He watched each log for its best cuts, sawing at optimum angles in relation to crooks in the logs and the grain of the wood, and avoiding or minimizing defects such as knots, splits, and decay. A good sawyer cut the best possible grades of lumber at the fastest possible speed; the output of a mill depended not only on its number and kind of headsaws but also on how quickly the sawyer could make decisions and move the carriage past the saw. It took training, practice, intelligence, and mental agility to become a sawyer. A really good one could feed a log into a band saw so fast that instead of making dust, the saw at times would strip "strings" of wood from the log.[26]

Another highly skilled employee in the sawmill was the saw filer. He too influenced the quality and quantity of the mill's output. The filer sharpened saws, hammered warped ones, and set the shape and angle of the saws' teeth. He "rolled" band saws to cup them from side to side so that they would not fly off the pulley wheels in motion. In smaller mills he also sharpened the planing mills' cutter knives. In mills like Fourche River there was a separate filing room in the planing mill, and another highly skilled man worked there.[27]

The sawyers, filers, and superintendents who planned production were the highest paid employees in the mill. Well below them on the pay scale were the foremen, and skilled workers such as the mill's carpenter, electrician, and blacksmith. Not far below the middle group were most of the work force classified as laborers, the ones who pushed boards onto conveyors or pulled them off; fed them into machines or took them away; stacked them or unstacked them. Lumber stackers and boxcar loaders worked on a piecework basis, paid according to how many thousand board feet they handled each day. Other day laborers were paid a low daily wage. This system endured for the next half century, not only at early mills like Fourche River and Saginaw but also at every other big mill that came later to the Ouachitas.[28]

For laboring folk in mills thoughout the region, the work was hard. Hess Maxey, who fed lumber into a planer, recalls: "I got two dollars and fifteen cents a day for feeding that big sizer. Ten hours. It was a high speed machine, 250 feet a minute. I've put three carloads of two-by-twelves through there. . . ."

Hard work. Lester Miller stood beyond a headsaw and shoved the lumber coming from the saw onto conveyors, to the edger for boards with an uneven edge or directly to the trimmer for those without. All day he stood next to the shotgun feed, the big steam cylinder that pushed the carriage. In summer the job was so hot that his sweat filled his shoes, ran over, and puddled on the floor.

All day Maxey pushed boards into his planer, with the machine screaming so loud that he had to communicate with his fellow workers by hand signals. All day Miller stood beyond the headsaw, his ears bombarded by the piercing sounds of the bandsaw as it sliced through logs, by the explosive puffs of the shotgun feed's exhaust, and by the constant roar of all the other machinery.

But it was a living. A job. Even a kid could get a job. In 1915 John Halkum went to work when he was twelve years old, with his fifteen-year-old brother. "We led jennies pulling carts of lumber from the yard to the planer. We led jennies by the bridle. They put us together and would pay us seventy-five cents for both of us. Seventy-five cents for a ten-hour day."

Many found their life's work in the big sawmill. Others used the sawmill as a stopping place along the road to somewhere else, maybe to something better. Whatever the case, in the Ouachitas around the turn of the century, people began to see that sawmill work for all its drawbacks was better than trying to exist on a hardscrabble farm.

————

Just as the lumber-making technology, job classifications, and levels of pay were pretty well settled by the time the Fourche River mill opened, so also were the corporate structures, financial arrangements, and the economic environment that would govern the lumber industry for the next fifty years.

Though many small and medium-sized sawmills remained as partnerships, built by two men or by several who put up the money, by 1900 the big lumber companies had become corporations, so that instead of partners there were stockholders having limited liability. Those who made money at sawmilling often invested their profits as partners or stockholders in other sawmills, and some of the wealthiest lumbermen held stock in many mills. Usually the controlling stockholder in a big sawmill was president of the company with headquarters in a city that served as an important distribution center for lumber: Chicago, for Fourche River, and especially St. Louis or Kansas City for other companies with mills in the Ouachitas. One of a small group of minority stockholders lived at the mill and managed it. The major stockholder provided general direction and oversight, and the sawmill manager was usually left alone to run the mill.

As lumber companies grew larger, they often needed more money for

Courtesy Earl Page

The Saginaw Lumber company, acquired and expanded by A. J. Neimeyer in 1895, operated the first sizeable mill to cut timber from the Ouachitas, and generated profits that helped Neimeyer establish a larger plant at Little Rock in 1907. Saginaw's mill was on the east bank of the Ouachita River, which was used as a storage pond for logs dumped from trains that came to the west bank. A ferry carried vehicles from the sawmill area to homes on the west side of the river.

"Nothing Makes Money Like a Sawmill"

This adage was coined by Garland Anthony, the long-lived elder of an Arkansas lumber family whose many sawmills included several along

expansion than was available from business associates who had earlier provided capital. Beginning in 1904, the same year that Fourche River started up, bond issues served as a way of borrowing to purchase large blocks of timberland. Lenders (bondholders) put up the money, and as the sawmiller cut his timber, for each thousand board feet he cut he set aside a fixed amount of money to pay the interest and principal of the bonds. Bond issues were usually arranged so that bondholders were repaid in ten years or less, including interest at a generous six percent.[29]

It wasn't long until lenders accepted lumber company bonds not only for purchase of timberlands but also for expansion of sawmills and logging railroads. Bonds were secured by mortgages on standing timber and other assets that could be converted to cash in case of default. Practically every one of the larger operators in the Ouachitas floated a bond issue at some time, and several of them borrowed "to the hilt," mortgaging timberlands, timber cutting rights, sawmill sites, buildings and machinery, railroad trackage, cars and engines—nearly everything those companies owned.

A big mill had to be operated for at least ten years to pay its own cost and insure a profit to the owners. Usually a mill was sized so that it took about twenty years to cut the available timber. By the end of twenty years the mill was paid for, the machinery was worn-out, the timber was all cut, and everybody got out—hence the term "cut out and get out." For a long time the system worked, at least in a narrow economic sense. Companies throughout the industry paid off one bond issue after another, interest and principal, and the bondholders were happy. Often there were large profits after all expenses were paid, so that the partners or stockholders prospered.

But the lumber industry was doomed to have bad years as well as good ones. For every company the goal was not only maximum output but also continuous production: employees needed steady jobs, investors wanted high dividends, and lenders expected full interest and recovery of principal. Even before the turn of the century, everything was in motion; literally thousands of sawmills, large, medium-sized, and small, were making lumber. Their total capacity to produce lumber far exceeded the country's ability to make use of it. Sawmilling had come to resemble farming, another area where thousands of entrepreneurs tended to over-produce on the slightest hope of making a profit.[30]

Lumbering was to experience periods of feast and famine that ran with the booms and depressions of the nation's building industry, which in turn was affected by the state of the national economy. In 1893, for example, a financial panic brought a depression to the building industry so that lumber prices dropped and mills closed. Eventually the economy turned around, and for several years the lumber market kept improving. By 1907 southern pine prices were the highest ever, averaging $17.34 a thousand board feet.

By 1908, however, the industry was in another depression and southern pine had skidded down to $12.50. Low prices remained until late in 1915, when World War I stimulated a boom in which the market sky-rocketed. By 1920 the average price was $46.86, spelling lush prosperity for lumbermen. But in 1921 it plummeted to $22.17 a thousand. The next year it rose to $29.29 a thousand, and for several years through the early 1920s the industry remained healthy, though the $46.86 level of 1920 was not seen again for many years.[31]

Bad times had many bad effects, some of them obvious—unemployment—and some not as easily seen as resulting from a sour economy. During hard times, mill operators had to keep on making lumber, even at a loss, to pay overhead costs, including the interest and principal on bond issues. But much of this lumber could not be sold, and it accumulated and rotted in sawmill yards. With profit margins so narrow, mills also tried to cut costs by taking only the parts of trees easiest to process and yielding the highest-grade, best-priced lumber. Stumps were cut high, the top log of each tree was left in the woods, and there was much waste of timber in other ways as well.[35]

———

Thus the turn of the century in the Ouachitas was a time of encounter between a rural, traditional people and a nationwide, expanding industry. The years around 1900 marked a broad, symbolic boundary between old and new eras in the history of the United States. The nineteenth century was an age of westward expansion and agricultural settlement, and by 1910 the nation's rural population had reached a maximum. The century was also an era of industrial pioneering and railroad development, when the nation's railroad mileage had achieved transcontinental limits. During the nineteenth century the lumber industry grew to im-

the southern edge of the Ouachitas.[32]

Sharing Anthony's belief in sawmilling as a way to wealth were many others who succeeded in the lumber business, or tried to. One was William Blake Barton, who wrote in his memoirs that around 1900: "I moved back to my home town, Cove, Arkansas . . . and I put in a small sawmill. I only had $300 of my own and I borrowed $200 more. I hired a good sawmill man to do the sawing. . . . Labor and timber was cheap and we got busy. . . . I soon began to learn something about the sawmill business and in three months after we started I had made $2,000."

Before long Barton had cut the area of timber close to town that made him the two thousand. Then, he wrote, "My brother-in-law had a tract of timber about six or seven miles out of town that he wanted me to cut. I moved the mill out there. That was a failure as the cost of hauling the timber and a decline in price made me lose most of the money I had made."[33]

Barton kept on sawmilling and prospered in the long run, becoming the wealthiest man in Cove. The sawmillers who survived their reverses often did become well-off. Those who did not became invisible, pursuing other lines of endeavor.

But successful or not, lumbermen could appreciate and share a laugh about another old saying, "If you want to go bankrupt, get into the sawmill business."[34]

mense size; in 1910 lumber was America's largest manufacturing industry in terms of employment, with 700,000 workers. In 1899 the South replaced the Great Lakes region as the nation's leading lumber producing area, and national production continued to rise. From 1904 to 1913, as agricultural and industrial development peaked in the northeastern, central, lake and prairie states, the nation's production of lumber each year exceeded forty billion board feet.[36]

Rural population, railroad mileage, lumber production—those were reaching all-time highs. As the new century began, fundamental change was underway. Wood and coal would soon be overshadowed as the nation's principal sources of motive energy by petroleum and electricity. The new energy would inspire a deluge of innovation, transforming a subsistence economy into a consumer economy and creating a society in which resources of information would be shared and used in ways never before imagined.

———

In 1906 the railroad mentioned by McRae in his letter to Samuel Barney became a reality. Planning to cross the midsection of the Ouachitas, the builders of the Gurdon & Fort Smith Railroad laid track up the Caddo River into the country that McRae had urged his prospective client to visit. Although Barney apparently did not buy timberland, others did. Along the Gurdon & Fort Smith (which in a few years would become part of the Missouri Pacific) three large sawmills were soon under construction. Elsewhere in the Ouachitas, three other substantial mills were being built. From 1906 to 1909 the last extensive virgin forest east of the Rocky Mountains was opened to widespread, large-scale cutting.

The boom was underway, a boom in sawmilling that carried some to their fortunes and swept thousands to new destinies, that removed the old growth virgin forest from the land for all time, that gave the people of that land a new livelihood and, symbolically, a convenient stepping stone on their path from a rural past towards a more modern society.

2. Getting Started

T. W. Rosborough stood and watched the teamsters digging his log pond. A revolving parade of men with mules and fresno scrapers moved along the levee and into the pit, picking up loads of dirt in scraper buckets, walking onto the levee again, dumping their buckets, and going back into the excavation.[1] Rosborough estimated how much levee had been built since his last visit three days ago, and mentally calculated how long it would take to finish: about five weeks. It had to be wide enough for both the railroad and skidway for dumping logs, and high enough for some deep-water storage.

(As Rosborough watched, he was being observed, furtively, by one of the teamsters, fifteen-year-old Carney Bardwell, who had been hired with his mules and was drawing man's wages, fifteen cents an hour, a dollar fifty a day. Carney looked out of the corner of his eye, and thought about the role of the man standing beyond the pit: *Mr. T. W. Rosborough. . . . He's the one that makes things happen. Whatever he does—he sure does it in a big way.* Carney glanced again and saw that the man was leaving.)[2]

Rosborough walked past the site of his planing mill, now following a line of survey stakes toward the tracks of the Gurdon & Fort Smith Railroad. Marking the alignment of a railroad spur into the mill, the stakes had been set by L. D. Williams, a log hauler. Rosborough had learned that Williams was experienced as a surveyor, and had asked him to lay out a line for this short stretch of railroad track. He now noted that Williams' work appeared to be satisfactory.

Rosborough glanced at his pocket watch, continued along the line of stakes—then stopped and looked over to the next hill where several carpenters were framing his new house. Bigger, the head carpenter, had told him that it would be ready in ten weeks. *Gracious damn, he'd better be right. I need to live here. There's too much going on—*

At that moment Rosborough heard a train whistle and resumed walking briskly to a signboard—ROSBORO—beside the Gurdon & Fort Smith tracks. Within a few minutes he flagged the evening train, climbed aboard and began traveling south on his way home to Prescott.

The year before, in 1906, Rosborough and three partners from Kansas City had organized the Caddo River Lumber Company. The man with the largest financial investment in the company was M. R. Smith, who also had lumber interests on the West Coast. Although president of Caddo River, from the beginning Smith had left most of the company's management to others. W. E. Cooper, a lumber salesman with a wide acquaintance among wholesalers and retailers, had a minority interest in Caddo River and was responsible for selling the firm's output of lumber; he was also secretary of the corporation. Lee Wilson, another minority owner, kept the account books in the Kansas City office and served as treasurer. Rosborough, who was probably the second largest stockholder, became vice-president and was to build and operate the sawmill in Arkansas. And now, as Carney Bardwell realized, T. W. Rosborough was making things happen, beginning to build the mill.[3]

Thomas Whitaker Rosborough was a big man over six feet tall, well filled out and weighing more than two hundred pounds. He had an erect, almost military bearing, and was always well dressed, in suit and tie even on his visits to the mill site. His appearance called for proper attention and respect.

Close up, the man was even more formidable. Rosborough knew what he wanted and was not to be argued with. His employees could see it in his face, in the determined line of his mouth, his strong nose, ruddy complexion, and startling blue eyes. They could feel it in his voice—softly accented, southern, but a heavy voice, demanding, insistent. Plainspoken; blunt. And loud. One man remembers that when Rosborough "throwed his voice—he'd just jar the acorns."

Rosborough expected his people to work. He expected them always to be on time. He fired people as readily as he hired them. At the Caddo River Lumber Company, Rosborough's word was law.

Those whom he employed to build his sawmill learned these things and some of the man's habits, too. Rosborough's nervous energy surfaced at times as stammering—uh-uh-uh—as if he were hurrying to say something but couldn't put it together fast enough. He also used an expletive, "Gracious damn," when excited, whether angry or not. But "Hell's fire!" was a sure sign that Mr. Rosborough was mad. In time, however, Rosborough's people would know his gentler side.

T. W. Rosborough's strong personality derived from obvious physical attributes, but just as much from family background and life history. He was born the son of James Thomas Rosborough, a captain in Robert E. Lee's Army of Northern Virginia, and owner of a thousand-acre plantation on the Red River near Texarkana, Texas. James Rosborough had met T. W.'s mother, Martha Parish, at the plantation home of his stepfather, Willis Whitaker. The young lady had come to Texas all the way from Vermont to be a private tutor for Whitaker's children. When the Civil War broke out she remained with the family and embraced the southern cause. Soon after the war she and James Rosborough married. T. W. was born on September 7, 1868, their second child, who would be the only boy among seven sisters.

When T. W. Rosborough had this portrait made about 1910, he was on his way to becoming a major figure of the big-sawmill era in the Ouachitas.

Courtesy Jessie Williams Diamond

On the family plantation young Rosborough became familiar with farm life and the black people who worked and lived on the land. At the family's spacious town house in Texarkana, with its prominently displayed Confederate flag and portrait of General Lee, he received his first schooling from his Yankee mother. She was deeply religious and the family was Episcopalian, so that T. W. at an early age became a member of the Episcopal church. Rosborough, however, would never be particularly religious. In his younger years he liked to have fun, going to dances and perhaps indulging in a few enthusiastic excesses.

In his teens he was sent north to a military school near Chicago, and towards the end of this period he transferred to a preparatory school at the University of the South, an Episcopal institution at Sewanee, Tennessee. After a year in that school and a semester at the university, he dropped out, never to return. It wasn't because of his grades; he had done well enough in all subjects and made high marks in mathematics. But during the last grading period at Sewanee he had collected an unusually large number of demerits for conduct, so it appears he was simply fed up with school.[4] He came home to work in a business owned by his father, the Bowie Lumber Company.

Rosborough—by that time a tall, lanky youth—was made the lumber company's timekeeper, which permitted him to observe the entire operation. After two years at Bowie Lumber Company, Rosborough, twenty-one years old, bought a sawmill of his own for eight hundred dollars. The mill, located on the Cotton Belt Railroad twenty miles west of Texarkana, could cut fifteen thousand feet of lumber a day. Rosborough proudly named it the T. W. Rosborough Lumber Company and got busy learning how to log with oxen and make a sawmill pay. The year was 1889. Much later, he would affirm that it was then that he was bitten hard by the sawmill bug.

After four years he sold his first sawmill and bought another in Louisiana that could cut thirty-five thousand feet a day. He had hardly assumed ownership when the depression of 1893 hit, and lumber prices plummeted. Rosborough lost the mill but was able to pay off his creditors. He then got jobs as a lumber salesman, first at Grandin, Missouri (where he learned more about sawmilling at a big mill there), and later at Wichita, Kansas.

In 1899 the Choctaw, Oklahoma & Gulf Railroad was built across Arkansas and Rosborough moved to the little town of Havana on the new railroad to operate a planing mill. He was past thirty years old by that time, unmarried, room-and-boarding as he pursued his itinerant career in lumber. In Havana he lived with the hospitable family of John Mitchell, the town's doctor, but after two years there moved back to Wichita to become a partner in a wholesale lumber business. Then he went to Kansas City as a lumber wholesaler—still single, still unsettled.[5]

Around 1905, he came back to the town of Prescott, Arkansas, where his sister Elizabeth lived. She had married William N. Bemis, one of a family that had been in lumbering for generations, ever since the eighteenth century. Originating in Massachusetts, they came through western New York to Iowa, and in the 1870s appeared in northeast Texas where they met the Whitaker and Rosborough families. In 1891, James H. Bemis, William's father, and Benjamin Whitaker, one of James Rosborough's half-brothers, established the Ozan Lumber Company at Prescott. Whitaker soon left Ozan for other ventures, but James Bemis and his sons remained. By 1905 they had purchased timber, logged it, and extended the company's logging railroad, the Prescott & Northwestern, from Prescott northward into the southern edge of the Ouachitas.[6] The Ozan Lumber Company—or at least the acreage in timber that Ozan now owned—became large enough for Rosborough to come in and take part. Apparently he first worked for Ozan, though that is not certain. What is certain is that the Bemis family became one of his steadfast and lifelong supporters.

When he moved to Prescott, T. W. Rosborough found that the Bemises were logging about as far north, forty-five miles, as they could go with their railroad. They were out of the flatlands and into the Ouachitas where the line had to wind among the hills, so that the Prescott & Northwestern was now being called by another name: the Pea Vine. A few miles beyond the end of the track, a chain of east-to-west mountain ridges prevented any extension of the railroad farther north. Over those crests, however, more timberland belonged to Ozan. Though beyond reach of the P. & N.W., it was within easy reach from the new Gurdon & Fort Smith Railroad lying to the east.

Rosborough and the Bemises talked things over. Rosborough wanted to get back into sawmilling, his first love. He wanted to build a sawmill on the Gurdon & Fort Smith and cut the timber beyond the mountains. The Bemises agreed to cooperate.

Surprisingly, the Bemises did not become full partners with T. W. in this undertaking. Perhaps they were too much committed to their mill at Prescott, which still had several years' supply of timber south of the mountain barrier. In any case, Rosborough had to look elsewhere for financial backing, and thus formed a corporation with Smith, Cooper, and Wilson from Kansas City. Together they would build a sawmill, acquire some of the Ozan timberland to get started, and would buy more as they began to make money.

After Caddo River was organized as a corporation, Rosborough needed to find a site for the sawmill. He arranged to meet with civic leaders from the town of Amity, located on the Gurdon & Fort Smith directly east of the timberlands that the company would buy. To these men he described his plans for building a lumber manufacturing plant, stating that he would like to buy land at Amity for the mill. The town would benefit from having mill workers who would spend their wages with the local merchants.

"We would rather you not locate here," the town leaders told Rosborough. "We do not want a sawmill. We won't sell you land to build a mill." They did not want transient mill workers, nor did they want blacks. There were no black people in Amity, only a lingering hostility said to have stemmed from an incident in the past when a black person— or someone having Negro ancestry—had caused trouble there while masquerading as a white.[7]

So Rosborough began to look farther along the railroad to the north, and four miles beyond Amity he found a perfect site. Beside the railroad was a level area large enough for the mill, bordered by a creek that could be dammed for the log pond. Houses would have to be built for his employees, but there was room for those, too.

He had no problem buying the two farms that he wanted for the mill site; reportedly, he offered the owners ten dollars an acre, at that time considered more than a fair price. He purchased the land in the name of the Ozan Lumber Company, probably because Caddo River at the time did not have funds. (Caddo River bought the land from Ozan in 1908 after the mill was in operation.)[8]

Rosborough named the new mill and town after himself, simplifying the spelling to Rosboro "for trade and postal purposes," as he later put it. The Caddo River Lumber Company was named for the pretty little river flowing a couple of miles to the north. By 1907 T. W. had established a small sawmill at Rosboro to cut timbers for his big mill, while two carpenters built houses.

In July of that year, Rosborough filed Caddo River's incorporation papers with the state of Arkansas, after the company was incorporated in Missouri. With authorized capital of $450,000, Caddo River would not be the largest lumber company but certainly held a place of second rank.[9] Assuming that stockholders paid in the entire $450,000 in capital, the construction and operating budget may have been approximately as follows, based on prevailing costs:[10]

Sawmill with one band saw, dry kilns, sheds, and planer	$150,000
Housing, commissary, etc., for employees	50,000
Timberland for first several years of operation of mill	100,000
Locomotive, flatcars, etc., and railroad construction	50,000
Mill hands' wages and other initial operating costs	100,000

It was assumed that the mill would be operating with the company selling lumber and making money, before the $450,000 was entirely spent.

As it turned out, 1907 was the first in several years of depressed prices for lumber, and Rosborough and his fellow stockholders must have had some uneasy moments. He did have one advantage, however: the Bemises would hold timberland until he was ready to buy it. (In later years, they actually waited to be paid for timber until after it was cut and marketed as lumber.) Caddo River did not need to have so much money tied up in timberland as, for example, the Dierks Lumber and Coal Company. Timber that Herman Dierks purchased shortly after 1900 would not be cut until the 1930s or even later.

During 1906 and 1907 Rosborough bought timberland or timber cutting rights. From Ozan Lumber Company he first purchased nearly fourteen hundred acres of prime timberland extending three miles west from Rosboro. He paid $14.00 an acre, a high price that may have reflected the fact that the timber was so close to the mill that costs for transporting the logs were lower. To "block in" land that he purchased from Ozan, he bought small tracts. Several of these averaged above $10.00 an acre, and for timber from one tract he paid $1.50 per thousand board feet; by this time the price of stumpage was more than the $1.00 a thousand that McRae had quoted Barney.[11]

In four succeeding purchases from Ozan, Rosborough got about 2,400 acres of timberland and timber for about $1.35 a thousand (assuming an average of five thousand feet per acre). One of these four purchases included timber cutting rights on 200 acres, and the Bemises must have debated about how much time to allow Rosborough to cut the trees. Sellers of cutting rights for timber always required buyers to remove the timber within a specified time: five years, fifteen years, or at the most maybe twenty-five years. Finally the Bemises agreed on a figure and, with a chuckle, wrote it into the timber deed: Rosborough would have ninety-nine years to cut and remove the timber. They would give their brother-in-law a little extra time.[12]

Caddo River then had another neighborly relationship to settle, with the Dierks Lumber and Coal Company, whose timberlands lay just to the west. In May 1908, Hans Dierks drew up a contract between Dierks and Caddo River that began

. . . whereas the parties to this contract are engaged in buying timber in the northern part of Pike County, Arkansas, and they wish to establish a line between them across which neither will buy timber, it is therefore agreed that the following line be established. . . .

The document then described a boundary following land survey lines and the Little Missouri River. Caddo River would purchase no timber to the west of the boundary and Dierks would buy none to the east. Caddo River would sell to Dierks any land or timber they might own or acquire west of the line, and vice versa. Any sale of land and timber under the agreement would be made at $3.50 per thousand board feet of stumpage, based on a timber estimate made by an independent appraiser.[13]

Though this contract may seem to imply that the companies were bent on dividing the territory for conquest, there was nothing illegal about it. Lumber companies frequently made such agreements to delineate areas where they could reasonably expect to block timber and log it by railroad. Limits were often drawn along natural barriers, such as the chain of ridges between Caddo River and Ozan, or the Little Missouri River between Caddo and Dierks. Within any given area that could be logged to one mill, the lumber company owning the most timberland usually prevailed over others having only small holdings.

A month after their dividing line contract was signed, Dierks sold to Caddo River nearly thirty-five hundred acres of timberland and about one thousand acres of timber cutting rights that they owned in Caddo River's area east of the Little Missouri. The price averaged about $7.00 an acre, suggesting that Caddo River did well in this transaction, especially if they were to pay $3.50 a thousand board feet as stipulated in the dividing line contract, for timber in that country averaged considerably more than two thousand feet to the acre.[14] Perhaps in this sale it was not the Bemis connection but the Kansas City relationship that favored Caddo River. With corporate offices in the same building, Caddo River's M. R. Smith and the Dierks brothers surely knew each other and must have been on cordial terms.

Rosborough's block of timberland, most of it still with Ozan and other lesser owners, extended west from Rosboro for approximately twenty miles. From four miles in width at its east end near Rosboro, it widened to twelve miles in the west along the Little Missouri River. To the south lay the ridges bordering Ozan's territory, and to the west lay the Little Missouri and Dierks. An even more imposing natural boundary lay to the north, a line of mountains forming the southern front of one of the most rugged areas in the Ouachitas. Within these limits Caddo River would operate in an area of some 150 square miles. Rosborough could expect to cut most of the timber from portions that he could reach with his railroads, maybe 100 square miles or 65,000 acres.

———

Evidence suggests that Rosborough met and courted his future wife, Winifred Melville, while he lived at Prescott. Possibly introduced by the Bemises, Winifred was English-born, with reddish blonde hair, a nice figure, and a friendly personality. She and Rosborough were married in

June of 1906. The wedding took place at Arkadelphia, a town forty miles up the Iron Mountain Railroad from Prescott toward Little Rock. They may have eloped, gotten off the train there, married, and caught the next train for a honeymoon farther north. Winifred was twenty-seven at that time. Rosborough was ten years older and already much involved in organizing the Caddo River Lumber Company—two reasons why apparently there was no elaborate wedding.[15]

By 1907, along with responsibilities for mill, town, and timber, Rosborough was overseeing the design and construction of his new residence. It was a large bungalow having spacious rooms with ten-foot ceilings, undoubtedly a finer home than any of the country folk around Rosboro had ever known. T. W. and Winnie would have not only a dining room but also a screened porch off the kitchen where they could take meals in the summer. The kitchen itself was provided with ample storage cabinets and a service pantry. There was inside running water in the kitchen and a bathroom—even a second lavatory in one of the bedrooms where Rosborough could shave and tie his necktie in the morning. Next to the lavatory was a feature quite unknown in the rural Ouachitas, a walk-in clothes closet. The house also had such luxuries as papered walls, and a living room wainscot paneled in "curly pine" lumber having an elaborate whorled figure. At the back of the house was a screened sleeping porch where the Rosboroughs could retire on hot summer nights in hopes of catching a breeze. The screened porches, the high ceilings, and some shade trees around the house were the principal means of relief from summer's heat.[16]

In August 1907 the Rosboroughs' first baby was born in Syracuse, New York, where Winifred had gone to be with her sister, Rita, and receive better medical care than existed at Prescott. Surely Rosborough was also there for the birth of his son, Thomas Whitaker Rosborough, Jr.[17] Soon afterwards the family returned to Arkansas and settled into their new home.

Within view of that house, carpenters were putting up dozens of buildings. Teamsters carted loads of material, men with mules hoisted timbers into place for mill sheds, and men and mules pulled heavy crates of machinery from the railroad siding to the new sawmill. Before very long, Rosborough would begin to make lumber.

Other lumbermen would, too. Along with Caddo River, five other companies were building large sawmills in the Ouachitas.

A. J. Neimeyer had looked beyond his mill at Saginaw for another opportunity and found it in the hills west of Little Rock. There he was able to buy sixty-eight thousand acres of timberland from the Iron Mountain Railroad for $7.00 an acre. The area had been bypassed by others who thought it would not yield more than two thousand or twenty-five hundred feet to the acre. On a tip from a friend, Neimeyer looked the country over—and hastened to the railroad people to buy their land. He then hired a timber cruiser to go in and prepare a closer estimate. As Neimeyer expected, the cruiser told him that the land aver-

Courtesy Joe F. Maxey, Daisy Maxey Scoggins, and Geraldine Merriman

aged more than five thousand feet per acre.

Neimeyer's acreage contained nearly 320 million board feet of pine and 80 million of oak, in an area that began only ten miles west of the new Arkansas state capitol building and extended for another twenty-five miles farther west. His agents started buying adjacent tracts and soon the holdings totaled eighty thousand acres. By the summer of 1907 Neimeyer was having two band saws installed in a new mill on the south edge of Little Rock, to be known as the A. J. Neimeyer Lumber Company. Neimeyer was also building a logging railroad named the Little Rock, Maumelle & Western (L.R.M. & W.), which would be chartered as a common carrier.[18]

The Fort Smith Lumber Company had by then cut all the timber within reach of their little mills along the Rock Island Railroad. Extending their Central Railway of Arkansas for six miles beyond the Rock Island to the village of Plainview in the Fourche LaFave valley, they built a sawmill there having one band saw backed by a gang saw to increase production, and in 1908 started up the mill. By that time the Fort Smith Lumber Company owned timber in the hills along the Fourche River, and they started to build a railroad from Plainview into their holdings.

Far to the west and beyond the Dierks timberlands in Oklahoma, the Pine Belt Lumber Company began cutting on the southern edge of the

Timber Family

At Hot Springs, Arkansas, in 1907, the families of recently married John and Mary Maxey line up for a street photographer. John's first wife had died in childbirth, leaving him with six children. Mary's first husband had succumbed to kidney failure, stranding her with five young mouths to feed. John made a bare living by hauling rough lumber by wagon from little mills in the country to a planer in Hot Springs. When he and Mary married they put the four oldest boys, two of his and two of hers, to hauling logs and lumber; they could help support the family.

A few years later, the family arrived at a logging

camp operated by the Caddo River Lumber Company. (In the meantime John and Mary had produced four more children of their own.) John Maxey owned mules and a wagon and became a contract log hauler for Caddo River ("He had the sorriest old mules and harness of anybody").[33] He worked hard but drank hard, too, and gambled long and regularly in the camp's penny ante poker games ("Some days he was loaded with money and some days he was broke").[34] Mary, a tiny woman four feet ten inches tall, stayed busy trying to manage John and bring up the children. She and John eventually ran the big boardinghouse at Mauldin, Caddo River's logging town.

Fourteen children in this family lived to maturity. Every boy, and every girl's husband except one, found employment with the Caddo River Lumber Company as log cutters, log haulers, and sawmill workers. But in the next generation—John and Mary's forty-three grandchildren—only five of the boys went to work in the timber industry, and only a few of the girls' husbands. Among the other grandchildren are an accountant, a banker, a beautician, a bookkeeper, a carpenter, a cattle trader, a chicken farmer, a dress shop owner, military men, school superintendents, teachers, a telephone operator, a union officer, and a welder.

Ouachitas. About 1909 they started up a mill at Fort Towson on the Arkansas & Choctaw Railroad, and laid their own tracks northward into the timber. The company's owners lived in St. Louis and Oklahoma City, too far away it seems in retrospect, for them to know that their timberland would yield little more than three thousand feet per acre in what would prove to be rough, rocky terrain.[19]

Barely four miles up the Gurdon & Fort Smith Railroad from Rosboro, still another big sawmill began operations within months of the start-up of Caddo River's plant. The A. L. Clark Lumber Company had closed a mill at Gilmer, Texas, and moved to Arkansas to cut over the country north of Rosboro, farther into the heartland of the Ouachitas than any of the other big mills had penetrated. A. L. Clark also generated a new town. His lumber company built two blocks of white frame houses for their supervisors along Gilmer Street or Company Street (more often called Silk Stocking Row), and another street of smaller homes for the rank and file on Clay Street (called Candy Street because the houses were covered with boards painted red with white batten strips between them). The company put up little unpainted houses east of the sawmill for black employees, laid out a downtown area with a commissary, and sold lots to other business people and home builders. In 1908 the community was incorporated as the town of Glenwood.[20]

The largest of the six mills built at that time was at Graysonia, on the Gurdon & Fort Smith about fifteen miles south of Rosboro. The principal owner, William Grayson, had been born near Manchester, England; emigrated to St. Louis, Missouri, as a young man; and in 1873 began to manufacture wooden eaves troughs, or gutters, from southern yellow pine. Before long he started making wooden iceboxes as well, and the business became the St. Louis Refrigerator & Wooden Gutter Company. Grayson used so much pine lumber that in 1876 he bought a small sawmill on the Iron Mountain Railroad at Hope, Arkansas. His enterprises grew rapidly, and within eight years he owned three Arkansas sawmills to supply both his plant in St. Louis and a wholesale lumber business that he had organized. Grayson became one of the largest lumber manufacturers in the South and one of the major lumber wholesalers in the entire country, selling not only from his own mills but also from many others. He grew very wealthy, and was worth several millions.[21]

A young man named Nelson Wesley McLeod bought out the smaller stockholders in Grayson's company in 1898, and became a partner in running the business. McLeod was a native of Maine who had come west to Kansas, managed a string of lumberyards in Nebraska, managed A. J. Neimeyer's interests at Texarkana, and continued to advance in lumber sales and financial management until he was able to buy into the St. Louis Refrigerator & Wooden Gutter Company. Four years later, with Grayson and McLeod the only stockholders, the name of the firm became the Grayson-McLeod Lumber Company. Grayson was nearly sixty years old, a heavy man with pale blue eyes and a drooping mustache who preferred to stay out of the limelight and tend to manufacturing.

McLeod was in his early forties, a direct, forceful, persistent man whose specialties were sales and finance.[22]

Shortly before the turn of the century the company had started buying timberland in the southern foothills of the Ouachitas, acquiring some with government scrip, purchasing a large acreage from the Iron Mountain Railroad, and buying a still larger part from homesteaders and dealers in timberland. For seven or eight years Grayson-McLeod continued to buy, until they owned more than a hundred thousand acres containing six hundred million feet of pine timber. Their holdings lay in a broad swath west of the town of Arkadelphia and reached for thirty miles across two counties. In 1907 the company acquired a mill site and began to build the sawmill and its town.[23]

Grayson-McLeod's mill was even larger than Fourche River's. It had two of the heaviest band saws, plus a gang saw that could swallow a squared log and slice it into many boards at one pass; in all, the mill could produce 150,000 board feet a day. To handle the great volume of lumber coming from the sawmill, there were automatic stacking and unstacking machines, replacing an entire crew of human lumber stackers. In the shed where kiln-dried lumber was sorted, boards were separated by length, width, thickness, and grade into a series of bins. Each bin held a stack of lumber fifty-two inches wide and twenty-five inches deep

The Fort Smith Lumber Company's single-band mill at Plainview, Arkansas, was one of six large sawmills built in the Ouachitas between 1907 and 1909.

U.S. Forest Service photo, courtesy Ouachita National Forest

that could be handled as a single unit. These "packages" were picked up by electric hoists traveling on an overhead monorail and delivered to the planing mill or storage sheds. The system of monorail tracks was more than a mile in length. The idea of handling lumber as unit packages, with electric powered equipment, instead of moving it by push-buggy and restacking it by hand, was an innovation that made the mill one of the most labor-efficient of its time, and presaged the unit handling procedures in the lumber industry today.[24]

In other respects the Grayson-McLeod mill was like all others of its day, developed around the nineteenth-century technology of steam power. Most of the sawmill machinery was run from one steam engine that produced a thousand horsepower. As the piston moved back and forth (with so little vibration, it is said, that a silver dollar could stand on its edge on top of the engine), the heavy flywheel pulley turned. From the flywheel, some eighteen feet in diameter, a wide leather belt stretched from the engine room into the sawmill to turn a smaller pulley spinning on a shaft that extended the length of the building. From additional pulleys on this "line shaft," leather belts stretched to the drive pulleys of the band saws, edger, trimmer, and conveyors. The main belt from the steam engine into the sawmill was several feet wide and a half inch thick, laminated from the hides of more than a hundred steers. The belts, steam engine, and line shaft would all soon be made obsolete by the development of electric motors powerful enough to run sawmill machinery.

The town of Graysonia, where nearly eight hundred people lived alongside the mill within a broad bend of the Antoine River, had nearly two hundred houses, three hotels or boardinghouses, a post office, and an ice plant capable of producing twenty-five tons of ice a day. There were separate schools, churches, and recreation buildings for whites and blacks. The white section of town also had a poolroom, a cold drink house, and a barbershop equipped with an electric fan and hot and cold baths.

A few months after the mill started up, an Arkadelphia newspaper editor came to see Graysonia and strolled into the town's new commissary. He found it to be a huge, high-ceilinged room, wide and exceedingly long, with narrow balconies that stretched back along each side. Wandering down broad aisles, he looked into glass display cases filled with men's shoes and ladies' hats, and surveyed counters and shelves stocked with ready-to-wear and yard goods, hardware and groceries. Behind every counter stood a salesperson. On one of the balconies were stacks of skinny-legged wooden chairs, a row of dressers with fancy mirrors, and many other pieces of furniture.

Scattered around the interior were artificial palm trees with tall straight trunks and bushy tops, a touch of elegance. At intervals in the middle of the aisles were cast-iron radiators to warm the building in winter, and above each one was a ceiling fan to circulate heat, or to stir the warm air of summer. Here and there along the aisles were cuspidors.

Back in the grocery department was a separate room for flour, holding

Courtesy Mr. and Mrs. James Rosborough Bemis

as much as a freight car load at one time. At the rear of the building was a meat market, screened against flies, where Mr. Bethea, the butcher, sliced and sawed for waiting customers. Bethea offered smoked side bacon, smoked ham, shoulders of pork, and quarters of fresh beef. For his ham and bacon, hung in a long storeroom, he had gone to nearby farmers and purchased a hundred hogs.

The commissary also carried feed for draft animals and livestock, replacement parts for the mill, equipment for the loggers, and everything else from baby dresses for the newborn to funeral goods for the deceased. Cavanaugh C. Jackson, the manager, was understandably proud of his establishment. He told the newspaper man that his commissary had a stock that cost $30,000 and did a business of more than $10,000 a month.[25]

In 1910, not long after the editor's visit, *American Lumberman* reported that "Graysonia has been made what many sawmill towns are not—a habitable neighborhood . . . with opportunities for recreation and self-improvement. . . ." The *Lumberman* also noted that the Grayson-McLeod Lumber Company had "timber resources to cut for twenty years. . . ."[26]

———

All six of those big mills—at Rosboro, Little Rock, Plainview, Fort Towson, Glenwood, and Graysonia—were built within the span of three years between 1906 and 1909. The older companies in the region were

At Graysonia, slabs from the sawmill (right) were worked up into barrel staves, while sawdust, shavings, and other scraps were conveyed to the fuel house (left) to be stored until burned under the boilers of the power plant (center).

Ways of Waste

"When the A. L. Clark Lumber Company was here, they didn't think they would ever run out of timber. And so they cut just any way they wanted to. Cut the best and leave the rest."[27]

Clark ran out of timber and closed his mill at Glenwood in 1921, but even after World War II, lumber companies generated huge amounts of waste. About two-thirds of the

wood which grew in the tree was discarded. It was left as stumps, limbs, and tops in the forest, or removed as slabs, edgings, trimmings, sawdust, shavings, and cutoffs in the sawmill and planing mill.

Many of the larger mills were able to recover a portion of their waste, converting slabs, for example, into plastering lath. Graysonia sawed slabs into as many as ten thousand barrel staves each day. Caddo River, Dierks, and others had "reworking plants" where pieces of waste wood were fashioned into ladder rungs, toy parts, mop handles, cantaloupe crates, or anything else for which there was a profitable outlet. But the hundreds of small mills existing in the Ouachitas could not afford to do this.

Every mill generated so much refuse that it became a major operation just to get rid of it. That which could not be made into marketable products or given away as firewood was burned under the mill's boilers. What could not be used as boiler fuel was conveyed to a waste burner, an open pile or a silo-like structure where a fire burned year-round, day and night. At small mill sites, sawdust was heaped into piles that often remained for decades after the mills had moved on.

As long as timber was abundant and lumber was cheap, it was not economically possible to prevent waste. In 1915, William L. Hall, speaking for the

expanding too, and building their railroads farther into the timber. By 1909, eleven lumber companies were logging by railroad in the Ouachitas. Five of their sawmills were large enough to have one band saw, and five more were equipped with two.

The year 1909 that marked the climax of lumber's most frenetic period of expansion into the Ouachitas also happened to be the all-time high year for lumber production in Arkansas, the South, and the entire United States. Arkansas manufactured 2.1 billion board feet, becoming the fifth ranked state in the nation. The South produced 16.3 billion feet, while the entire United States reported production of 44.5 billion feet.[29]

It was an exciting time for lumbermen, especially in the Ouachitas where they were building sawmills and establishing cutting rights around much of the region's perimeter. About that time, however, a significant change took place in the status of the public domain that still existed in the Ouachitas' central core, for there the public's cutting rights were given precedence.

On December 18, 1907, President Theodore Roosevelt issued a proclamation based on an Act of Congress on March 3, 1891, the original authorization for the president to create national forests. Roosevelt "reserved from settlement or entry and set apart as a public reservation, for the use and benefit of the people" most of the public land remaining within the Ouachitas Mountains in Arkansas. The new reservation was to be known as the Arkansas National Forest.

Roosevelt acted on the advice of his Forest Service chief, Gifford Pinchot, who in turn was following the recommendations of the man whom he had sent to inspect the public land, William L. Hall. After his journey through the region, Hall provided his chief with a graphic description of the federal unappropriated lands in the Ouachitas, stressing their lack of value for agricultural homesteads and the existing and future potential as a source of timber. Thus Hall, in recommending that the public domain in the Ouachitas should remain in public ownership and management, triggered the creation of the first national forest in the South, which, in 1926, was renamed the Ouachita National Forest.[30]

Roosevelt and Pinchot operated at the forward edge of a new movement called conservation. Both men were well aware of a growing public belief that the nation's natural resources had to be protected for the use of future generations as well as the present, and both believed in taking direct action to defend the resources on public lands. They set aside the Arkansas National Forest for the same reasons that they created many other reserves during Roosevelt's administration: to protect navigable streams (such as the Ouachita River) from being damaged by erosion in their upper watersheds, and especially to insure a perpetual supply of timber.

Pinchot's U.S. Forest Service had become a full-fledged land managing agency only in 1905, hardly ready to take on management of another national forest, given such thin resources of staff and operating funds. On creation of the Arkansas National Forest, about all that Pinchot could do was send a qualified supervisor to Arkansas with instructions to become better acquainted with the forest and its needs for management.

T. W. Rosborough soon heard about the creation of the national forest but probably felt that it was not his concern (though it would be, very much so, in later years). He faced several problems related to getting a sawmill in operation, including one in the area of employee welfare. Some of the whites who lived around Rosboro were threatening the black people he brought in to work at his new mill. While there is no record of exactly why whites feared the presence of the black workers, probably their anxiety was based on both economic and social factors. Blacks would take jobs that whites might otherwise have, and the blacks' behavior might somehow disturb the whites. There had not been any blacks living around Rosboro, and some of the whites preferred to keep it that way.

Rosborough had handpicked his black workers, relying on the knowledge of the Bemises and others to employ those who had sawmill experience. Blacks were to work only at the mill, not in the logging operation, for loggers had to live in camps in the woods where blacks would be even more vulnerable to harm from neighboring whites.

The first black employees to arrive at Rosboro had to live in tents. Since threats kept circulating, Rosborough built a high board fence around them, with gates that could be locked against intruders, and employed trustworthy white men to stand guard over the compound at night.[31] After a while the threats died down and the workmen and their families moved into the new houses in Rosboro's black neighborhood. This section of town, typical of others like it, was called the Colored or Negro Quarters, Colored or Negro Town, or just plain Nigger Town. At Rosboro the Colored Quarters lay east of the mill, just beyond the Gurdon & Fort Smith Railroad, with little unpainted houses close to the tracks.

By the time the first black families moved in, the rest of Rosboro had taken form. Farther up the railroad and across the tracks from the Quarters, a depot, boardinghouse, office, and commissary had been built. To the west stood Rosborough's residence, and homes for the higher paid people at the mill. South along the road toward Amity were three- and four-room houses, much alike, for the white workers. Except for the Rosboroughs, the town's residents used outhouses, and fetched their water from wells drilled in each neighborhood. Electric lights and buildings for a church and a school would come later.

Rather than put any finishing touches on the town, Rosborough wanted to complete the sawmill, for it was needed to generate income. He also needed to start building a logging railroad, but first he wanted to talk to L. D. Williams, the log hauler who had done a satisfactory job of laying out the spur into the mill site.

Rosborough's first impression of Louis DeElliot Williams must have been that the man was just another rustic. Williams had grown up on a farm about twenty-five miles south of Rosboro and had gotten only a grade school education before becoming a log hauler, with wagon and mules, at various sawmills along the southern edge of the Ouachitas. When he came to Rosboro he was in his early thirties, six feet tall with

U.S. Forest Service, remarked that lumbermen would bring out of the forest and sell all the material they could handle without loss. When prices were low, there was twenty-five or thirty percent more waste left in the woods. They were forced to leave in the woods or burn at the mill anything that could not be sold for at least its cost of manufacture.

Hall then suggested that waste could be eliminated by utilizing the small and odd-sized pieces, by working up all species of trees, and by combining the harvest for all uses. Said Hall, "Some of the large sawmills might profitably add box factories. . . . Others should put in pulp mills . . . {or} preservative treatment plants. . . ."[28]

Except for a few reworking plants that existed at the largest mills, no effective means to stop waste existed until the 1950s when lumbermen began to install machinery to convert their refuse into chips for making pulp and paper. Then, as the prices of timber and lumber continued to rise, sawmillers everywhere equipped themselves to sell pine and hardwood waste as chips. In addition, new markets developed for wood treated with preservatives, and large mills began to harvest and utilize the entire stem of the tree.

By the 1980s, every one of William L. Hall's suggestions voiced in 1915 had been put into practice.

The sawmill that T. W. Rosborough built at Rosboro in 1907 was a typical single-band mill of its day. Logs were pulled from the pond up the incline into the second floor of the mill. The penthouse atop the sawmill contained the filing room where saws were sharpened. At left is the boiler house with its high smokestack.

straight black hair and a black mustache that covered a scar on his lip. He was not very talkative.

Rosborough found, however, that Williams would readily discuss business matters, and he did know how to survey for a railroad. Also, Williams did not smoke or drink. In fact, L. D. seemed not to socialize at all; he spent his after-work hours at home with his wife and five children. His wife, Effie, was more of a talker and social person, but her main interests were home and children, garden and cow, and the Baptist church. Rosborough saw a stable family life which indicated that Williams might be a good man for the long pull.[32]

He talked with Williams. The mill was to be running before long, and there was only a small amount of timber close enough to be hauled to the mill by wagon. A railroad had to be built farther into the timber west of town, and construction had to be started as soon as possible. Rosborough wanted Williams to lay out and oversee the building of the railroad.

L. D. agreed to take the job, unaware, at the time, that he would be logging with the Caddo River Lumber Company for the rest of his long working career.

3. Growing Up

L. D. Williams proved fully capable as a railroad locator and surveyor, and Rosborough quickly learned more about him. Williams could do figures in his head faster than most men could do them on paper, and Rosborough respected such ability; he himself liked to do mental arithmetic. Perhaps, thought Rosborough, Williams could estimate timber, as well as plan and coordinate the logging.

Rosborough needed someone to run his woods operation; he had no time to do it himself. Every phase of logging—building railroads, cutting logs, and transporting them—had to move in the proper sequence to keep timber coming to the sawmill without letup. Otherwise, the mill would face a shutdown. Rosborough decided to make Williams logging superintendent, in overall charge of getting raw material to the mill.

Again Williams proved capable and the logging proceeded without any major problems. The railroad main line and spurs were pushed farther and farther west from the mill and before long a small army of loggers and railroad builders were working for the company. Many of the new employees had worked in logging elsewhere. Many more, though, came from farms along the company's railroad.

One of the locals who went to work for Caddo River was a youngster named Virgil Smalling. His father was a farmer who had become one of the lumber company's log haulers, leaving Virgil and his brothers to take care of the farm. Recalling those days, Smalling says: "We farmed there for a year or two . . . and finally, I wanted to work on public works. I wanted to do something. I didn't want to farm. I just kept on belly-aching and quarreling about wanting to work and I was too young and Daddy wouldn't let me work."

Eventually Virgil's father talked to one of the lumber company bosses. As it happened, there was another boy about his age, the son of Tom Boyd, the railroad construction foreman, who also wanted to go to work. The boss said he would talk to Boyd.

"Well, he seen Old Man Tom, and told him to pick me up, and put me to work and put his boy to work but don't let us tote no crossties, nothing like that. [Tom Boyd was told to] make us peddle spikes for them to drive down or something that was light work that we could do, and marking off for the ties to be laid down. And I went to work in the steel gang, building railroads down through Pike County. I went to work for them when I was a little over thirteen years old. And it wasn't long until we could do any of it. Old Man Boyd kept us busy for a year or two, and then we went to catching all of it, doing everything."

Many on the steel gang were not much older than Virgil. Glen Roberts, who went to work for "Uncle Tom" Boyd when he was seventeen, remembers the crew: "Just boys . . . most down to eighteen. The old man liked to work boys because the boys didn't argue with him. Boyd was strictly boss. He'd fire you, too. But the old coot, he'd fire a guy, and hire him back in a week or two."

Tom Boyd was rough-talking and "bad to get drunk," as one man recalls, but he was likeable, and he got the work done. "All right, lay your hands on it!" he hollered, and ten of his boys hastened to a pile of rails beside the tracks, dragged one off the pile, and lined up in pairs along the rail, each pair holding a set of big tongs called scissors. "Lay your hands on it—" The ten stooped, lifted the rail with the scissors, stumbled forward and dropped it on a push car. Soon the greenhorns in the crew learned the motions. They weren't hard to learn, just god-awful hard work—and the push car was soon fully loaded with rails.[1]

Next the crew attacked a pile of crossties, with one or two of the younger boys helping to lift them onto the shoulders of the older ones. Each carried a tie eight feet long, as much as two hundred pounds of green oak if it was new, somewhat less heavy but often wet and dirty if it was salvaged from another dismantled railroad spur. The boys staggered to the push car with their ties, and in a few minutes had them stacked on top of the rails. Now the car was moved up to the end of track.

Several of the crew unloaded the ties, dropping them along the grade, while others scraped and scooped with shovels. Once the ties were aligned and bedded, it was time to put down rails.

Ten men slid a rail off the car and with scissors carried it forward and lowered it into position. At the order "Joint back!" they shoved the rail against the end of the one already in place, and a younger boy quickly ran bolts through the angle bars that tied the rails together. At the same time, another rail was jointed back alongside the first one. Two pairs of spikers moved in, a left-hander and a right-hander for each rail, and with ten-pound mauls they hammered down the spikes, one inside and one outside each rail for each crosstie. Behind the leading hammer man, a boy held the gauge to make sure the rails were the right distance apart. Archie Taylor, who started driving spikes for Boyd when he was eighteen years old, recalls that the hammer men on the two rails would "both try to get out to the end at the same time, so they could roll this push car up, and slide us off a rail. And that's the way we kept two rails going, side by side."

For every mile of rail put down, there was a mile taken up, after the timber in an area was cut. Though the main line to the mill remained in

Courtesy Fred M. Dierks

place for years, many spur tracks into cutting areas lasted less than six months, sometimes less than three. Taking up a railroad was, if anything, more disagreeable work than building one. A former crewman remembers: "We pulled the steel first. Took five sets of scissors pulling that steel, two men on a scissors. Ran with the rail to the flatcars. Saved all the spikes. Then we picked up them ties and carried them up there. That was the awfullest job, pickin' up them old muddy ties. Had to pry them out, belly 'em up again' your belly. . . .

"Oh, it was a hard job. That was the hardest work I guess there was."[2]

Apparently Tom Boyd was the only foreman with Caddo River Lumber Company who consistently employed boys younger than eighteen for heavy labor. From all accounts, however, a constant parade of farm boys sought and at times got jobs with other lumber companies. Dierks hired workers as young as eighteen, and the A. L. Clark Lumber Company employed them as young as fourteen to maintain their railroads. Caddo River eventually refused to keep anyone on the job who was not twenty-one, but would relent and employ a minor if he were "manualated," meaning that his parents had signed a waiver preventing them from suing the company if their minor son was killed or injured at work. (As it happened, a number of Caddo River's employees were killed or seriously injured on the job, but none of the accidents involved minors.)

The steel gang performed only the last act in building the railroad, a

A railroad spur on Dierks timberland in Oklahoma, around 1930. Lumber companies ran spurs up the bottoms of valleys, for easier construction and the advantage of moving logs downhill to the tracks. Spurs were temporary, and construction was only good enough to prevent engines and cars from derailing too often.

process that, in all, could take several years.

After Rosborough and L. D. Williams decided to cut timber in a particular valley at a certain time, the railroad locator walked up the valley to mark a route. He tried to stay on the level bottomlands where ties and tracks could be laid without excavating or filling. Sometimes he would find a canyon so narrow that the railroad had to go along the bed of the creek. Such a place would be railroaded and logged in the summer when the creek ran dry.

The survey crew then laid out the alignment and grades for the track, and figured how deep the cuts and fills had to be. Surveyors usually camped near their work area.

The company contracted with local people to clear the path staked out by the surveyors. Lewis McCauley recalls that in 1914 he and his brother cut trees and brush and removed debris from the right-of-way for the Caddo River railroad, and were paid ten dollars an acre.

Then came a big crew of mule drivers to build the railroad grade. First the "powder monkey" set charges of dynamite, broke up rock, and blew out stumps. Wherever there was a cut in a hillside to be made for the railroad, men loosened the soil and broken rock with oversized plows, at times pulled by as many as six mules, with one man holding the handles while three or four others rode on top to weigh it down.

Behind the plows came drivers with two-mule teams pulling "wheeler slips," scoops balanced between two wheels as big around as wagon wheels, scooping up dirt and moving it short distances from high areas to low ones. If a wheeler slip got into heavy rock, the driver called for help from the "hook team," three big mules whose harness pulled a heavy chain with a hook. After attaching the hook to the wheeler slip, the driver gave a command and all five mules slowly dragged the scoop forward into the broken rock. Mules on the hook team often weighed eighteen hundred pounds each. Fred Jones, who worked on a grade crew, remembers: "They had some of the finest mules I ever saw. They were tremendous mules." Sam Anderson, another grade crew man, recalls that in all, the crew had at least twenty teams—forty mules.[3]

Besides the many mule drivers and the powder monkey, the grade crew employed a blacksmith who replaced plow points, repaired the wheeler slips, and kept the mules shod. An old man whom everyone called "the corral dog" fed the mules and doctored their scalded shoulders and sore necks where harnesses had rubbed. The water jack, or water boy, dipped a bucket in the nearest creek and brought it to the crew. Everybody drank out of the same dipper, which tasted of chewing tobacco.

The grade crew's foreman had to keep track of this menagerie, which at times was spread out for a mile or more along the right-of-way; one foreman always rode his little bay horse at a long lope to get from one part of the job to another. The foreman also had to see that his crew had lodging. Sometimes the men camped in abandoned farmhouses, but usually they stayed in tents that were hauled in wagons from one site to the next. When the company grew more prosperous, the tents had wooden floors and the crewmen and their families lived in them year round, with heating stoves and furniture. The crew built grade for about three miles in each direction from a campsite.

L. D. Williams tried to schedule operations to give a new roadbed time to settle, allowing two or three years if possible, so that it would be solid for laying track. During this interval the company sometimes contracted with local farmers to build drainage culverts along the new grade. Usually a contractor worked with a helper, cutting oak trees near the railroad and dragging the material to the culvert sites. The simplest culverts consisted of two logs for the sidewalls with short logs laid across for the roof. On main line railroads that would be used for several years, culverts were built from oak timbers hewn with a broadax and fitted and spiked together to form open-ended boxes under the railroad.

To cross larger streams and gullies, the company's bridge gang built bridges and trestles. After track had been laid to a construction site, the crew cut heavy timbers from nearby trees, and a locomotive moved them into place. At many streams, however, they avoided building bridges and simply laid timbers in the streambed, fastening railroad ties and rails to them. Floodwaters would flow over these "low water bridges" without damaging the track.

Every mile of logging railroad required nearly three thousand crossties, and Caddo River contracted with dozens of local men to make them. These tie-hackers, usually working in pairs, felled oak trees that stood near the railroad, cut them into eight-foot lengths, squared the logs with broadaxes, and piled the ties alongside the tracks. Tie-hacking was hard work and there may not have been enough men willing to do it, for eventually Caddo River used portable sawmills to produce ties, and also built a tie mill along the railroad at Rosboro. (The cluster of houses the company built at the Rosboro site came to be called Tie Town.) The company took up and reused crossties from one logging spur to the next, but they were not treated against decay or termites, and had to be replaced frequently.

————

Caddo River started out with a gear-driven Shay logging locomotive, very powerful for its size and able to pull loads up steep grades. The Shay, however, made a rattling noise like machine gun fire, so loud that it could be heard for miles, and the crewmen didn't like it. It was also disgustingly slow; fifteen miles an hour was about top speed. In 1911 the company purchased a conventional steam locomotive to replace the Shay. They used engine Number 2 (more often called the Two-Spot or the Deuce) to pull the log trains to Rosboro.

There was another reason for buying a faster locomotive. Rosborough's railroad had been chartered by the state as a common carrier, licensed to haul passengers and freight as the trunk lines did. An advantage in having a chartered railroad was that Caddo River could employ eminent domain if necessary to acquire right-of-way. The primary benefit was that the chartered railroad could share in freight revenues with trunk lines that carried lumber from the Rosboro mill to market. This revenue shar-

Baldwin Locomotive Works photo, courtesy John M. Martin

The Caddo River Lumber Company purchased this rod-driven engine in 1911 to replace a slower Shay locomotive for hauling logs from the woods to the Rosboro mill.

ing was based on the idea that Caddo River's short line performed an integral part in shipping the company's lumber from its original source to the final destination.

Rosborough had named his line the Caddo & Choctaw Railroad Company, perhaps imagining that someday the tracks would go all the way to the Choctaw Nation. (Actually the old Choctaw boundary, the Oklahoma state line, lay only fifty-five miles west of Rosboro.) In any case, he felt that his railroad would open Caddo River's cutover lands for development as farms and orchards. Already, Rosborough knew, his in-laws the Bemises were hauling freight car loads of peaches on their Pea Vine railroad. With agricultural development along the Caddo & Choctaw, he reasoned, towns also could develop.

So inspired, Rosborough decided to push things faster. He enlisted a few associates and in 1911 platted a townsite twelve miles west of Rosboro.[4] Soon Rosborough built a railroad spur into the site, which was named Cooper, and there he put up a railroad station.

In time he realized he was mistaken. Nobody bought Caddo River's hilly, infertile cutover land, and nobody came to live at Cooper. Rosborough gave up and had the little railroad station boosted onto a flatcar and hauled in to Rosboro, where it could be used as an office.

The only "towns" that did spring up along the Caddo & Choctaw were Caddo River's own camps for their employees. The largest of these communities, which was moved every few years as the center of logging activity shifted from one area to another, had a collection of little portable houses for log cutters and some of the railroad maintenance workers. It also had a small commissary (a branch of the main store at Rosboro) and a group of portable buildings used collectively as a boardinghouse ("the hotel") for single men. Elsewhere, along railroad spurs where timber was being cut, there were smaller camps of portable houses

Sidney Streator photo for *American Lumberman,* courtesy Forest History Society

Logging superintendent L. D. Williams sits atop a trainload of logs awaiting the trip to Caddo River's sawmill at Rosboro in 1913. Williams was responsible for moving a steady flow of raw material like this to the mill.

for the log haulers.

As it turned out, the Caddo & Choctaw carried most of its passengers for free. At least once a year, everyone who lived along the railroad was invited to ride to Rosboro for a big celebration. The annual Fourth of July picnic developed into an all-day affair to which people brought basket lunches. The company provided free ice water and band music and brought in notables who spoke on important topics of the day (mostly agricultural subjects, since nearly everybody had some interest in farming). The company programmed a baseball game between the Rosboro team and one from another mill town, and held races and contests for all who wanted to take part.[5]

As Caddo River prospered, Rosborough arranged for other kinds of excursions. Around 1920 all of the company's employees and neighbors along the railroad were invited to Rosboro to see a moving picture show. Horace Russell, who then was about seven years old, remembers riding there on a flatcar: "Everybody brought quilts and blankets or whatever they had, and they spread 'em on the edge, and you could either set up on the side and hang your feet off, or you could set back in the middle of the flatcar." Russell remembers that the engineer eased his train forward at ten or fifteen miles an hour, stopping frequently to pick up more passengers. Trash and cinders blew from the flatcars and locomotive; children cried because they'd gotten cinders in their eyes.

At Rosboro the crowd found a large tent had been set up for the movie. After dark, the movie began. "Some Western show," Russell recalls, "I know there was a lot of cowboys in it. They would run a reel, and then they had to shut it down till they put on another reel. They had a lady up there on a piano; she'd set there and play music while they changed the reels. . . ."

It was late by the time the movie was over and everyone got aboard the train again: "'Course all the kids were sleepy, and they had to make beds, pallets on the flatcars for the kids to sleep on. So there was really not much commotion going back, because most of the children were asleep. 'Course myself, I never batted an eye. I had to be sure that I didn't miss anything.

"'Course that was the talk for a long, long time after that, about that movie, and all those things that we saw in that movie. We were just children, but there were quite a few older people that had never seen a movie before."[6]

Aside from excursions to Rosboro, social activities at the logging camps were about the same as they were on a farm: Saturday night square dances, and Sunday services at neighborhood churches. Even at Rosboro, social life was limited. The company had built a church building where Baptist and Methodist preachers held services on alternate Sundays, and there was a schoolhouse where pupils gave programs and plays. Upstairs in the school, the Woodmen of the World held lodge meetings. Some of Rosboro's youngsters got together at home to learn the Charleston to music from a Victrola, but such things as dancing and card playing were not done in public. It is said that some of the leading women of the church saw to that; in any case, there was no dance floor available. Social life consisted largely of ice cream parties and similar events, or sitting on the front porch visiting with friends.

Beyond the mill and the railroad tracks, Rosboro's black people got along in a less formal way. Like blacks in Graysonia, Glenwood, and other sawmill towns, they had a Barrel House, a recreation building where they could drink home brew and dance without anyone objecting. Mr. Rosborough decreed, however, that whites were not to visit the Barrel House, or anywhere else in the Colored Quarters.

On the surface, relations between the races were amicable, but an undercurrent of resentment remained among whites in the country around Rosboro who felt that blacks had taken their jobs, and that Rosborough favored blacks. ("He'd turn white men away and hire a nigger," says a white who lived at Rosboro.)[7] Eventually some of the local whites became emboldened. One night, men on horses rode through Rosboro and dropped leaflets saying that the blacks were to get out, or they would get hurt. Rosborough promptly called the leaders of the black community into the lumber company office and handed them several rifles. If any

Bardwell photo, courtesy *The Looking Glass*

Bardwell photo, courtesy *The Looking Glass*

Rosboro Folks

On Sunday afternoons while the people of Rosboro were at leisure, Carney Bardwell and his uncle B. Bardwell, the town's unofficial photographers, made their rounds, took pictures, and sold postcard sized prints.

Portraits which the Bardwells made during the 1910s and 1920s suggest the social workings of a sawmill community of that period. Many of Rosboro's residents came from farms where they had known very little cash income, and wages at the mill opened for them a new world of consumer goods. The pay was small but food and housing were cheap, so that ladies could afford some dress-up clothes, young dudes could tote pistols, and a few people could own cars.

About half of Rosboro's people were blacks. Posing for these portraits beside the unpainted buildings of Rosboro's Colored Quarters, they are a varied group in hand-me-downs or Sunday best, packing guns or holding aloft a Bible.

While blacks were at the bottom of the economic ladder, a small number of whites, also from money-poor rural backgrounds, had begun to climb a few rungs. Logging superintendent L. D. Williams, his wife and six children belonged to the group in Rosboro having higher incomes.

Bardwell photo, courtesy *The Looking Glass*   Bardwell photo, courtesy *The Looking Glass*

outsider came into the Quarters to harm the blacks, he told them, they were to protect themselves.[8] ("Old Man Rosborough didn't go for that, beatin' his niggers," says a white who worked at Rosboro.)[9] In time the furor died down, but the blacks long remembered what Rosborough had done for them.

Rosborough, however, remained a person of his own time; he never attempted to change the prevailing separation of the races. He did feel responsible for protecting his black employees, one reason being that he wanted the best sawmill men he could find, regardless of color. He would probably have agreed with an observer who wrote in 1895 that "the average negro, unspoiled by education and life in the city, was, if dealt with properly, the best type of mill labor, as patient as an ox and as reliable as a steam engine. All he wanted was fair treatment, plenty of food, and a chance to frolic occasionally."[10]

One Rosboro resident recalls: "The niggers done most of the stacking of the lumber. Most of the work they done was drudgery work that white people wouldn't do."[11] That was true, but as a lumber journalist once explained, "There has never been as precise a separation of jobs into 'white man's job' and 'negro job' in the lumber industry as in many other industries."[12] Black men stacked the heavy green lumber, but whites at

Bardwell photo, courtesy *The Looking Glass*   Bardwell photo, courtesy *The Looking Glass*

times stacked lumber alongside the blacks, for the same pay. At Rosboro and in other mills, blacks as well as whites graded lumber, operated the edgers, and dogged and even set blocks on the carriages. All of those jobs required good reflexes and sure judgment. One southern mill superintendent noted, "Many Negroes, although unable to read and write, perform complicated operations that require quick mental calculations and exceptional skills. . . ."[13]

Rosborough realized that employing blacks made economic sense, but he also liked black people. Admittedly, he practiced a kind of benevolent paternalism that would today be unacceptable. McKinley Williams, a black who worked at Rosboro, recalls: "I never heard him say Negro—or 'nigger'—in my life. They were all his boys. If he didn't say 'my boys' he said 'my darkies'."

Though patronizing as "my darkies" sounds today, it does not have the demeaning tone adopted by an editor of the newspaper at the nearby town of Glenwood, writing in 1916, at a time when Glenwood's sawmill employed blacks:

> In regard to the negro population already here . . . they are that class of
> colored people known, even among themselves, as "white man's niggers" and

Bardwell photo, courtesy *The Looking Glass*

Bardwell photo, courtesy Velma Oden Merritt

Bardwell photo, courtesy *The Looking Glass*   Bardwell photo, courtesy *The Looking Glass*

give little trouble, often much less than others who should know better, and these negroes, while they still retain most if not all of the ordinary vices of their race, indulge these only to their own personal detriment and to that of one another and the white man is seldom his victim. The nigger here, as in the Carolinas and elsewhere south, with considerable mortality and fatality to his race, has learned the salutary lessons of politeness and general consideration of what he concedes to be the superior race, whose representations will make him a good nigger, if he starts in to be a bad one. That's understood fully by both races, and is part of the code of unwritten law.[14]

Rosborough, though conservative, was not cut from the same cloth as the Glenwood editor. He was of the southern gentry, with a Yankee mother and northern schooling, and besides, he had always known black people on his family's plantation. Blacks were aware that he liked them, did not think he took advantage of them, and regarded Rosborough with affection.

Blacks were no different from whites in believing that sawmill work was better than farm life or menial employment elsewhere. By stacking lumber and being paid by the thousand board feet, a black could make more money in less time than did many whites. D. C. Blackmon re-

Bardwell photo, courtesy Max A. Williams

members black lumber stackers at Glenwood: "They'd just throw that
stuff down there and kick it in place. They worked in a hurry. You'd see
'em goin' home about three o'clock."

Employees working for hourly wages on the production line in the
sawmill and planer had to hurry along at their tasks amid the noise of
machinery; they had no opportunity to express any individuality. But
black lumber stackers, in quieter areas of the outside yard, lumber sheds,
and loading dock, were able to develop a style. Floyd Kimble remembers
"Negroes loading boxcars, singing in rhythm, making a tune, bouncing
them boards. . . ."

Rosborough got up before daybreak. By seven in the morning, when the
ten-hour workday began, he was at the mill talking with the men. Later

he might visit the Rosboro school, or stop at the home of the new preacher to get acquainted; a good mill man looked after his people's welfare. On some days he went to the woods, dropping in on the railroad grade crew (where he always took a few minutes to pet the mules and rub their noses), or stopping to chat with workers on the steel gang, or going with L. D. Williams to look at timber. Sometimes he was able to stop at the Cooper townsite, where he ate dinner with Aunt Lizzy and Uncle Jim Williams, a farm couple who boarded some of Caddo River's logging employees. Aunt Lizzy's meals were sumptuous and Rosborough liked to indulge, as his expanding waistline showed.[15]

Every person he met during these rounds knew that Rosborough was the man in charge—*Mister* Rosborough. He had a way with people, though, a quality of charismatic leadership. He would sit down and visit with the humblest worker, whether white or black, and get acquainted with him, and learn and remember the man's name. Moreover, if someone became ill or had misfortune in his family, Rosborough circulated a sheet of paper, with his name first, on which every signer indicated an amount to be taken from his next paycheck, for the company to hand over to the needy person. Since health insurance and workmen's compensation were not yet available, people still helped one another as friends and neighbors in their own communities.

Rosborough's wife, Winifred, also took the same friendly, almost maternal, interest in people. Velma Merritt, then a young girl at Rosboro, remembers: "It made no difference how poor anyone was, if they needed help, she went and helped them. She carried food to the sick; visited the sick."

In an Arkansas sawmill town, Winifred lived a life far removed from what she had known in England and the East. Rosborough worked six days a week, but on Sundays, or in the twilight of long summer days, he took her for walks through the silent mill with Whit, their little son. Her sister Rita occasionally came down from Syracuse to visit, but otherwise all of Winnie Rosborough's world was close at hand. When Whit was four years old, she learned she was going to have another baby.

Then the worst happened. Winifred miscarried and hemorrhaged. Nobody knew what to do. On June 30, 1912, six years and two days after she and T. W. had married, she died. Winifred was thirty-four years old; Rosborough was then forty-three.

One of Rosborough's sisters, Nelle Beidelman, whose husband worked for Ozan Lumber Company at Prescott, came to Rosboro to help ease the transition. Rosborough talked to her about wanting to keep his son there with him. Who, though, could take care of little Whit?

Nelle went back to Prescott and presently returned with Halcy, a black girl not yet out of her teens. Halcy was about five-three, with dark skin and a big smile that made her cheeks dimple. Her formal name was Halcyon, a Greek word meaning calm, peaceful, or happy. She was quick to learn household procedures, and was talented as a cook. She also knew how to care for a lively four-year-old. Before very long, Nelle went home and left Halcy in charge.[16]

Rosborough tried to put Winifred's death behind him. He resumed his rounds of inspection, business trips to Kansas City and elsewhere, and his plans for improvements and expansion. As always, he was less interested in the routine, day-by-day operations which others could attend to.

No expansion of a mill was possible without timber, and Rosborough constantly sought more. In 1910, he and L. D. Williams had even gone to Florida to negotiate for timber, but the owners had wanted too much money and the deal fell through. About 1914, Williams also cruised an Arkansas timber holding south of Arkadelphia, but again the price was too high and Rosborough did not buy.

In the spring of 1915, fire broke out in the Rosboro sawmill while the crew was home at lunch. Flames spread; by the time help arrived, both the sawmill and its power house were beyond help. Firefighters managed to save the rest of the plant; the kilns, lumber storage areas, and planing mill were all located a little distance away from the sawmill.

Rosborough began immediately to rebuild. The company had money, probably both an insurance settlement and some capital, and Rosborough now had an opportunity to build a sawmill "like he wanted to," as one employee recalls.[17] The new mill was equipped with two band saws instead of one, and was framed with the heaviest cypress timbers that Rosborough could find, embedded in concrete and braced with cross beams. By Thanksgiving of the same year, the new sawmill was making lumber. Rosborough led visitors through the ground floor of the mill and told them to lay their hands on the supporting framework. Even with both band saws whirling and both of the heavy carriages rolling back and forth on the floor above, there was scarcely any vibration. (Rosborough boasted that his mill never got out of alignment, and that there was no other mill as stout and strong in the South. He regarded this sawmill as the best one he ever built.)[18]

Rebuilding the mill with doubled capacity, Rosborough revealed an innate optimism. The remaining timber in Pike County, including all that could be purchased from the Bemises and others, amounted to barely seven years' cut for the new mill. Had Rosborough already found another stand of timber?

If he had not secured a supply, he had sensed an opportunity. While the sawmill was being rebuilt, he asked L. D. Williams to let the logging crews build railroad grades in Pike County, and he then made Williams a timber cruiser and estimator. Williams was to work north beyond the end of the Gurdon & Fort Smith Railroad in adjacent Montgomery County.

The railroad had never been completed to Fort Smith; construction had been halted at the village of Womble (later renamed Norman) on the upper Caddo River about twenty miles north of Rosboro. A few miles beyond Womble, a low divide in the mountains separated the Caddo River's watershed from that of the Ouachita River. The Ouachita's drainage area included the entire northern half of Montgomery County, almost all in virgin timber. The Ozan Lumber Company owned several thou-

After the single-band saw-mill at Rosboro burned in 1915, T. W. Rosborough built this double-band plant "like he wanted to" and boasted about its strong construction.

sand acres there, which the Bemises would sell to Caddo River. Other lumber companies, timber speculators, and homesteaders owned more, but no single owner was dominant. That was Rosborough's opportunity.

By 1917, L. D. Williams had become a full-time timber cruiser and buyer and moved his family from Rosboro to Womble, leaving his younger brother, Celon (or "C. H.") Williams, a log hauling contractor, to take charge of logging in Pike County. L. D.'s early purchases of timber were small tracts, and for a while Rosborough may not have been sure of buying enough land in Montgomery County to carry on a logging operation. But in the summer of 1918, Caddo River was able to acquire, for nearly $400,000, more than thirty thousand acres of prime timber belonging to the Graham Lumber Company of St. Louis.[19] (Assuming five thousand board feet per acre, Caddo River paid about $2.50 a thousand for stumpage.) The Graham family had owned the land for years, and had probably hoped to build a large sawmill after completion of the Gurdon & Fort Smith across Montgomery County. When the railroad did not materialize, the family held on to the land and waited for a buyer.

Rosborough, of course, had decided to build his own railroad from Womble into the forest that lay beyond the Caddo-Ouachita divide. With the Graham timber in hand, it was time to start surveying for that railroad. A civil engineer named George E. Giles had been hired by Williams to survey for the company's railroads in Pike County, and Giles had already laid out all of the logging spurs that needed to be built there. Williams transferred him to Womble and explained that he was to survey toward Mount Ida, the county seat, for a main line railroad. Beyond the first few miles out of Womble, this main line was also to have spurs branching off into the nearest parts of the timber. Old Man Giles, with a survey party and his bulldog named Woodrow, set off from Womble into the forest.

L. D. Williams had become even more a man of the woods than Giles. He spent months roaming the back corners of Montgomery County, locating scattered parcels of Graham timberland and cruising them, walking through each forty-acre unit to take measurements of the timber that would become the basis for estimating board feet of stumpage. Since he was constantly on the move, the company bought him a car, an early model Ford with a brass radiator cover and what may have been a faulty ignition system. "You could hardly start it," one of L. D.'s sons recalls. "You jacked up the back wheels to start it."[20] L. D. drove the car anywhere it could be made to go, and when it could go no farther he continued on horseback. Williams looked at any timber that might be purchased; he sought out any owner who might be persuaded to sell. Caddo River bought timberland and timber cutting rights almost everywhere in the northern half of Montgomery County.

Williams boarded with farm families and slept on their front porches. It was a rough sort of life but he had always worked outdoors and was able to sleep almost anywhere. Rosborough had given him a big responsibility and Williams, with only a smattering of formal education, took pride in being able to carry it out. In fact, he had become a very loyal Caddo River Lumber Company employee.

About this time, L. D.'s loyalty was reinforced, for Rosborough and the other company directors voted to provide him with bonuses of company stock. To augment his small salary, he now could use his dividends for educating his six children, whom he was determined to see through college.

As the Montgomery County logging program began to take form, T. W. Rosborough married again. He had known his second wife, Urcy Mitchell, when she was about twelve years old, and had remembered her as a pretty child. Rosborough had boarded with the family of Dr. John Mitchell for two years around 1900 while running his planing mill at Havana, Arkansas. Urcy had grown up, gone to college, and become an attractive woman. She was slightly plump, nicely proportioned, with dark eyes and hair, a peaches-and-cream complexion, and a flair for wearing pretty clothes. Rosborough had renewed their acquaintance, courted her, and soon proposed marriage which she accepted. They were married at Havana in August 1916. Urcy was a month past her twenty-ninth birthday, Rosborough three weeks short of his forty-eighth.[21]

T. W. took his new wife on a honeymoon trip to the Pacific Northwest. When he saw Oregon's magnificent Douglas fir timber for the first time, he was deeply impressed.[22]

At Rosboro, Urcy settled into the family home and began to share with Halcy the upbringing of young Whit, now nine years old. Fortunately, Urcy liked her stepson.

Halcy had become a part of the household, an excellent cook whose accomplishments Rosborough appreciated, and practically a foster mother to his son. By the time Urcy arrived, Halcy was seeing a lot of a tall, good-looking fellow named Fred Wingfield. He had come to Rosboro to pull lumber on the green chain, and later began to take care of Rosborough's yard and horse and buggy. Lighter skinned than Halcy, he was said to be part Indian. Halcy and Fred married and moved into a little two-room house that stood behind the Rosborough home.[23]

When Rosborough bought his first automobile, Fred Wingfield became his chauffeur, since T. W. refused to learn to drive. Instead, he rode in the back seat where he could see out both sides and survey the passing woodlands. "If I can't make more money looking at the timber than sitting under the wheel, I'm not worth my salt," he said.[24]

Young Whit seems to have been little affected by the changes around him, and had begun to exhibit some of his father's ways with people. Guy Baker, one of Whit's childhood friends, says: "To have been raised affluent for that time, he was a good kid. Very friendly, a real nice kid. He was smart; he had a head full of sense."

People who lived in sawmill towns have remarked that lumber people were "democratic." Whit attended the public school at Rosboro and played with the other children. He gathered hickory nuts and trapped rabbits with them. His friends came to the Rosborough home at Whit's invitation to play on his swing, ride his Shetland pony, and share fresh cookies that Halcy always made. Sometimes they followed Whit on guided tours of the house.

When he became a little older, Rosborough arranged for Whit, Guy Baker, and another boy to spend a week with a family on a farm. Baker says, "Rosborough wanted him to be a regular boy, to play in the creek and get chigger bites."

Whit's friends, including Baker, sometimes persuaded him to experiment. "We'd smoke and we chewed pine needles to kill the smoke odor. He wasn't a naughty boy. But he had some good tutors.

"He lived in mortal fear of his father. He called him 'faddy'. Old Man T. W. would beat the hell out of him, if he smelled smoke on Whit. . . ." Perhaps Baker overstates, but Rosborough was a big man and must have seemed huge in Whit's eyes at that young age, and evidently T. W. believed in spanking.

Whit finished Rosboro's eighth grade in 1921, second in his small graduating class, and left late in the summer for military school. He had become a tall, slender boy, turning fourteen.

With Whit away at school, Rosborough and Urcy were in the house by themselves. At home in the evenings Urcy read to him. Then Rosborough retired early, and Urcy sat up for a while and sewed, with her little bulldog asleep at her feet.

––––––––

From 1918 when Giles started to survey for the railroad out of Womble, it was four years before the fifteen-mile main line was completed to the site that Williams and Rosborough had chosen for a Montgomery County logging center. When Caddo River began to lay track, local people speculated that it was the long-desired extension of the G. & F. S. to Fort Smith.[25] Before construction was complete, the farm depression

U.S. Forest Service photo, courtesy Ouachita National Forest

Rosborough bought this mill at Glenwood in 1922 from the A. L. Clark Lumber Company, improved it, and began cutting logs from Montgomery County.

of 1921 hit, and hungry tenant farmers came and camped along the railroad, hoping to get work.

Williams sometimes drove Rosborough along the railroad grade in his car to check on progress, and then both got out and walked. One of the workers recalls seeing Rosborough afoot, slogging along the newly built grade through heavy rain, wading in mud near the top of his rubber boots. Another time the man saw Williams drive his automobile off the end of the railroad fill, determined to take the car as far as it would go.

Rosborough once considered building a sawmill at Mount Ida, the Montgomery County seat, for it was centrally located, with housing, stores, and a school already established. Leaders in Mount Ida, however, reacted as had the leaders of Amity, years before: no sawmill, no blacks.[26] Rosborough decided to take Montgomery County's logs by railroad to the mill at Rosboro.

The country people did not want blacks, either. During construction, a contractor from Hot Springs brought in a crew of black men to work on the railroad grade, and started to set up a camp for them nearby. Some local farmers approached the foreman and told him that his black people would have to go or there would be trouble. So the blacks left.[27]

Caddo River purchased a site about four miles from Mount Ida for a logging center and named the place Mauldin, after the homesteader who had lived there. The site lay just south of a gap in a long ridge. It was possible not only to extend track to the east, but also to run a railroad through the gap and branch out from there to the northeast, northwest, and west. Log trains could converge at Mauldin then, from any of four large areas. Trains could be coupled together and moved south on the company's main line to Womble, and from there on the Missouri Pacific (the former G. & F.S.) to the sawmill.

By the end of 1922 the company had laid track to Mauldin; during the next year they built a logging town. The first employees lived in tents, but soon the company put up houses and a commissary, and hauled in two-room camp houses from Pike County.[28] Logging in Pike County west of Rosboro was finished; all the timber within reach of Caddo River's railroads had been cut. The company took up track and hauled the rails and ties from Pike to Montgomery County.

With the prospect of cutting Montgomery County timber for years, Caddo River bought another big sawmill. The A. L. Clark Lumber Company at Glenwood had cut the last of their timber. Instead of acquiring more raw material in Arkansas, A. L. Clark, who lived in Texas, had purchased timber on the West Coast. A man given to flowery oratory, he declared in a speech to fellow lumbermen that the South was his mother but that the great Pacific Northwest was his wife, and so he would move to Oregon.[29] According to the deed records of Pike County, Caddo River purchased Clark's sawmill on April 3, 1922, with its hundred-acre mill-site, all of Clark's houses (Silk Stocking Row, Candy Street, and Glenwood's black neighborhood), other buildings that Clark owned, and more than forty town lots in Glenwood, all for ten thousand dollars.[30]

Rosborough acquired a sawmill for a low price, but it was in pretty rough shape. He began to rebuild, adding a resaw and other equipment behind the band saws. At the planing mill he tore out the old steam power plant and installed electric motors. For storing rough lumber he built a huge shed, 300 feet wide and 450 feet long.[31]

Then there were two mills, each with two band saws, only four miles apart at Rosboro and at Glenwood, and a world of timber in Montgomery County waiting to be cut.

4. Second Biggest

In barely fifteen years Caddo River had grown from a brand-new lumber company with one single-band mill to a seasoned manufacturer having two double-band mills, four times the original sawmill capacity, and an increasing inventory of stumpage to supply both. Because of Rosborough's foresight in going after timber in Montgomery County, his Caddo River Lumber Company was also becoming the second biggest in the Ouachitas; only Dierks would be larger.

Caddo River had already outstripped several other lumber companies having problems with money, management, and—especially—timber supply. The first big sawmill that had cut Ouachitas pine, the Saginaw Lumber Company, was the first to cut out. Saginaw had exhausted its original timber as early as 1912, and a group of Wisconsin lumbermen operating as the Arkansas Land and Lumber Company had purchased the timberland to the north and west, blocking Saginaw from any expansion. So the operation closed down.

Arkansas Land and Lumber owned fifty thousand acres west of the Ouachita River. In January 1914 the company's owners started up a new sawmill at Malvern, with a logging railroad crossing the river and into their timber. The mill, with one band saw and a resaw, cut seventy-five to eighty thousand feet a day, indicating that the company's initial holdings of about 250 million feet of stumpage would enable the mill to operate for about eleven years.[1]

Arkansas Land needed more timber, but as their mill got underway, the lumber market was depressed. In November of that year, the company's president, Harry Howard Foster, wrote from Malvern to one of the stockholders in Wausau, Wisconsin:

> The exceedingly low price of cotton and the consequent depression among the farmers has opened up an opportunity for the Arkansas Land and Lumber Company that we would like to take advantage of, but we have found it impossible to move our product sufficiently fast to accumulate funds with which to do it, although a large amount of money is not necessary. Hardly a day passes but what from one or two farmers are in, from among the hills

west of us, offering to sell timber at prices that would range from $1.00 stumpage up to $2.00 stumpage, but owing to our financial condition we have staved them off as long as we could. . . .

We know of from two and a half to three million feet of timber that can be picked up at these prices now, which would probably take somewhere about $5,000.00, and we certainly know that $1.50 to $2.00 stumpage is a good buy. Have you any idea where we could get the $5,000.00. . . .[2]

During those years when Saginaw shut down and Arkansas Land started up, the owners of the big mill at Graysonia were groping for direction. William Grayson, the founding genius of the Grayson-McLeod Lumber Company, had died in 1910, leaving the company to his four sons, with Nelson McLeod as a minority owner. But as one observer says, "The Graysons had built a marvelous mill, but didn't know anything about running it."[3] The oldest son, George, lived at Graysonia and was supposed to be the manager, but he was addicted to other pursuits such as hunting, camping, parties, vacations, and the horse races at Hot Springs.

Soon after the elder Grayson's death, his successors merged the company with the Nashville Lumber Company at Nashville, Arkansas, and in 1912 bought out the interest of those who had owned Nashville Lumber.[4] Almost immediately, however, they turned around and offered to sell the Graysonia mill, town, and timber to the Arkansas Land and Lumber Company at Malvern. Since Arkansas Land did not yet have a sawmill, the company's owners considered using the Graysonia mill to cut their timber located west of Malvern. The idea did not seem practical because Graysonia was too far away from their timberland, and the owners of Arkansas Land decided against buying.[5]

In December 1915, though, the Graysons were able to merge with Ozan. The combination became the Ozan-Graysonia Lumber Company, consisting of the big double-band mill at Graysonia with its extensive timber holding and Ozan's double-band mill at Prescott having less timberland. The Graysons received $750,000 in bonds of the new company to make up for the difference in value between the two original companies, and with the Bemises they received equal amounts of stock.

The Graysons had at last achieved a union with men who knew how to run a sawmill. William Bemis, president of the Ozan Lumber Company and T. W. Rosborough's brother-in-law, became the president and general manager of Ozan-Graysonia. One of the Graysons who lived in St. Louis became first vice-president, and, at Will Bemis's behest, Rosborough was made second vice-president and assistant general manager. Since he lived only fifteen miles up the railroad from Graysonia, Rosborough was available to help until things were straightened out. (He acted as vice-president for a year, and then resigned to be replaced by his sister Nelle's husband, Lawrence Beidelman, who had been an officer with the Ozan Lumber Company.)[6]

After the merger, the Graysons withdrew from active management of the mill. Eventually, the Bemis family acquired most of the Ozan-Graysonia stock, so that the Grayson family owned only a token number

Courtesy Geneva Grayson

In duster and driving gloves, George Hardy Grayson, manager of the mill his father established at Graysonia, departs with his family and servants for a two-month vacation to Colorado, around 1912. He and his wife chose to live as big spenders, maintaining a large guest house, numerous servants, and a private tutor for their children.

of shares.[7] Although William Grayson had amassed a fortune, most of it vanished within one or two generations.

———

The Ozan-Graysonia merger in late 1915 coincided with the beginning of five good years for lumber, when mills throughout the Ouachitas went full blast to meet the heavy demands of World War I and the early postwar period. In 1921, however, four of the region's big mills—A. L. Clark, Fourche River, A. J. Neimeyer, and Pine Belt—shut down and went into liquidation. Though it was a terrible year for lumber, with market prices less than half what they had been in 1920, the mills closed for a different reason: each had run out of any profitable timber.

Their common predicament has been suggested by an employee of Pine Belt, Frederick Hauenstein, who wrote in his memoirs: "Pine Belt made money for a number of years, while their timber was within a radius of 20 miles. . . . But after they had cut their easy logging timber they began to lose money, and the farther they got into the hills the faster the money went and the deeper in debt until their credit was all gone. . . ."[8]

In the last years of the A. J. Neimeyer Lumber Company at Little Rock, the value of the company's uncut timber diminished more rapidly than the balance of their unpaid debts. Neimeyer's management reported on July 1, 1917, that the value of real estate (mainly the worth of land having unharvested timber) was $600,000; the total debts, $500,000. By January 1, 1921, cutting had proceeded so that the value of real estate was down to $200,000 but debts were $365,000. The following year, real estate (nearly all cutover land) was valued at $150,000; debts, $325,000. The mill was already closed and the company was in bankruptcy.[9] Under similar circumstances, the Fourche River Lumber Company had also shut down and gone into receivership.[10]

As mentioned before, the Caddo River Lumber Company bought A. L. Clark's mill at Glenwood. Dierks bought the remaining assets of both Pine Belt and Fourche River, kept some of the sawmill and railroad equipment and sold the rest, but held the timberland, even though most of it was cut over. In this way Dierks acquired forty-two thousand acres from Pine Belt and another large acreage from Fourche River. Pine Belt's land included some uncut timber adjoining that which Dierks already owned for the Wright City, Oklahoma, mill.[11] The Fourche River land included small uncut areas scattered through the hills north of Hot Springs, not in reach of any existing Dierks mill, but in 1923 when Dierks bought the land, the company had plans to move into that part of the Ouachitas.[12] Nobody, however, seemed to want A. L. Clark's cutover lands near Glenwood, nor A. J. Neimeyer's large acreage in the hills west of Little Rock.

What became of the owners and employees of these defunct lumber companies? When Neimeyer and Fourche River went bankrupt, who was most affected?

Probably none of the original owners was hurt. It appears that all the companies generated large profits in their early years, even after making payments on debts, and the net profits were distributed as dividends to the stockholders. In later years as profits turned into losses, bondholders probably were not repaid in full. Also, stockholders during the companies' declining years failed to recover all of their capital. About the liquidation of the Pine Belt Lumber Company, Frederick Hauenstein writes: "The St. Louis banks had been paid. The timber sale to the Choctaw Lbr. Co. [Dierks], together with the sale of our equipment, and lumber on the yards would furnish enough money to repay the stockholders almost what they had invested in the stock."[13]

But the original owners had already made their money. A. L. Clark went to Oregon and built another sawmill. F. A. Goodrich, one of the major stockholders in Pine Belt, moved to Burbank, California, and got into the nursery business.[14] A. J. Neimeyer went to Pasadena, California, and retired. That city had become a sunny retreat for rich old lumbermen, where even the great Frederick Weyerhaeuser spent his last years.

Hundreds of employees lost their jobs when the mills shut down, many of them undoubtedly suffering before they found other work. Without unemployment compensation, the jobless had to rely on help from family and friends. Some of them moved back to their farms; some found jobs with other lumber companies; some left the Ouachitas to find new means of livelihood. Their days with Clark or Fourche River, or with Neimeyer or Pine Belt, all became fading memories.

Courtesy W. Ray Hanley collection

Hot Springs, Arkansas, in 1920 was the only "urban" place in the Ouachitas. Timber families, migrating from Fort Towson in the fall of that year, traveled down the resort city's Central Avenue, observing its tree-lined Bath House row and array of tourist shops and hotels.

Job Seekers

The flow of early morning traffic on Central Avenue was back to normal. Stores were not yet open, and the only moving vehicle in sight was a streetcar.

Only minutes before, however, bystanders had idly watched an odd caravan coming along the avenue, eight large wagons drawn by mules, wheels

Although 1921 was bad for lumber prices, Caddo River did well in succeeding years. Rosborough was happy. At military school, Whit was making high grades in math, science, and mechanical drawing. He collected some demerits—mostly for tardiness—but made an A in company football. When he graduated in 1925, he ranked fifteenth among seventy-three in his class.[15]

About the time Whit finished military school, his father built a spacious new home on Silk Stocking Row in Glenwood, undoubtedly the best built residence in town. Now, with a house having three large bedrooms and two tiled baths, Rosborough could adequately entertain family members and business associates.

Behind the main residence, a two-car garage had quarters above for Halcy and Fred. Beyond the garage were the wash house, chicken house, and cow barn.[16] Halcy milked the cow and made butter.

On moving to Glenwood, Urcy Rosborough found a town with only a thousand people, but that was twice as many as Rosboro had and not all were connected with Caddo River Lumber Company. She started going to the Methodist church. At that time the Methodists were putting up a new brick building; Rosborough, in fact, had arranged for lumber company employees with mules and slips to dig the church basement. He had always supported the local churches, even to the extent of having Caddo River pay half the preachers' salaries.

A music major in college, Urcy could play the piano and sing; her abilities could be well used at church. As months passed, Rosborough's wife blossomed, becoming more involved in the Methodists' activities, and very supportive. She made sure that the preacher and his family had plenty of milk and butter. As the small congregation worked hard to complete their new buildings, she grew ever more sympathetic. Finally she took a large step. With $1,600 of her own money, it is said, she bought oak pews for the entire church auditorium.

Walter C. Yancey, the Methodist preacher, also conducted services at Rosboro twice a month, and if needed, Urcy went with him to play the piano. She encouraged his going to Mauldin, too, for services and revival meetings at which she played the piano. Brother Yancey was well regarded as a preacher; a fluent speaker, he was very good at explaining the Bible, and was the main force in completing the church building. A young fellow only a few years out of college, Yancey was good-looking, likeable, friendly, and a good talker given to complimenting people.

———

When Caddo River began to make lumber at Glenwood while continuing operations at Rosboro, the company moved up about even with Ozan-Graysonia as the second largest lumber manufacturer in the Ouachitas. Each company had two double-band mills. In January 1924, however, Ozan-Graysonia's sawmill at Prescott, the original Ozan Lumber Company mill that had operated since the early 1890s, ran out of timber and shut down. Caddo River then became second biggest without question.

The Dierks family had achieved an even more dramatic record of growth than Caddo River with the pair of companies they owned, the Dierks Lumber and Coal Company in Arkansas, and the Choctaw Lumber Company in Oklahoma.

The sawmill at De Queen, Arkansas, that the Dierks brothers had purchased in 1900, burned nine years later. It was not rebuilt, since construction was underway for a double-band mill that started up in 1910 at the new Dierks town of Bismark (now Wright City), Oklahoma. From Bismark, Dierks extended the short line railroad eastward for sixteen miles to the site of a second new town, Broken Bow, where two years later they opened a single-band mill for pine and another single-band mill for hardwood, both of which were later enlarged to double-band mills. (Broken Bow was named for the town in Nebraska where the Dierks brothers had opened their first retail lumberyard.) In 1918, Dierks began to produce lumber at a new, all-electric, double-band mill at Dierks, Arkansas, the site of a former logging camp for the De Queen mill. At last there were three big pine mills (not to mention the hardwood mill at Broken Bow) to cut the timber that Dierks had begun to buy in Arkansas and Oklahoma soon after 1900.

As Dierks built logging railroads into the southern Ouachitas during the 1920s, they continued to buy Ouachitas timberland; holdings of the

rumbling and hoofs clopping on the pavement and car tracks, some wagons with rude boxes arched over with canvas, others having little more than heavy wheels attached to axles and a center pole. Riding on mules or in the wagons were men and youths in overalls, women in long dresses, and one small boy, all craning their necks and sightseeing, pointing at the buildings, and talking to one another.

The caravaners had passed along tree-lined Bath House Row with its elegant bathing-halls— Victorian castles, Spanish palaces—that looked across the avenue to a row of curio shops, rooming houses, hotels, and offices. Farther up they had rolled past the magnificent Hotel Arlington: a six-story tower surmounted by a gazebo topped by a flagpole from which an American flag fluttered in the breeze, then a block-long frontage of four stories with an awninged verandah overlooking the street, then another six-story tower with gazebo and flagpole. After Central Avenue the caravaners continued up Park Avenue past other hotels and boardinghouses, past towered mansions and on to the wooded countryside. Thus, in the autumn of 1920, did a band of simple working folk drive through the famous, cosmopolitan resort city of Hot Springs.

———

Some days before, the Pine Belt Lumber Company at

Fort Towson, Oklahoma, had closed their logging camp, putting all the loggers out of work. One of the log hauling contractors, Dan Angel, learned that jobs were available with the Fourche River Lumber Company near Bigelow, Arkansas. Angel and another contractor built boxes of rough pine lumber on several of their log wagons, stretched canvas over the arched bows, piled in bedsteads, cook stoves, tables, chairs, and clothing, climbed aboard with brothers, sisters, in-laws, and other kin, and a few who were not family, and, with eighteen people in all, started out for Fourche River.

Along the way they camped out at night and cooked over open fires. Arriving at Hot Springs one evening, they bedded down at a wagon yard and the next morning proceeded through the only "urban" place in the Ouachitas, admiring the pretty buildings and enjoying the one stretch of pavement they encountered on the entire trip of two hundred miles. Two or three days after leaving Hot Springs, they arrived at Fourche River's log camp. The men and older boys went to work in the woods and the women started housekeeping in tents.

Within months, however, Fourche River shut down and everyone had to look for work once more. Dan Angel went one direction and his youngest

defunct Pine Belt and Fourche River Lumber Companies were only two among many acquired. Dierks also purchased active enterprises that owned timber. One was the Cove Lumber Company, founded by William Blake Barton around the turn of the century. Barton had a planing mill on the Kansas City Southern at Cove, Arkansas, and several portable mills that were cutting timber from thirteen thousand acres of company land. In October 1925, Dierks bought the whole works. For Barton's ninety-five percent interest in the company, Herman Dierks wrote him a check for $233,750.[18]

Why could Dierks expand while other companies having similar beginnings could not?

First, the profitable Nebraska lumberyards had helped pay for the early sawmills and timber purchases. The company also had salesmen in Kansas City who could wholesale any lumber that the Dierks yards could not absorb, so that Dierks always collected at least the wholesaler's percentage. In addition, family members owned controlling interests in a large sawmill in east Texas and another in Louisiana, which supplied their lumberyards before the Oklahoma mills started up. They later disposed of those two mills, but both provided funds, at least indirectly, for expansion into the Ouachitas.

Besides having ready money, Dierks had managerial depth. The family was large enough so its own members could oversee and promote all of its major operations through thirty years of expansion from 1900 to 1929. As Hans and Herman Dierks became less active in the business around 1920, the second generation was already in charge. Hans's son Herbert looked after the sawmills, while his other son, Harry, managed finances and ran the Nebraska yards. Herman's son, Fred, followed his father into logging and timber buying and proved as able as his father had been. Peter's son, DeVere, was in charge of sales and marketing. As family members and stockholders in jointly beneficial enterprises, these men were strongly motivated to see that Dierks made money.

A key to making more money was to get enough timberland to expand operations. Herman Dierks and his son Fred, with strong support from other members of the family, exercised a single-minded passion for acquiring timber.

The Dierks operations were probably better managed at all levels than most of the smaller lumber companies. If nothing else, the large size of Dierks permitted hiring people of greater ability. The Pine Belt Lumber Company, for one, had employed an inept surveyor who put the main line railroad up a hill with a grade so steep the log train couldn't climb it.[19] Dierks, on the other hand, could afford to hire capable surveyors. And, while the small lumberman was of necessity a jack-of-all-trades, without capability for long-range planning, Dierks could employ people to handle day-to-day operations while higher management took time to choose the wisest course.

Problems, however, were developing. The Dierks empire had grown so rapidly, with mills being built, companies bought, and members of the family investing various amounts of money at different times in several enterprises, that the whole structure had become complicated. Furthermore, in Oklahoma, where politicians held to the populist idea that land should belong to small farmers rather than to large companies, the state constitution forebade corporations from owning land. To avoid this restriction, individual members of the Dierks family held the Oklahoma timberlands in their own names. The family's interests in Arkansas were designated as the Dierks Lumber and Coal Company, while the mills in Oklahoma became a separate corporation, the Choctaw Lumber Company. The two companies had essentially the same owners and officers, but kept two separate sets of books.

Before long, bookkeeping problems would be overshadowed by more serious concerns.

Even while buying smaller lumber companies and more timberland within reach of their existing big mills, Dierks in the 1920s began to acquire two large new blocks of timber in the heart of the Ouachitas as a basis for two more double-band sawmills. Each would have its own logging railroad and mill town. One, the Pine Valley Lumber Company on the upper Kiamichi River in Oklahoma, started up in 1927. The other, the Dierks Lumber and Coal Company's mill at Mountain Pine near Hot Springs, Arkansas, opened the following year.

The mills and towns of Pine Valley and Mountain Pine were very much alike, though apparently they had not started out that way. The

brother Jim and several others went elsewhere to haul gravel. Then some of them lived in tents again and hauled logs for the Fort Smith Lumber Company until that too soon played out. Next they hauled lumber to a planing mill at Hot Springs, then moved to still another tent camp to haul logs.

Finally, about 1924, many of the original group found jobs with the Caddo River Lumber Company in Montgomery County. Together again, Dan and his brother hoped the job might last for a while.

Hardwood Mills

Ignoring the dangers of whirling, unshielded saws, belts, and pulleys, eight men at Big Fork, Arkansas, in 1913 operate a por-

Courtesy Verla Fagin Standridge

table mill to cut "head-
ings," short boards or
staves for the ends of barrels. From stave bolts (the
pieces of oak in the left
foreground), a sawyer at
the far left cuts the rough
staves. Two men at the center operate an edger that
slices bark from the staves,
and the young fellow in
shirtsleeves at the right
stands before a trimmer
saw used to square the ends
of boards and cut off defects
such as knots. Completed
staves are stacked on the
wheelbarrow at the right.
In the background are the
boiler and steam engine
that power the mill; one of
the men at the far right is
the fireman for the boiler.[17]

Before fiberboard and
paperboard containers were
developed, many commodi-
ties were stored and shipped
in wooden kegs, casks, and
barrels which were mainly
made of oak. Barrels for
aging whiskey were (and
still are) made of the highest grade of straight-
grained white oak. During
the early decades of this
century there were small
mills throughout the Oua-
chitas cutting hardwood
staves for barrels.

A far greater volume of
hardwood, however, became
railroad crossties. Men eked
out a living "hacking" ties
by hand with broadaxes
until lumbermen moved
portable sawmills to the
woods to produce ties.
Every town on a trunk line
railroad had its tie yard,
where the railroad company
or a private operator purchased ties from small mills
in the hinterlands. In the

idea of the Pine Valley mill originated with Fred H. Dierks, Herman's
son, when he visited the Buschow Lumber Company on the Kansas City
Southern at Stapp, Oklahoma. The Buschow brothers from Kansas City
had built a modest sized single-band mill at Stapp with a narrow gauge
railroad extending into their timber. The operation was profitable, and
when Dierks learned there was a large tract of pine for sale in the
Kiamichi valley, just to the south, he took an option to buy the timber.

Fred and his cousin DeVere Dierks planned to become partners to
build a sawmill, about the size of the Buschow mill, to cut the Kiamichi
timber. Other members of the family, however, became concerned that
the Dierks companies would be losing two young, energetic men who
were probably undertaking a venture beyond their means, and they persuaded them to let the mill become a family supported project.[20]

Maybe as a result of the optimism that prevailed during the 1920s, the
original plan developed into an elaborate design for a much larger mill, a
twin to Mountain Pine. Everybody seemed to forget that Mountain Pine
had access to more than a hundred thousand acres of timber including
some of the finest pine in the Ouachitas, but Pine Valley had much less.
It lay in an isolated valley of limited area, flanked by high mountains,
near the western end of the pine belt where most of the trees were short-
bodied, having fewer logs per tree.

Even so, the Pine Valley project was pushed along in tandem with
Mountain Pine. As the timberlands were purchased, and drawings for
the mills and their towns were completed, the Dierks family had cause to
feel confident. Their lumber business had enjoyed a long run of favorable
years; except for 1921, lumber prices had been good ever since 1915. The
Choctaw Lumber Company had made a profit every year since the Wright
City mill had opened in 1910. Now, in the mid-1920s, everything was
making money. The Dierks family seldom had borrowed to finance the
business—there always had been profits to plow back, or someone in the
family had extra cash to invest—but with both Pine Valley and Mountain Pine under construction, more money was needed. In 1926 Dierks
successfully arranged to issue six and a half million dollars worth of
bonds.

Pine Valley, at the end of a fifteen-mile railroad branching off from the
Kansas City Southern, was developed as a self-contained town with commissary, drugstore, post office, barbershop, doctor's office, and school. A
hotel, or boardinghouse, offered sixty-eight rooms, a spacious lobby, and
a dining room—"the finest mill town hotel in the South," proclaimed a
reporter for The Dierks Industries Co-Operator, a monthly newsletter for employees.[21] Over one hundred houses, some of them architect-designed,
comprised "the finest company houses which we have seen in any of the
Dierks Industries communities." A movie house, which also served as an
auditorium and church, could seat five hundred, and had a stage with
dressing rooms and an orchestra pit. The commissary offered the services
of a tailor and would deliver ice made in Pine Valley's own ice plant. Pine
Valley even had a jail, a concrete pillbox with two cells, one for whites
and the other for blacks.

The sawmill was the most modern of any built during that time. All the machines were driven by electricity supplied by a 1,500-kilowatt turbine. The planing mill was floored with an acre of concrete instead of wood. The newsletter reporter wrote that "this plant is said to be the finest of its kind in the world. From this standpoint of efficient lay-out, there is no counterpart for Pine Valley."[22]

Still, Pine Valley was a sawmill town: Silk Stocking Hill, a white neighborhood below the hill, and the Colored Quarters. Black people lived in a community north of the sawmill with their own school, boardinghouse, Barrel House, and tiny Baptist church. For blacks and whites too, the largest number of houses were three-room shotgun dwellings, with outside hydrants and privies, that rented for about three dollars a month. Compared with older sawmill towns, though, Pine Valley was a little better; even the smallest house had a coat of white paint. The company sponsored a baseball team, the Lumberjacks, and not long after the mill started up a high school was opened, with a football team called the Pine Valley Panthers.

Three prominent smokestacks rose two hundred feet high and could be seen far up and down the Kiamichi. The mill's whistle could be heard even farther, sounding like a summons. Valley farmers quit farming and came to work at the mill; before long it seemed that everybody in the upper Kiamichi worked for Pine Valley Lumber Company. As Bill McBride, a longtime resident, says: "The wages were cheap; the work was hard. But actually it was about the only thing there was in this country to do."

Isolated, Pine Valley lay below Winding Stair Mountain to the north and the long, brooding ridge of Kiamichi Mountain to the south. The nearest sizeable town was Mena, Arkansas, thirty-five miles distant over terrible roads. There was only one telephone line, and one dependable means of transportation to the outside world. A flange-wheeled Model T truck, converted to a bus, traveled the railroad and made connections with the Kansas City Southern. It carried luggage on top and mail in the back, along with meat and produce for the store. On the day before payday, men rode the bus with high-powered rifles, guarding the company payroll.

The people of Pine Valley lived modestly on their low wages, in a close-knit community. Through 1928, however, the mill even had to run three times a week in the evenings to keep up with orders for lumber, and reports to the Dierks *Co-Operator* began to take on a new flavor. Ordinary working folk at Pine Valley were buying cars, usually Fords, but also several other kinds. People were driving the bumpy, unpaved track to Mena, fording the creeks to go to dances. Women sought the beauty shop: "Pine Valley has been struck with a 'permanent wave'. All the ladies of Pine Valley who have not already got one are now on their way to Mena after one. Each one comes back with harrowing tales of stiff necks, long hours and scorched scalps to which none of the future victims pay any attention," said one reporter.[23]

And from Mountain Pine, whose mill started up in 1928, a reporter

early twentieth century when railroad mileage was near its maximum and before wood preservatives were widely used, the railroads' need for replacement ties was tremendous. All of the better quality ties produced by the Caddo River Lumber Company at their hardwood mill at Mauldin were sold to the Missouri Pacific and other trunk line railroads; many of them were shipped west for use on the Great Plains. Caddo River used inferior quality ties on their own logging railroads. Crossties were cut from the knotty interior parts of hardwood logs, while hardwood lumber was produced from the outer portions having fewer knots. Mauldin's hardwood mill operated from about 1923 to 1931, as long as there was a supply of timber.

The largest hardwood mill to depend largely on the Ouachitas as a source of timber was operated by Dierks at Broken Bow, Oklahoma. In the 1920s this mill was rated at sixty thousand board feet a day.

The Ouachitas, though, were never as good a source of hardwood as the lowlands farther south. In the mountains, only the moist, fertile bottomlands along streams produced top grade hardwood trees. On dry hillsides, hardwoods were often stunted and defective so that they were passed up by loggers. Shortleaf pine, which does thrive in dry environments, was the predominant lumber tree of the Ouachitas.

Courtesy Joel A. Walker

Henry Walker personally surveyed the line for his narrow gauge logging railroad up the canyon of Buck Creek near Moyers, Oklahoma. After a flood in 1915 destroyed much of the track, he rebuilt the railroad as it appears here, with expensive timbered floodwalls. Failing to take notice of mounting costs and a dwindling stock of timber, Walker soon had to sell his logging company, and never recovered financially.

wrote: "The Yo-Yo craze at last has reached us. . . . With the air full of the whirring insects life and limb is endangered. . . . Everyone is going by with a funny little thing running up and down a string. . . ."[24]

————

While Pine Valley and Mountain Pine were getting underway, two other mills were cutting out. The Fort Smith Lumber Company, having extended their logging railroad to the far limits of their scattered timberlands and cut everything possible, in 1928 closed down their mill at Plainview, Arkansas. The next year the Wisconsin and Arkansas Lumber Company, owner of the Arkansas Land and Lumber Company since 1921, closed their mills at Malvern.[25] These companies were repeating a pattern seen throughout the South during the 1920s when many of the large timber firms cut out and either went out of business or moved to the West Coast.

After 1929, only four companies having single or double-band mills remained in the Ouachitas: Buschow, Caddo River, Dierks (Dierks Lumber and Coal in Arkansas, and the Choctaw and Pine Valley Lumber Companies in Oklahoma), and Ozan-Graysonia. The Malvern Lumber Company did not cut out but replaced its single-band mill which burned in 1918 with a smaller plant. Caddo River remained second biggest, with two double-band mills, but now Dierks had five.

For several years, though, T. W. Rosborough had thought about an-

Frank J. Gibbs photo, courtesy Forest Heritage Center

other mill, and now he moved forward with his plans, despite an unsettling experience.

Perhaps Rosborough heard the rumor from Fred Wingfield, or perhaps from Effie Williams, L. D.'s wife. Or perhaps he heard it from one of them, and on his questioning the other said the same thing: *Open your eyes.*

Urcy was confronted with it upon her return from a trip. She found Rosborough waiting for her, and he got quickly to the point. She had checked into the Marion Hotel in Little Rock, and Preacher Yancey had been there with her. The man who had brought their drinks to the room was not a bellboy but a detective employed by Rosborough.

He told Urcy he was going to leave for a few days, and when he got back he wanted her gone. He would be filing for divorce.

And so it was done. Rosborough had made up his mind and Urcy moved away. Yancey reached an understanding with his family and they also left town. At the next conference meeting of the Methodist church he surrendered his minister's credentials and was allowed to withdraw from the conference under charges. It is said that Rosborough filed the charges.

Rosborough was shocked. Embittered. He told Beuford Cole, his as-

Below the long bulk of Kiamichi Mountain, Dierks built the Pine Valley sawmill, touted as "the finest of its kind in the world."

Groundhog Mills

Throughout the big-sawmill era, untold numbers of small sawmills also operated all over the Ouachitas. These lesser mills— often called doodlebug, groundhog, jerkwater, peckerwood, or whippoorwill mills—were usually moved from one "set," or setup, to another to be close to the timber, and cut from three to ten thousand board feet a day. Mills at first were steam-driven and supplied only the local needs for lumber. In the 1920s, as tracts of virgin timber

became smaller and more
scattered, and the internal-
combustion engine grew
more dependable, the num-
ber of mills increased enormously. Some were still
powered by steam, but
many more were run by
gasoline engines from tractors, or from automobiles
(high-horsepower Buicks
and Cadillacs were favor-
ites), or even (in one case,
at least) from an airplane.
By the 1930s such "tractor
mills" were everywhere,
cutting remnants of old
growth and beginning on
second growth.[26]

The typical small mill
employed from three to six
men and logged tracts from
five to two hundred acres—
farmers' woodlots, second-
growth tracts, and other
areas too small or too re-
mote for the big mills to
bother with. A mill would
cut from a few thousand to
several hundred thousand
board feet at one "set."
Travel between sets aver-
aged four days: one day to
dismantle the mill, one day
to move, and two days to
set up again.[27]

Some small-mill opera-
tors air-dried or smoke-
dried their lumber, but
most of them hauled green
lumber to the nearest railroad where they sold it to
operators of "concentration
yards." These establish-
ments collected lumber from
mills within a radius of
about twenty miles, graded
it, seasoned it in dry kilns
or by air-drying on the
yard, edged and trimmed
the boards if necessary, and
finished them at a planing
mill. Some of these com-

sistant in charge of the Rosboro mill, that, after all, he had given Urcy a high social position.

The people of Glenwood had been rocked on their heels, and those in the Methodist church were demoralized. Eventually, however, life went on and little was said about the affair, least of all by Rosborough's own family. His strong-minded, deeply religious sisters no longer acknowl- edged Urcy's existence.

Occasionally one or another of Urcy's old friends in Glenwood or Rosboro would hear from her. She always had two questions: *How is T. W.? How is Whit?*

————

The divorce took place in 1927. Rosborough was fifty-nine and had an- other sawmill on his mind, one that he wanted to build for Whit, who was at college studying engineering.

Rosborough had looked north of the Ouachita River basin being logged for the mills at Glenwood and Rosboro, and had seen more tim- ber in the hilly watershed of the upper Fourche LaFave. This new area lay to the west of the country logged by the Fort Smith Lumber Company, and west of that to be cut over by Dierks at Mountain Pine. The area remained open to timber buyers and there was enough acreage to support a large mill. Rosborough had L. D. Williams work the Fourche drainage as well as the Ouachita, buying small tracts and also cruising larger holdings purchased previously by Rosborough or by the Kansas City office.

In 1924, as Caddo River continued to buy timber, there was a major shift in the company's ownership. M. R. Smith, who had been the largest stockholder since the firm's organization, sold his interest to William F. Ingham, a Kansas City lumberman long involved with small mills in the Ouachitas. Will Ingham was Rosborough's age and a native of Nebraska. On trips to the South to buy lumber while he was a man- ager of retail yards, Ingham had learned about sawmilling and got to know many mill operators, especially small ones. Like A. J. Neimeyer and the Dierks brothers, Ingham had developed a string of lumberyards in Nebraska but soon moved his headquarters to a major distribution center, locating in Kansas City.

Around 1898 Ingham had teamed up with his brother Sidney to buy his first sawmill, on the KCS Railroad in the Ouachitas at Vandervoort, Arkansas. Not long after, the two brothers incorporated as the Ingham Lumber Company to sell lumber from mills owned by others, and to buy and sell timberland. Will and Sid Ingham, together or separately, also became partners in many small and medium-sized mills, helping to fi- nance them and sell their lumber. From 1900 into the 1920s there were Ingham-financed mills in western Arkansas, southeastern Oklahoma, northeastern Texas, Louisiana, Mississippi, and Alabama. But when Will Ingham bought the controlling interest in the Caddo River Lumber Company and assumed the presidency, that became his largest lumber investment in the South. He and his brother then divided their interests so that Sid moved out of the mills in the Arkansas-Oklahoma area and took over those in Mississippi and Alabama.

Will Ingham is remembered as being a six-footer with white hair, a tall, dignified looking man whose quiet ways impressed one of the Caddo River manager's wives as "all business, rather cold . . . no fun about him."[30] Like Smith before him, Ingham's interests lay in other lumbering

Bert Hiltebrand photo, courtesy Eloise Goodwin Plaster

Partly hidden by massive pine logs, a portable sawmill's crew and their children pose for a traveling photographer near Mena, Arkansas, about 1910.

The mill's boiler and machinery were designed to be hauled by wagon from one "set" to the next.

panies had their own portable or stationary sawmills, and all bought lumber from independently owned mills. Concentration yards existed along railroads throughout the region.

Small-sawmill activity probably peaked during the 1930s when hundreds of such mills operated in the Ouachitas. One planing mill operator on the Kansas City Southern, for example, had fourteen little mills supplying him with lumber. Overall, the small mills may have surpassed the region's big mills in output.[28] Even companies such as Caddo River and Dierks at times used portable sawmills to clean up timber that was beyond reach of their large mills.

After the 1930s the little mills, especially the portable ones, became outdated. Roads were improved and trucks hauled logs for longer distances to medium- or large-size mills that produced better lumber at lower cost. The remaining virgin timber was owned by the leading companies or by the government, and the larger mills paid higher prices for standing timber than their neighbors could afford. With economics against them, operators of small mills went out of business.

Courtesy A. V. Pirtle

Stacks of lumber air dry at a yard on the railroad at Mena, Arkansas, around 1950. "Concentration yards" like this bought rough lumber from small sawmills, seasoned it, and then finished it for sale to out-of-state buyers.

Frank J. Gibbs photo, courtesy Forest Heritage Center

Smoke kilns (or "Arkansas dry kilns") are used by a small operator to season his own lumber near Mena, Arkansas, in 1928. Two kilns are in operation and a third is being assembled in the foreground. Green lumber was stacked so that a fire of green slabs could be built within or under it. Heat and smoke dried the lumber, but someone had to be present at all times to keep the fire going—and to keep the stack from catching fire. In about a week the boards were dry, though drying was uneven and they were dirty to handle. Surface discoloration from smoke was removed when the lumber was planed.

ventures, including timber on the West Coast. He only visited his Arkansas mills about once a year.[31]

Caddo River, then, was watched more closely by one of his longtime associates, Hal Shaffer. For twenty years Shaffer had managed Ingham sawmills in western Arkansas, Oklahoma, and Texas, and in 1922 had become secretary-treasurer of the Ingham Lumber Company in Kansas City. When control of Caddo River was acquired, Ingham sent Shaffer to Arkansas for a close look at the timber buying activities of L. D. Williams. He wanted Shaffer to make sure that when Williams bought timber, Caddo River Lumber Company was getting full value. Shaffer was to go everywhere with Williams. Before he was to complete any purchase of timber, Williams was first to get Shaffer's approval of the offered price.

It was not easy to live as L. D. Williams did, boarding with farmers and often sleeping outside, riding horseback or walking through the forest to look at timber, and trying to bargain with backwoods people who easily became suspicious of outsiders. Shaffer was not a local; he was a native of Kansas, tall, slender, rather handsome, with a natural wave in his black hair, hardly the rough-hewn type that Williams was. Hal Shaffer, however, had lived in small towns of the Ouachitas, such as Hatfield, Arkansas, when managing sawmills, and had known country people. He also had a friendly, moderate, mild-mannered approach, and an outgoing disposition that caused people to like him. He was able to

U.S. Forest Service photo, courtesy Ouachita National Forest

Sawmill shacks at a small mill in Scott County, 1924. These are similar to the one lived in by Gertie and Jeff Barnett.

Sawmill Shack

Jeff and Gertie Barnett of Scott County, Arkansas, began their married life in the early 1920s as farmers, but they didn't like farming. "We had plenty to eat," says Gertie, "but we had no money. Farmers had to be careful to save enough money to pay their taxes." Jeff went to work as a log hauler and team boss for a Baptist preacher named Johnson who ran a portable sawmill. At Johnson's mill, the Barnetts lived in a "sawmill shack," a one-room house of rough lumber with a roof of thin boards bent into a shallow arch that was supposed to shed the rain.[29]

Gertie recalls her responsibilities when the mill finished cutting at one "set": "The men wanted to be logging just as long as they could to finish up the timber . . . and we would want to get moved as quick as possible . . . so me and this lady, her name was Mrs. Hampton—me and her always lived right close together—we would move our furniture out in the yard, and me and her would tear down these houses. As we tore down the houses, we would mark what was the siding and what was the roof and everything . . . front and back and all, and they

strike up a conversation with anyone, even the womenfolk who were normally shy about talking. And in one respect he was just like L. D. Williams: he could lie down and sleep almost anywhere.[32]

Traveling with Williams, Shaffer learned that L. D. often stayed with a rural family for several weeks so that he could get to know, and be known by, everyone in the neighborhood, and gain the community's confidence. Williams occasionally promised jobs with the lumber company if a man would sell his timber. The basic strategy, though, was simply to offer the going price for stumpage. (One of L. D.'s sons remembers him saying: "Don't ever try to cheat anybody. Give them the worth of their land.")[33] Today, the prices he paid seem ridiculously low—around ten dollars an acre—but in the mid-1920s those were the prevailing rates.

Before his tour was over, Shaffer had come to like and respect Williams, whom he saw as the salt of the earth. Ingham, who was conservative in money matters, was apparently satisfied with Williams' land buying and Shaffer's judgment. Even more conservative than Ingham about spending money, Shaffer from then on held the Caddo River purse strings.

In addition to purchasing small tracts of timber, Shaffer and Williams looked at the western end of the fifty-mile-long strip of land assembled by Frank Drummond and Paul D. Rust. Some of the Drummond-Rust land lay within reach of Mauldin; the remainder of the western part could supply the sawmill that Rosborough wanted in the Fourche River watershed. The Dierks Lumber and Coal Company hoped to get the *would know just exactly how to put it up. . . ."*

The men came and loaded the house material on log wagons, set the furniture on top, tied it down, and moved all to the next sawmill set where late that afternoon they put up the houses. Gertie recalls they would "then move our furniture into the houses and be there that night . . . they could just throw it up right quick."

The Barnetts' furniture consisted of a table and chairs, a wood-burning cook stove and a food storage cabinet, all placed at one end of their single room, and a bed and a chest for clothes at the other end. Instead of glass windows there were planks that could be pushed aside in warm weather. "Then in the winter time they had to be closed . . . we burned coal oil lamps to eat lunch by."

One winter Gertie boarded some of the sawmill workers, feeding them at her table and making the beds in their bunkhouse. Each man paid seventy-five cents a day for three meals and a bed. "That was the coldest winter I ever went through in a sawmill house," Gertie says. The green lumber of the house had shrunk so much that a dropped table knife could slip through one of the cracks in the floor. "I could spill water on that floor and it would freeze . . . be ice. I had on heavy clothing. Right in the house, I wore a long coat

rest of the Drummond-Rust timber for their projected mill at Mountain Pine.

After buying land in this area around 1905, Paul D. Rust had become part owner of a large and profitable longleaf pine mill in Louisiana.[34] About 1915 Drummond and Rust deeded their individual holdings in the Ouachitas to a corporation they had formed, the Yell Lumber Company (named for the county which had the largest portion of their land). Rust, the predominant owner, became president.[35] Rust may have been interested only in timber speculation (as U. L. Clark had been with his Detroit Timber and Lumber Company in years past), but there are indications that he planned to develop a railroad logging operation.

Much of the Drummond-Rust timber was of high quality and the landholding was blocked out so that it could be logged from one long east-west railroad. But there was a problem. Just to reach the timberland from the nearest trunk line railroad, the Rock Island, would require tracks for more than twenty miles, or from the next nearest trunk line, the Missouri Pacific at Norman, a railroad nearly forty miles long through Montgomery County. It appears that Paul Rust wanted to go through Montgomery County. A railroad from the Rock Island, though shorter, would only have crossed "worthless" cutover land of the Fourche River or the Fort Smith Lumber Company. One through Montgomery County, however, would have put Rust in the best position to buy and cut the virgin timber there.

If that were Rust's plan—and it seems a logical one—Caddo River spoiled it. While he was preoccupied elsewhere, Caddo River acquired the best route for a railroad from the Missouri Pacific through Montgomery County, and by the early 1920s they were buying timber all over the northern part of the county. Rust had been blocked.

When he realized what had happened, Rust got busy. Evidently he wanted revenge. He could see also that his way of getting even with Caddo River could be quite profitable. Rust and his agents moved into Montgomery County and, between August 24 and October 12, 1923, bought dozens of small acreages at carefully chosen locations. The speed with which they moved and their accuracy in pinpointing the areas suggest that Rust must have known the county's topography very well, as if he had studied it in planning his own future logging operation. Moreover, the prices he was willing to pay must have astonished the landowners. He paid in cash as much as fifteen, twenty-five, nearly *forty* dollars an acre for parcels along certain creek valleys. The land did not have to be fertile or have timber and the pieces could be as small as a strip thirty-five yards wide. It just had to be where Rust wanted to acquire land.

L. D. Williams soon learned Rust's strategy. The newly purchased land blocked every suitable route for logging railroads that Caddo River would need for access to half of the company's timberlands in Montgomery County.[36] Speaking of Rust's maneuver, Bill Wingfield of Mount Ida recalls: "He hired my father to buy land to block Caddo. Rust bought maybe 160 acres in a gap above Mauldin. My father had me put a barbed wire fence across it."

Yes, Rust would now talk with Caddo River about selling them his land—at *his* price.

Caddo River dickered with him for months, after L. D. Williams and Hal Shaffer had looked over Rust's scattered tracts, estimated their value for timber, considered alternate routes for railroads, thought about the possibility of buying a lot more of his land in Yell County, and weighed every other possible plan of action. Eventually, though, Caddo River had to buy. The price is not known; the recorded deeds say "one dollar and other valuable considerations," the stock phrase used when the seller or buyer wants to avoid revealing a price. Vernon Williams, a son of L. D., says: "I remember Mr. Shaffer talking about how expensive the timber was. They didn't dare tell anyone else how much they had to pay. They finally had to pay Rust's price, or somewheres near it." Caddo River bought land from Rust in two separate transactions, one in March 1925 for about seven thousand acres,[37] the other on June 29, 1926, for nearly four thousand acres more including pieces Rust had acquired in 1923 to block the Caddo River railroads.[38]

Meanwhile, in October 1925, Dierks purchased the rest of the Yell Lumber Company timber, in the largest land purchase in the Ouachitas since the United States bought the entire region from France as part of the Louisiana Purchase, nearly eighty-eight thousand acres of timberland plus nearly six thousand acres of timber cutting rights. As recorded in the deed, the price totaled $532,078.64, averaging about $5.70 an acre.[39]

Then, on June 28, 1926, one day before Caddo River bought the railroad right-of-way land from Paul Rust, Dierks sold Caddo River the entire west end of the landholding previously purchased from Rust, comprising forty thousand acres of land and timber for $250,000. The average price per acre in this transaction was about $6.19, so that Dierks made a profit over the $5.70 per acre they had paid Rust the previous fall, but not an exorbitant one.[40]

On the next day, Caddo River concluded its second transaction with Rust. It can still be debated whether, after the sale papers were signed by both parties, they told Mr. Rust that they had just purchased forty thousand acres of his land from Dierks at a very reasonable price. Caddo River and Dierks had both rented offices in the R. A. Long Building in Kansas City. Dierks later moved across the street into their own building, but the principals of the two companies remained in friendly contact. Now, as in Pike County, they laid out a boundary between their respective areas of operation. Caddo River would buy and cut timber in Montgomery County. For their Mountain Pine mill, Dierks would buy and cut timber in Garland County, adjacent to Montgomery on the east.

———

Thus Caddo River accumulated timberland in parcels large and small. One means they employed for acquiring some of the smaller tracts was provided by a federal law known as the Timber and Stone Act, originally passed by Congress in 1878 to enable homesteaders to acquire woodlots for their own use. In addition to his homestead, any person could enter a

and cooked." To keep the place warm she acquired a wood heating stove. "That little King heater, you put pine knots in that thing and it would get to dancing. Oh, it just danced. . . ."

In spite of the rigors, Jeff and Gertie followed Preacher Johnson's sawmill around Scott County for seven years—one year moving thirteen times. But in 1931 Jeff got a regular job with the Caddo River Lumber Company, and that ended their living as nomads.

claim for up to 160 acres of unappropriated federal land, unfit for culti-vation, and having timber but not minerals. As amended in 1892, the act applied to lands in any of the so-called public land states, including Arkansas. The entryman was to swear that he was appropriating the land "to his own exclusive use and benefit [and] has not . . . made any agree-ment or contract . . . by which the title . . . should inure . . . to the benefit of any person except himself. . . ."[41]

Congress had passed the act in the same spirit as the Homestead Act —with an intent to help the small farmer. Resource historian John Ise, however, estimates that only a fraction of one percent of the area acquired under the Timber and Stone Act remained in the hands of the original entrymen. Congress made little or no provision for the lumber industry to directly acquire forest tracts extensive enough for large-scale, long-time production of lumber for the general market. So lumber companies, at least in the western states, latched on to great expanses of public land by hiring hundreds of "dummy" entrymen to file on land under the Timber and Stone Act and then convey title to the companies.[42]

In the Ouachitas, it was easy enough to buy land at low prices from legitimate homesteaders who failed at farming. But there were also many small-scale speculators who filed on homesteads and on Timber and Stone claims with the intention of selling their acreages as tim-berland. Whenever feasible, lumber companies arranged for individuals to enter claims later to be sold to the companies. At Caddo River, T. W. Rosborough saw there were scattered parcels of government land in the area where the company was buying timber, and arranged for trusted employees and members of their families to enter claims. The entrymen, who paid the government a $10.00 filing fee and $2.50 an acre for the land, included Rosborough; Beuford Cole, Rosborough's assistant at the Rosboro mill, and his wife; and the L. D. Williams family.

For Williams, the proceeds from selling Timber and Stone claims to the company were a timely blessing. During the 1920s, L. D. and Effie Williams had five children to see through college (one was already through), and his salary remained low, reportedly only $160 a month. (Even at that, he was one of the company's higher paid employees, whose salary was equivalent to the pay of a mill sawyer.) At different times from January 1921 through November 1925, L. D. and his wife, separately and also jointly as an "association of persons" as allowed by the law, and six other members of the family took up separate Timber and Stone claims, ranging in size from 40 to 160 acres and totaling 1,200 acres. Each relative sold his or her claim to the Caddo River Lumber Company for at least the going price of stumpage. Usually the sales were completed even before the government formally issued patents to the land.[43]

Vernon Williams recalls that he and his twin brother Virgil, both engineering students, borrowed a team of mules from the grading fore-man at Mauldin and rode across the mountains in a wagon to survey their claims. "We had to be on the land and swear it wasn't fit for agricultural purposes," he says. The tracts were located in the backwoods of Yell and

Scott counties where there were no roads, but eventually they reached their claims, surveyed the boundaries, and drove home. "It didn't take long to prove up. A lawyer [employed by the company] in Mount Ida took care of the paperwork. We just signed the deed and then the land was sold to the Caddo River Lumber Company. We used the money to finish college," he recalls.

Vernon and Virgil had each filed on 160 acres. At $2.50 an acre plus the $10.00 filing fee, each claim cost $410.00, which was paid to the government. Caddo River paid each of the boys $1,600 for his 160 acres. The payment of $10 an acre may have been the going price for land at the time, or it could have been more, as a bonus to the family of a key employee.

――――――

By the middle 1920s, Caddo River's timber buying reached into Yell and Scott counties as well as Montgomery, and in the latter the company's logging operation was far larger than that of Pike County in earlier years. Mauldin had become the largest town in Montgomery County—not a full-fledged town, exactly, but much more than a temporary logging camp. It was Caddo River's headquarters for supplying two big sawmills with timber, and it had become a population center with both social and economic influence over the surrounding area.

5. Mauldin

The Caddo River Lumber Company located Mauldin where their long-line logging railroads in Montgomery County joined the main line toward Glenwood and Rosboro. Near the intersection, the company put up the principal buildings of the town: office, commissary, boardinghouse, doctor's office, school, and church. Not far to the east, where two small streams were dammed to supply water for boilers, they built a sawmill to produce hardwood crossties, and a repair shop for the engines and flatcars of the log trains.

The company brought some of the employees' homes from log camps in Pike County, two-room portable houses that were set off the flatcars and left close to the railroad. They built many more dwellings on-site, most of them shotgun houses with living room/kitchen/bedroom all in a row. (The doors in these dwellings were supposedly placed in a straight line, so that when they were opened, a person could shoot a shotgun all the way through the house without hitting anything.) These were homes for the families of ordinary employees such as section hands (paid $2.50 a day in the 1920s), steel gang workers ($2.65), and tong hookers ($3.00).

Higher paid employees including foremen ($3.75), locomotive engineers ($4.50), and log loader operators could have four-room houses. Delzie Williamson, wife of a locomotive engineer, recalls that her four-room dwelling had a kitchen sink, but that she had to carry water into the house from a well in her yard, and the sink drained through a pipe to a ditch outside. Everybody in the smaller houses used outhouses and took their baths in washtubs, as did Delzie and her family.

L. D. Williams had a larger house, as did his brother C. H. Williams, now a train master in charge of the operation and maintenance of the railroads. The Williamses, the company's doctor, the commissary manager, and a few others enjoyed inside running water supplied from a tank on the hill above the sawmill. But there was only one flush toilet in all of Mauldin, at the house where T. W. Rosborough stayed overnight during his visits once a month.

There was no electric utility closer than Hot Springs, and the company installed a generator powered by a steam engine at the hardwood sawmill. The mill, office, commissary, kitchen and dining room at the boardinghouse, and some of the better homes had electric lights which went out at nine every night when the generator shut down. Most people used coal oil (kerosene) lamps.

For some reason the company did not choose to put the houses at Mauldin in one concentrated area. Instead, they were scattered for nearly two miles along the railroad, or clustered on short streets here and there running at right angles to the tracks. People had more elbowroom that way, but families that lived at opposite ends of Mauldin saw little of each other.

The town's focal point, doubling as emporium and social center, was the company store. Inside the long wooden building candy and tobacco attracted the townspeople, along with notions and hardware; beds, dressers, and rocking chairs; overalls, shoes, yard goods, and thread; canned fruit and vegetables, dried beans, salt pork, and baloney. There was an icebox for the baloney and in later years an electric refrigerator for ice cream, but the town's generator was small and could be run only part time, so there was not enough refrigeration to keep fresh meat and vegetables.

In the commissary's back storeroom were many sacks of flour and sugar. Outside were new Lindsey log wagons, barrels of kerosene, and two hand-cranked gasoline pumps (one for red gas and one for white). Between the store and the railroad was an ice house for storing the blocks shipped in from Glenwood. A feed house was filled with bales of hay and huge sacks of oats—each holding five bushels and weighing 160 pounds. ("When a guy could take one of those sacks by the ears and sling it up on his shoulders, he was a man.")[1] Feed was carried out the side door onto flatcars to be taken to log haulers and the railroad grade crew for their mules.

The commissary manager, his several clerks, and two delivery men kept busy waiting on customers, assembling and carrying orders to people around town, and filling requests from numerous camps along the railroads. Few of Mauldin's families owned automobiles and no one had a telephone, so two or three of the store clerks, going from house to house during the morning, solicited orders for groceries and other items to be delivered that afternoon. Also each morning, Mack Baker, one of the delivery men, traveled the length of the town in his Model T truck, delivering ice.

Mauldin's buildings were of simple board-and-batten construction, and the commissary and most of the others in the central part of town were painted with shiny enamel, boards red and battens white, like Glenwood's Candy Street. So on leaving the commissary with his load of ice, Mack Baker traveled through Candy Town, or Stri-ped Town, first passing the striped office, a small square building of three or four rooms where a dispatcher controlled railroad traffic and a bookkeeper kept records of time and pay. Past the company office and a post office, he

The Hotel at Mauldin (left) contained a dining room, while the Bunkhouse (right) accommodated single men.

Courtesy Nettie Rowe Taylor

Bertha Ketchum (left) and her three helpers pause after setting out another meal in the dining room at Mauldin's Hotel.

Courtesy Tina Palmer Smith

Courtesy Daisy Maxey Scoggins

In front of Mauldin's "striped" hotel, a log cutter and one of Mrs. Ketchum's dining-room girls indulge in a little mild flirtation on a Sunday afternoon.

Loggers' Hotel

FOUR A.M. Bertha Ketchum took the poker hanging by the stove, opened the door, stepped out into the chilly darkness, and walked across the yard. She could just make out the circular silhouette of the saw, suspended . . .

Claaang! Claaang! Claaang! Claaang! Claaang!

From upstairs and in the other building she heard groans, and bumps. Through a window she saw a match flare up— somebody lighting his coal oil lamp. She went back into the dining room.

In a few minutes the men, now dressed, began to file in and take seats, and more kept coming until they were jammed shoulder-to-shoulder on benches flanking two long tables. Their places already were set, plain tableware on white oilcloth with dishes of butter and jelly every so often, and Mrs. Ketchum and her three helpers were bringing in bacon, eggs, cornflakes, hot biscuits, milk, coffee. Everybody started eating as soon as food arrived.

Within fifteen minutes the men were through, walking back to the bunkhouse to build a fire in the heating stove and get warmed up. A little before five they would pick up

arrived at the Hotel or boardinghouse, where he left ice for the dining room and kitchen. Just north of the Hotel was another striped two-story building, the Bunkhouse or Bull Pen, with sleeping rooms for boarders.

Continuing east, Baker passed the church that Rosborough had built, where Baptist, Methodist, and Presbyterian preachers carried the lessons of the Bible on different Sundays, though most of the congregation were Baptists. Next to the church stood the school, a two-story white building having a one-story annex and a bare, rocky play yard. (The lumber company also supported the school, which during the 1920s was one of only three grade schools in Montgomery County having full nine-month terms. Usually there were nearly a hundred pupils in Mauldin's eight classes, and sometimes the first and second grades were so large they were split into morning and afternoon groups. The older children rode a bus to high school at Mount Ida—if they went at all. Boys often quit school after the eighth grade, or when they reached their teens, in order to go to work.) At the school's annex, Baker might have seen "Miss

their lunch buckets, and
the log cutters and others
would walk over to the
toolhouse to get ready to
go to work.

Bertha Ketchum, the
stout, matronly woman
who ran the larger of
Mauldin's two boarding-
houses, rose and worked
with her crew from three
o'clock, cooking breakfast
and seeing that the men's
lunches were made. (Tina
Smith, one of Mrs. Ket-
chum's lunchfixers, remembers: "We'd make a jelly
sandwich with butter.
We'd fry an egg and put it
with cucumber pickles and
bacon in a biscuit. Put 'em
a piece of pie—apple,
apricot—and then a piece
of cake. Sometimes, four or
five Viennas in a little
can. Sometimes an apple or
an orange. Sometimes have
peanut butter and crackers.
We'd have baloney sand-
wiches. You never did hear
nobody complain about how
she fed.")

After breakfast one of
the girls gathered dishes,
washed them in a No. 3
washtub filled with soapy
water and rinsed them in a
tub of hot water replenished
from a kettle on the massive
wood-burning cook stove.
The others peeled potatoes,
rolled out piecrusts, and
prepared other things for
supper. Today there would
be big half-moon fried
peach pies.

Mrs. Ketchum went to
talk with the housekeeper
who cleaned the men's
rooms, those on the second
floor above the dining room
and on both floors of the

Jessie" Diamond, L. D. Williams' schoolmarm daughter, washing and combing some unkempt first-grader; she kept a pan of water on the wood heating stove for that purpose.

Beyond the school were unpaved side streets with striped houses where the bosses lived—including L. D. Williams and his brother—and where the doctor's home and office were. Then Baker came to the striped sawmill, with its elevated open dock where men "doodled crossties," rolling the ties out of the mill on a conveyor, sorting the 6 x 8s from the 7 x 9s and the good ones from the rejects, and shoving the several kinds onto their respective skidways for loading into gondola cars below. From another sorting conveyor at the lower level of the mill, men loaded hard-wood lumber onto buggies to be pushed to the lumber stacks in the drying yard. Baker made his rounds of the sawmill to put ice in the kegs of drinking water.

Beyond the sawmill Baker stopped to leave ice at the machine shop where several men worked on locomotives and log cars, and then drove into Mill Town or Red Town, the red-painted shotgun houses belonging to sawmill hands and railroad workers. After making the rounds in Red Town, he turned back, for he had come to the east end of Mauldin at U.S. Highway 270.

West of the commissary, Baker visited other homes scattered along the railroad for about half a mile. One woman recalls that when she lived at the west end of Mauldin, every passing log train "jarred the houses—they were not over twenty feet from the track."[3]

Baker was only one of several providers of town services. Mauldin had a barber, and the company employed a doctor who ran what was essentially a first aid station. Medical service was deducted from each employee's wages ($1.80 a month, one man recalls) and as a result, people came to Dr. Watkins with all kinds of minor problems. In the 1920s the practice of medicine was still rudimentary and lumber company doctors were often of dubious ability. Watkins sewed up saw cuts, pulled teeth without benefit of anesthetic, and at times set broken bones, but he had instructions to send the seriously ill or injured to St. Joseph's Hospital at Hot Springs. Mack Baker took them there, over forty miles of unpaved highway, in his Model T.

During a time when even Mount Ida, the county seat, had open-backed privies behind the town's stores and school, it is not surprising that people's health was none too good. At Mauldin the company employed a scavenger to shovel excrement from outhouses once a week and haul it away in a wagon. There was spillage, and a swarm of flies trailed the old man's wagon as he trundled from privy to privy ("The stinkin'est thing I ever saw in my life," a resident says).[4] One former resident of Mauldin recalls that three of his family there came down with ty-phoid fever one year. Another remembers that after a farmer sold con-taminated headcheese at Mauldin, "it shut down the school, the town, everything. . . ."[5]

Many of Mauldin's people had come from farms where they had eaten fresh and home-canned vegetables and fruit, and lean meat. When they began to live on canned goods, salt pork, and baloney from the commissary, they became ill. The women, especially, began to suffer from pellagra, a disease associated with diets deficient in niacin (a B vitamin), and in protein. For a time, local doctors did not know what they were dealing with. Finally the company hired a new doctor who prescribed brewer's yeast, a source of B-complex vitamins, and the pellagra began to disappear.

People in Mauldin either became sick or developed immunity or were lucky and escaped infection, and life went on. Beyond discussing the state of their health, they talked about others who had somehow touched their lives. A year after Rosborough's divorce, some still gossiped about Urcy and Preacher Yancey, recalling how she had come with him to Mauldin one time to "convert the heathen." But attitudes toward Urcy had become settled. She would always be a "loose woman" in the eyes of the men who talked about her; someone claimed that she had now gone off to become a prostitute. Among women in Mauldin, Urcy was not mentioned, at least not in public.

Off-color stories made their rounds. There was once a woman in the Mauldin camp who had some brozine (brass tokens that could be spent only at the commissary, so that their existence was not well known outside the town). A man came to her door peddling watermelons. She wanted one but told him, "I don't have any money, but I can pay you in brozine." The peddler got red in the face and stammered, "I'll have you know I'm strictly a virtuous man."[6]

In 1928 there was the Depriest affair. Two brothers, Jack and Sol Depriest, and their grown sons and daughters had come to Mauldin from the logging camp of the Fort Smith Lumber Company. Before that they had worked at a sawmill in southeastern Missouri. As logger Henry Overby recalls, "The Depriests were all big strong fellows, good workmen—but rough and tough, good people to let alone." Jack, who hired on with Caddo River as a filer with a saw gang in the woods, bore a scar on his jaw from a fight he had had in Missouri. His brother Sol, who rolled logs to the carriage in the hardwood sawmill, was a giant of a man who weighed more than three hundred pounds and could roll logs with his bare hands. Kenneth, one of the sons who operated the log hoist at the mill, had in some past fracas gotten his toes shot off. Another son, Carl, was a brakeman on the log train and was described as "pretty bad to fight."

The Depriests stayed out of trouble, however, until two of the sons had accidents, one not long after the other. Jack's boy "Little Ed" Depriest broke his leg while logging and had to have it amputated, and then sued the company for a cash settlement. One of Sol's sons, Arthur, who was a tong hooker, was killed when he fell between moving log cars on the railroad.

The company then gave each remaining male Depriest a termination notice and a letter of recommendation so that he could get a job somewhere else, and let all of them remain at Mauldin until they could make arrangements to leave. But Caddo River had fired every one of them—

Bunkhouse across the tracks. The rooms were small, about nine feet square with one or two narrow steel beds to a room. Some of the occupants were messy. ("Just as filthy as a pig," one former resident recalls. "They didn't care what was in the room or how it looked or nothing a-tall about it.")[2] The housekeeper was to make beds and keep the place swept and as clean as possible.

Most of the men who lived here were loggers or railroaders who were away at noon. Several who worked at Mauldin's hardwood sawmill or at the commissary came in for a hot lunch. When lunch was ready, one of the girls went out and banged again on the discarded circular saw that served as dinner gong as well as morning awakener.

After the lunch dishes were cleared away, Bertha Ketchum and her girls went to work in earnest to prepare supper. As always, there was to be meat. And mashed potatoes, and English peas or corn that came in gallon buckets (even in 1925 there were bulk-canned institutional foods), or maybe baked beans, and canned fruit. And always a big bowl of prunes.

By five the men were in from work and ready to eat, and when somebody banged the saw, they came as hungry as ever. After supper the girls washed the dishes, reset the table and mopped the floor. Soon it was nine o'clock and bedtime. Some of the men in the Bunkhouse lingered around the heating stove but most went to their unheated rooms and crawled under blankets. The three dining room girls retired to their own big room next to the kitchen.

Bertha Ketchum took a final look around and then opened the door of the two-room apartment off the kitchen where she and her husband and their eleven-year-old son lived. She was thinking of tomorrow, which would be Saturday. After work tomorrow night, should the girls make ice cream—though it was cold outside now— or should she take them to the picture show at Mount Ida?

Jack, Sol, Kenneth, and Carl, and Sol's son whom everyone called "Bug" who worked on the lumber yard at the sawmill, and even George Ward who had married Jack's daughter Ruth and was a locomotive engineer.

Sol and one or two of his sons found jobs at the newly-opened Dierks mill at Mountain Pine. Jack and several of his family sold their household goods, pooled their money, and bought a secondhand Buick and a secondhand Ford sedan. Soon afterward they rolled out of Mauldin and headed for the brand-new sawmill city of Longview, Washington, leaving Mauldin's people to talk about what had happened, and why.[7]

At times, conversation also turned to the company's attempts to bring blacks to Mauldin. Caddo River's managers knew that local people did not want blacks around, but there were occasions when there was heavy work to be done—loading crossties, laying railroad steel, straightening old crooked railroad rails—and the company sent black workmen to do those jobs. Apparently the men who loaded crossties were not harassed, even though they stayed at Mauldin overnight in cars on a railroad siding. (They came "once in a great while" during the time the hardwood mill operated from about 1923 to 1931.) But those who came to lay steel remained only one night before being sent back in the morning, and the crew who came to straighten rails were also forced to leave before they finished their job. "They would not allow black people in Montgomery County," one old resident recalls.[8]

———

The commissary was more than the commercial center of Mauldin; it was also a hub of everyday social life. On summer evenings many of the loggers congregated on the store's front porch to drink "sody pop," roll cigarettes, chew tobacco or dip snuff, and swap funny stories of the Lum-and-Abner variety. ("It was just like going to a show every night, hearing the things they'd say. . . .")[9] Children came to listen and eat Eskimo Pies. On paydays the crowd at the commissary became even bigger. Farm boys living outside Mauldin jumped on the log train returning from Glenwood and hopped off at the commissary. ("Just to be there, you know. We didn't have much to do. . . .")[10] Automobile salesmen, mainly from Glenwood, came and tried to sell cars.

The ladies who worked on projects for Mauldin's school and church knew that the commissary was the place to go to raise money. With a freezer of ice cream or a batch of homemade candy, they would set up shop on the porch and ask everyone to buy some to support their latest worthy cause. Often their best customers were log hauling contractors who had just received paychecks.

The church ladies, still raising money, promoted pie suppers, and held elections at a penny a vote to choose the Dirtiest Man, who received a bar of soap. Church activities also offered a time for young couples to go on dates. Most socializing, however, took place among friends who held parties or square dances in their homes on Saturday nights, and fish fries at the nearby Ouachita River on Sundays.

Mauldin residents were neighborly but lacked the intense spirit of community common to other sawmill towns. People could not get to-

Mauldin residents outside one of Red Town's shotgun houses. Here as elsewhere in Mauldin, houses had hand-pump wells in front and outdoor privies in back.

gether easily. The town did not have recreation facilities (and those at Mount Ida were less than four miles away). A number of Mauldin's families had come from nearby farm communities to work and went home on weekends instead of staying in town. Other families, and especially single men, were transients; they did not remain with Caddo River very long and so did not develop social ties. Many of the single men who did stay were fun-loving types who picked up their paychecks and left town for the evening or weekend.

The sawmill town of Graysonia, while having fewer people than Mauldin, was compact in its layout, equipped with a recreation building, and isolated from other towns. The residents patronized an outdoor movie theater and the circus during the summer, and indoor movies and Lyceum entertainments during winter. At Mauldin, somebody set up a tent and showed silent movies for a dime, but only a few came to see the show and the movie man had to fold his tent.

During its existence Mauldin was actually larger in population than the county seat. The 1930 census shows that Mauldin had 896 people; Mount Ida, 512. Mount Ida was a trade center, however, and not governed by rules of the Caddo River Lumber Company. Moreover, one of its leading citizens, Gip Bearce, regularly sent his truck and driver over to Mauldin on Saturday evenings to pick up anyone who wanted to ride back with him at no charge. Sometimes Bearce's driver had to make two

*Caddo River's log hauling
contractors owned portable
buildings so employees and
their families could live
close to the timber cutting
areas along the railroad
spurs. Several of the railroad maintenance crews
also lived in camps of this
kind, convenient to areas
where they worked. The log
haulers, especially, moved
frequently—once a year
or more often—to be nearer
the felled timber.*

*Each portable camp
house measured twelve by
twenty-four feet and had
two rooms. One, with a
wood cook stove, served as
kitchen, dining room, and
living room; the other,
with a wood-burning
heater, was usually the
parents' bedroom. Camp
houses were built with unpainted board-and-batten
exteriors and exposed two-
by-fours inside. Some had
ceilings, others did not.
None had closets; clothes
were hung from a broom-
stick nailed across a corner.
A small family lived in
one of these houses; a large
family occupied two. The
double houses had an open
deck or roofed hallway between their two buildings.*

*In camp, the women
kept house much as women
did at Mauldin, rising at
four a.m. to see their men
off to work; then garden-
ing, cooking, canning,
quilting, mending, and
sewing. On wash day, they
carried their soiled clothes
outside to a workbench
where there were two gal-*

or three trips, the truck heavily loaded each time, to accommodate all who wanted to go.

Bearce owned a department store, one of Mount Ida's cafes, and a building where he showed silent movies (with a projector powered by a Delco generator that popped noisily in the background). Bearce fixed up an abandoned building as a boxing arena, and one of his friends orga-nized boxing bouts and wrestling matches, with fighters coming in from Hot Springs, Little Rock, and elsewhere around Arkansas. Each of these attractions had its price, of course, but Bearce always offered a free ride home at the end of an evening.

Most Mauldin residents who traveled to "Mount Idy" on Saturdays bought supplies—prices there were lower than at their own commis-sary—and went to the movies. Most of the men had families and had neither the money nor the inclination to go carousing. But with some of Mount Ida's Saturday crowd, bootleggers did a lively business in moon-shine. As the evening progressed, drinking loosened inhibitions, and tightened aggressions, and invariably somebody got into a heated argu-ment and started a fight. If their friends took sides and started fighting too, sometimes there were three or four street fights going on at once. Often some of the Bunkhouse boys from Mauldin took part in these affairs and ended up in the county jail.

Footloose loggers also drank and brawled in a rural dance hall at Whitetown, six miles from Mauldin in the opposite direction from Mount Ida. Recalling the wild Saturday nights, Henry Overby says "so many of the Mauldin boys got into fights there that they renamed it Sock City."[11]

If a Mauldin boy had a car he could go to Hot Springs, which in the 1920s and 1930s was a wide open town. A young blade could dance at Fountain Lake, or gamble (or at least watch the high rollers) in the casino at Belvedere. And, as a former Mauldin resident recalls, "All of Central Avenue in Hot Springs, all the buildings, all the upstairs . . . girls used to be hangin' out those windows. . . ." There was Ma Harper's, where a lad could find home brew (despite Prohibition), and a willing female companion. There was also Gracie Goldstein's—and she was *the* madam in Hot Springs. ("She used to walk down the street, boy, dressed like Diamond Lil, with a great big Great Dane dog on a leash.") Gracie catered to the classy trade, but she would take in a boy from Mauldin if he had saved up enough nickels and dimes.[12]

Traveling prostitutes dropped in at Mauldin once or twice, and un-doubtedly there was other illicit sex, but liquor and gambling were by far the larger preoccupations. The company fired men who appeared drunk in public, whether on the job or not, but making, selling, and consuming home brew and wildcat whiskey remained a part of life for many who lived in and around Mauldin. Such activity was sub rosa, of course, but at times the evidence of it surfaced. Once a commissary employee discovered that several bags of sugar in the back storeroom had collapsed and were nearly empty. Somebody had crawled under the building at night, bored holes up through the floor and into the sugar

Courtesy Gerlene Angel Wiley

For many a log-camp family, a two-room house was home.

Courtesy Gerlene Angel Wiley

Without any real hazards from traffic, camp children played in yards that also served as the camp's main thoroughfare.

Girlfriends in a flivver pull up before a Dierks camp house near Mountain Pine in 1930.

Courtesy Vina Short Van Pelt

vanized tubs, a rub board, and a wash pot. The women built a fire under the pot, heated water and boiled the clothes, rubbed wet soapy clothes on the board, rinsed them in the tubs, fished them out, and hung them on limbs and bushes, or on a wire strung between trees. They carried water from a nearby creek or spring, or from a well in the camp area.

At times no school was within walking distance of camp, and children boarded with relatives at Mauldin or elsewhere to attend. Few camp people owned cars and the logging railroad served as their link to the outside world. Every week or two, the women sent their grocery lists to the commissary at Mauldin, and the company store delivered groceries (and ice, for a few having iceboxes) on a flatcar, or in a trailer pulled by a motor-car. Local farmers visited the camps to peddle vege-tables or fresh meat, and the company's time checker brought mail from the Mauldin post office.

Camp people were young and liked to have fun. In summer after work, every-body got out and played games; even grownups ran races and played hide-and-seek with their children. On weekends camp folk pitched horseshoes and played the fiddle, competed at checkers or poker, had parties and rooster fights. Sometimes everybody in camp walked to a Satur-day night square dance at

sacks, and drained their contents into a washtub that he then carried away to his brewery or distillery.

People from one nearby community smuggled their potent elderberry wine into Mauldin. ("You put it up just right, it'd knock your ass on the floor in just a little while.")[13] Two brothers from Sock City peddled their whiskey around town in milk bottles painted white. Others were even more cautious: "If you wanted whiskey, you almost had to know some-body that knew the bootlegger. They wouldn't let you know who was actually selling it. You'd give 'em the money . . . and they'd tell you you'd find it in a hollow stump so many feet off the road or something like that, and you'd go and there it would be. It wasn't bottled, seldom ever bottled. Usually in fruit jars or a gallon jug."[14]

Fred Jones, who once lived at Mauldin, recalls that in Montgomery County "one sheriff would be strong against liquor and the next one would be very tolerant and didn't look for the whiskey stills much. They'd have tolerant sheriffs and then ones that would run the price of whiskey up a little." Jones also believes there wasn't as much drinking in Mauldin as in places outside town, at picnics or on Saturday nights in Mount Ida where imbibers could be among their peers and blow off steam without risking their jobs.

Though it was also against company rules to gamble, there was a penny ante poker game somewhere around Mauldin every weekend. In bad weather, players got together in a vacant house along the railroad. In good weather they assembled in the woods on a ridge just south of town, maybe twenty-five men in all, four or five groups sitting on the ground. ("You'd go down there on Saturday after payday, and that hill was just covered up with fellows playin' poker. The log haulers—you take those Maxeys, they was some of the best log haulers and they were also poker players.")[15]

Stakes were low because many of the players didn't have much money, although several of the log hauling contractors could produce sizeable rolls of bills. The largest amount of cash ever accumulated by a man at one game was pulled in by Mike Risenhoover, a sometime log hauler from the next county. Risenhoover quietly showed up at a game in the woods one chilly Sunday morning, drew two pistols and announced that he was collecting everybody's money. Reportedly, he made off with seven hundred dollars—after handing back a dollar or two to those who had already lost all their money at cards. The players were even less able to cope with the bandit because they had been drinking moonshine pretty liberally to stay warm.

Cash wasn't always available for betting purposes, and gamblers had to resort to ingenious substitutes. Loggers played a card game they called Drink-or-Smell, using whiskey instead of money to reward the winner. A jar of moonshine would be opened on the table and the winning player could take a drink. Losers were only allowed to sniff the contents.

And at one poker game in the woods, a participant lost what little money he had and pulled off his new shoes to bet them—and lost again. He walked home barefoot.

Jack Gaston, an early settler on the South Fork of the Ouachita River between Mauldin and Norman, was a farmer all his life and the man for whom the Gaston community was named. When one of his boys got a job at the sawmill, Jack gave him quite a dressing down: "I've never had, at any time in my life, ever worked at anything that [when] I got tired, I couldn't sit down and rest. You're not going down there and work around there." Jack did not believe in working by the day or by the hour, but the old man could not convince the next generation. The following day the boy returned to work at the sawmill; he wanted a regular paying job.[16]

Eventually, several of Jack Gaston's sons worked for the Caddo River Lumber Company. One of them, Charlie Gaston, gave Caddo River the right-of-way for their railroad through the Gaston community, and because of that the company hired all five of Charlie's sons. The oldest, Grady, was at one time the company's time checker, with duties directly opposite to his grandfather Jack's ideas about work.

Grady began each working day at Mauldin's toolhouse, or carbarn, when the crews left on railway motorcars to ride to their jobs in the woods. It was his job to see personally that every day laborer was working, and that the foremen "didn't carry dead men." At the toolhouse he checked the bridge crew if the men would be working very far beyond the end-of-track, and learned the names and faces of any new employees. He checked foremen's time slips for the previous day against his own record of having seen the men at work. When all the crews had departed, Grady told the dispatcher at the office which direction he would be going first on the railroad. He had his own motorcar, a one-cylinder "pop-john," and the dispatcher had orders to make sure the tracks were clear for him.

On a typical day, Grady went put-putting along the railroad, mindful that there might be a locomotive not far behind him with a string of empty flatcars. He rode out the line westward from Mauldin and visited a section crew who were replacing crossties. Several workmen lifted up the track with heavy railroad jacks, shoveled dirt to expose the ends of the decayed ties, impaled them with picks, and dragged them from under the tracks. Several others inserted new ties and tamped the fill around them with shovels having such short handles that the men were forced to work stooped over. Gaston picked up the foreman's time sheet.

Returning to Mauldin on the railroad, Grady had to stop at every intersection where a spur came into the main line, to telephone the dispatcher to make sure the next section of railroad was clear of traffic. (If somebody was coming, Grady would move his motorcar onto a siding.) Time after time, he got off his motorcar to call in on the crank-operated telephones.

At one intersection he stopped, threw the switch, and rode up the spur to see a log loader crew (loaderman and four tong hookers) and the locomotive crew (engineer, fireman, and brakeman) who pulled flatcars into position for the loader. Nearby, a log hauling contractor was bringing logs on his wagons to the railroad, and Grady walked over to the

a local farmhouse. There, one or two rooms were cleared of furniture and the dancers formed a square in each room, with the farmer calling the dances. Elders sat and watched; children talked or slept; men hung around outside to sample home brew or wildcat.

Also in the summertime, camp people visited "picnics" held in Mount Ida and elsewhere around Montgomery County, week-long festivities with fiddling, guitar-playing, and dancing; hamburgers, lemonade, and homemade ice cream; and an occasional rodeo. At Easter, camp women organized egg hunts for the children. On July Fourth, at least one of the hauling contractors provided cold drinks, watermelons, and a freezer of ice cream for his families; others rode the flatcars to community picnics at Norman or Rosboro. Before Christmas, camp children were lured away for a walk in the woods while parents brought in a Christmas tree, decorated it in an empty house and put gifts there for the children and everyone else in camp. They covered the windows and locked the door before the children returned from their walk. The kids, of course, peeked through cracks and knotholes and spied some of the glitter, and could hardly wait to see it all.

Plain and crowded though the camp houses were—parents and three small children, maybe, in two rooms—camp people regarded these buildings as home. In the wintertime, especially, as wood stoves held off the chill there was a pervading sense of coziness and comfort. Even today, people have beautiful memories of being young and happy together in those little camp houses.

contractor's camp, delivered mail he had picked up at the Mauldin post office for the camp families, and received letters to be mailed.

Then he rode back to Mauldin, switched to another line northward, and followed that until he located Tom Boyd's steel gang at work on a new spur. It was to be a long one with shorter spurs branching off, so a section crew was at work along the newly-completed track, putting up a phone line. Where the line crossed an old field, two or three men dug postholes, another two or three worked in the nearby woods cutting trees for poles, and still others moved the poles and set them in the holes. Grady noted the working men by name and resumed his ride.

Presently, in another direction from Mauldin, he found that a locomotive had derailed. C. H. Williams, the train master, was supervising an effort to pull the engine back on the tracks. Grady observed the men who were on the engine crew and the section crew, and left them as they pried ties and rails back into line with big crowbars.

For most of the day, Grady shuttled along first one line and then another, checking five or six section crews, the steel gang, several locomotive crews, and two or three loader crews. (And, if they were only a short walk beyond the end of the tracks, he also visited the grade crew, the bridge-building crew, and the men who operated a steam shovel making cuts for new railroad.) Near day's end, he returned to Mauldin—trying to get in ahead of the log trains—and stopped at the machine shop, the sawmill, and the hardwood lumber yard. The machine shop employed only three or four men, but the mill and yard had twenty or twenty-five.

A section crew pauses along the portion of Caddo River's railroad system that they maintained. Each of these "snipe gangs" had a railway motorcar to transport themselves, tools, and supplies to work sites.

Courtesy Dixie Gaston

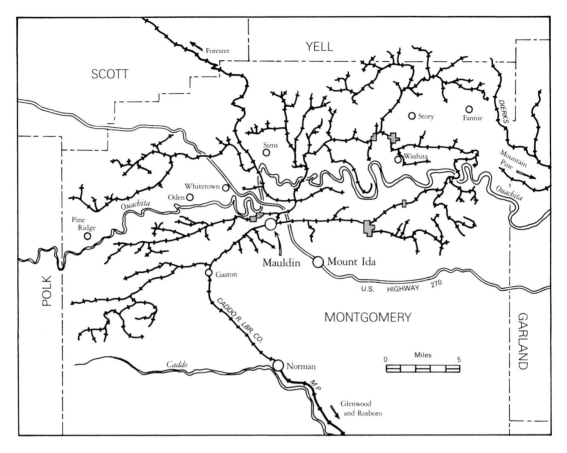

From 1922 through 1936, the Caddo River Lumber Company developed this many-branched system of logging railroads covering the northern half of Montgomery County. Shorter spurs were usually in place only a few months, enough time for the company to remove timber from small watersheds that the lines penetrated. The longer railroads stayed in use for several years, and the main line from Mauldin to Norman existed for fourteen years. Several spurs at the eastern end of the system entered the area now beneath Lake Ouachita, a reservoir completed in the 1950s. One spur at the extreme northeast reached within half a mile of a Dierks railroad from Mountain Pine. Shaded areas on the map indicate acreages purchased by Paul D. Rust in 1923, which blocked construction of Caddo River's railroads until the company purchased the land from Rust.

During this "average" day Gaston traveled about a hundred miles on his pop-john; picked up foremen's time sheets; delivered and collected mail at log haulers' and section crews' camps; and picked up grocery orders. He visited and checked on more than two hundred workers—and those did not include the railroad survey crew, main line section crew, office help, commissary employees, carpenter crew, sawmill watchman, scavenger, log cutters, log haulers, crosstie stackers, and salaried employees who were also a part of Mauldin.[17]

Moving day at Lyn Maxey's log camp. Ladies and children pose for one of the Tarkington brothers, traveling photographers.

Moving Day (at a log haulers' camp, about 1925)

The night before, somebody pulled the chickens off their roost and put them in a coop. Early in the morning, menfolks laid tall cabinets on the floor, took down stovepipes and removed the legs from stoves, took mirrors off dressers and laid them on beds, and pushed the beds and stoves to the side of each house that would be downhill, the side away from the railroad. The women tied other furniture to nails in the walls, took everything off the walls, packed

Caddo River at Mauldin was an industrial organization having hundreds of employees with many specialized skills, all contributing to a planned, coordinated effort to keep a steady flow of logs to the sawmills.

Even the basic process of cutting and hauling logs required special skills and planning. Before anyone could begin to cut down a tree, a crew of surveyors had to mark off the property to be logged. One surveyor hiked ahead and cut a line-of-sight opening through the brush while two more men on foot followed with measuring chain and compass. The crew found the corners of each section of land, one mile square, and then divided it into sixteenths: forty-acre squares that were one-fourth mile or 1,320 feet on a side. After they had marked every corner of each forty-acre block, Mauldin's saw boss, Walter White, assigned a saw crew to cut that area.

White usually had three crews at work, each employing sixteen to twenty log cutters, a saw filer, and a crew boss. When White's crews gathered at their toolhouse at Mauldin around five A.M., they were a large crowd of men. Many were restless single fellows, here today and gone tomorrow, and often there were vacancies on the crews and newcomers at the toolhouse looking for jobs. Rank beginners first had to learn the lingo of the woods: anyone who cut pine logs, for example, was called a "flathead," named for the flat-headed grub that chewed its way through the inner bark of pine trees. After Walter White assigned new men to crews, and allocated the areas to be cut, it was nearly six and the flatheads, filers, and crew bosses climbed onto motorcars and headed out the railroads to work.

Each crew had a railway motorcar (or a pickup truck with flanged wheels) and an open trailer with a long box to carry the crew's axes and two-man crosscut saws. Crew members rode on the motorcar (or in the truck) and on the trailer, sitting on both sides of the saw box. In the summertime the ride to or from work was pleasant enough, though a wise man always sat upwind at the front of the trailer to keep from getting freckle-faced, since many of the flatheads dipped snuff and spat. In winter, without any cover from the wind, the ride was frigid. Men wore their rain slickers as windbreakers and hunkered down as best they could.

Before seven o'clock the crews arrived at their work areas. If a crew was to begin cutting a new forty-acre block, the foreman first marked the boundaries between strips of timber for his men to cut. For a crew having eight saws (sixteen log cutters), he divided the forty acres into eight strips, each 165 feet wide and running all the way back through the forty. The foreman stepped off 165-foot distances along one side of the forty and with a compass, blazed enough strip line to get each pair of log cutters started; later he would come back and extend the lines. Whenever possible, strips were laid out so they ran uphill from the railroad tracks, which were along the bottom of the valley, rather than across the hill.

Each pair of men on a saw was assigned a number according to seniority; the last pair hired got the high number. The men with the number 1 began to cut trees as soon as the foreman had blazed the lines for the first strip. Those with the high number got their strip lines run last, about thirty minutes later.

To fell a tree, a pair of log cutters first notched out the undercut on the side where they wanted the tree to fall, made the back cut until the tree began to lean, and then got the saw and themselves out of the way as the tree came down. Next they worked along the prostrate trunk, one trimming off limbs with an axe while the other measured the tree into log lengths. Then with the saw they bucked, or cut, the trunk into logs. To keep the saw from getting gummed up with pine resin, it was occasionally brushed with kerosene from a pop bottle having a tuft of pine needles pushed into its neck. Finally, the stump was marked with the partners' saw number, and a chip was laid on top that later the crew boss would remove to show that he had scaled the board footage of the logs they had cut, as the basis for figuring their pay.

Logs were cut at even two-foot intervals between ten and twenty feet long, depending on the usable length of the tree's trunk. Some logs turned out to be ten or twenty-footers, but most were twelves, fourteens, and sixteens. One of Caddo River's log cutters of later years, Jeff Barnett, recalls: "One day . . . we drawed the prettiest strip I ever saw . . . four and five sixteens in that old yeller pine. Wasn't a limb on 'em till you got right up to the top. You wouldn't have to trim, just measure off the logs to cut. That shore was pretty timber."

their dishes in washtubs, and carefully stowed the coal oil lamps. The men left with the teams and log wagons for the next camp site, with one of the boys walking not far behind them, leading the cow.

Even before the log haulers departed, the snipe gang—section crew—arrived and several of them cut two young pines for skid poles, and snaked them into camp with a pair of mules. The snipes had already jacked up the first house when the train came. While the train's crew positioned a flatcar alongside the house and uncoupled their locomotive from the cars, the section hands pulled two cables underneath and hooked them to the floor sills at the corners away from the railroad. Now they fastened these hook lines to a main line which they pulled across the flatcar, through a pulley tied to a tree, and down the tracks to the locomotive, where they fastened the end of the cable to the back of the engine.

Meanwhile, others peeled the two skid poles and set them in place, from under the house up to the bed of the flatcar. Easing down the jacks, they let the house rest on the lower ends of the poles. Hurriedly, one man picked up a grease bucket and brush and daubed the poles; then the section foreman gave the signal.

Slowly the locomotive moved forward, pulling the cable tight—and with a

Barnett remembers that one day about that time he and his partner worked at top speed to cut twenty-five thousand board feet of logs: "We went to the woods and run. We hit the ground a-runnin'. We kep' runnin' till they scaled us off at the end of the day."

Most of the log cutters had to do with less. John Gwathney, another experienced cutter, found trees that were short, so it was hard to cut even twenty thousand feet a day; he recalls averaging around twelve thousand a day. Robert Lyons, a log cutter at Mauldin, found that his output was even lower: "If I had a good buddy who could swing that ol' crosscut saw, we could make ten, twelve thousand. Most of the days we only made three, four thousand—just barely got by. If we hit big timber, we did good. If we hit a patch of poles, we didn't do so good."

The company expected each pair of cutters to produce a minimum board footage each day—eight thousand feet, one man recalls—but because timber was "patchy" and since some men were not good producers, not everyone could cut as many logs as the company wanted.

During the day the crew's saw filer made the rounds and sharpened each crosscut saw. In the afternoon the crew boss began to scale the day's cut of logs, using a calibrated measuring device, the scale stick, to find the number of board feet in each log, and noting the footage in his tally book. The company paid each pair of cutters a set rate per thousand feet they cut, divided evenly between the two cutters. Robert Lyons remembers that in the early 1930s depression the rate was seventy-five cents a thousand board feet, so that he and his saw partner each got thirty-seven and a half cents per thousand feet that they cut.

Though log cutters sometimes stopped working when it rained, more often they did not. They needed the pay and the company wanted a steady flow of logs. Says Robert Lyons: "The only time we'd be laid off would be when the timber would freeze in the wintertime. Freeze so hard you couldn't saw it. But outside of that, they worked the year around. Never did rain too hard and the sun didn't shine too hot. Go or else. When you lost a day, then you had to miss something to eat. 'Cause it took just about all a man could rake and scrape to buy something to eat."

Without letup, the log cutters advanced from one forty to the next, cutting the pine. As one man recalls, "They could go through a forest and really lay that timber down."[18]

———

Walter White shuttled his saw crews from one area to another so that always there was felled timber waiting for each of more than a dozen log hauling contractors. Charlie Wilkerson, Caddo River's team boss, assigned each contractor his working area and negotiated the payments for hauling logs. Felbert Vaught, who contracted to haul logs for Caddo River in 1931, recalls that he was paid $1.45 a thousand board feet for hauls up to one-fourth mile, and $1.65 for one-fourth to one-half mile. Haul distances were from where the trees had been felled to the nearest railroad spur.

Each contractor owned his wagons and teams, as well as houses and other buildings where he and his employees lived along the railroad near the area being cut over. In addition to wagon drivers, a contractor might have men to skid (drag) logs with mules where the terrain was too rough for wagons; a swamper or brush-cutter to clear roadways; perhaps a blacksmith to repair wagons and shoe the mules; and a water boy to refill the two-gallon oak kegs of drinking water that the wagon drivers carried with them. The contractor paid his employees by the day. One wagon driver, Audie Shaw, remembers being paid $3.00 a day by a contractor in 1927.

By the time that Caddo River began to log in Montgomery County, the hauling contractors had replaced their four-wheel wagons with specially designed, heavily framed carriages, "low to the ground" between eight massive wheels having wide steel tires. Like eighteen-wheel tractor trailers on today's highways, these wagons were built to haul heavy freight. An eight-wheeled wagon, itself weighing more than a ton, could easily transport five tons of logs if pulled by a team of four good-sized mules.

The wagon driver usually worked alone, even when loading logs. He used his two leader (front) mules to pull long chains that he looped around a log, and when the mules walked ahead and pulled, the log rolled up a pair of skid poles onto the bunks of the wagon. If a driver had good mules and knew how to handle them, he could "cross haul" logs onto his wagon with a minimum of physical effort.

After loading, he took his leader mules and hitched them in front of his two wheeler (rear) mules that had remained hitched to the wagon. Then the mule skinner threw binding chains around the load of logs and tightened them, branded the ends of the logs with his contractor's identifying number, climbed onto his left-hand wheeler mule (which was saddled), and urged his "four up" team ahead. A good driver handled his mules so that the wheelers did most of the pulling and his smaller leader mules did not get tired, since the leaders' main job was to load the wagon.

Eight-wheel wagons were hinged at the middle, so the rear truck of four wheels could turn and tilt independently of the front four, making it easier to travel on rough, meandering haulways through the woods. Fortunately, most of the log hauling was downhill. At times, however, the going was steep and drivers had to lock their wheels, chaining them to the frames of the wagons so they would slide and act as brakes. On the steepest pitches, as many as six of the eight wheels were chained. Then and at all times, mule skinners had to exercise great skill in maneuvering four big mules and several tons of logs and wagon among trees, stumps, and rocks to get where they needed to go.

At the railroad each driver dumped his logs alongside the tracks, using a cant hook to loosen and roll them off his wagon and down the skid poles to the ground. Later, the company's log scaler came along and measured the board footage of the logs as the basis for paying the contractor.

Drivers carried long whips of plaited cowhide to make their mules

everything had sprung out of shape and couldn't be made to fit back together.

move and, especially, to entertain themselves. A virtuoso could crack his whip like a rifle, or delicately pop horseflies off a leader mule's behind— supposedly without hurting the animal. Mule drivers were proud of their expertise. Henry Overby, a log cutter, remembers "the mule skinners bragged about their ability to handle their teams, saying they could herd four mules, drive two, and make one mule climb a tree backwards."

Mule drivers could brag, and so could the fast, closely coordinated teams who loaded logs onto the trains. At Mauldin, Caddo River usually operated two log-loading derricks with a third one available if needed. Each crew had instructions to load eighteen flatcars (or, at least, all available logs) each day. When they had done that, they were free to go fishing, even if they were through by early afternoon. Naturally, the loader crews didn't waste time.

Each crew consisted of a loaderman, who operated the steam-powered log loader, and four tong hookers. The steam loader could pick up a log, swivel around with it, and drop it on a flatcar. The loader could also propel itself on tracks along the decks of the cars, and across the gaps between cars, to make room for new stacks of logs. Two of the tong hookers stood next to the logs piled on the ground, each man holding a sharpened tong attached to the end of a cable from the derrick. When loading, each man hooked one end of a log; then, as the loaderman lifted it, the tong hookers used pull-ropes attached to the tongs to keep the log aligned with the flatcar. As soon as it fell onto the car, the tong hookers jerked their ropes and released the tongs, and the loaderman reeled out the lifting cables and swung back to pick up another log.

Virgil Smalling, who had worked on the steel gang in Pike County, became a tong hooker at Mauldin. He says: "It wasn't so hard after you got on to it, but it's fast work. That loader boy would sling that tong at you and you had to slap [it] on to a log and he'd give that log a fast pickup and he was gone with that log, throwing it with that loader. Just as soon as we knowed that log was far enough out there until it would land on that car, we jerked them tongs out of there and turned that log loose and he'd be right back and we'd have another one. It was fast work." Another tong hooker remembers loading two stacks of logs on a flatcar in eight minutes, including time to roll the loader back to make room for the second stack.

The loader crewmen worked without talking, but watched each other's movements. Occasionally the loaderman asked for a large log, or a small one, to fit into the stack on the flatcar, but usually he just hurried the tong hookers, moving logs as fast as possible and swinging back to them for more. The work was so fast that the four tong hookers took turns from one flatcar to the next; while two worked with the tongs, the other two performed less demanding tasks such as helping to reposition the loader.

In hot weather the tong hookers burned out, got cramps, and perspired so much they could be tracked by their sweat-drops in the dust. Smalling says: "You'd get hot and you couldn't hardly cool. And where

A pair of flatheads with a crosscut saw slice into an old-growth shortleaf pine in the Ouachitas.

Frank J. Gibbs photo, courtesy Forest Heritage Center

Every saw crew had a filer who sharpened the two-man crosscut saws.

Courtesy Henry Overby

them log wagons would go along there and all the dust would dry and your face would be sweaty, that dust would just fill your face full."

Logs were often dumped on both sides of the tracks. When the crew cleaned up one side the loaderman yelled "Over!" and swung the tongs to the hookers; they grabbed the cables and stepped onto the tongs, and the loaderman would swing them up and over the train and down—into a hole of water, if that's where the logs were. Smalling recalls, "I've been set right off in the water, in Rainy Creek when it was cold, and when it was about knee deep, getting them logs. And britches legs would freeze.

"We didn't lose no time for rain, snow, nor nothing else. We had to go. The sawmill was going. It never let off on account of the weather. And we had to keep logs for that sawmill. I never did know a [Caddo River] sawmill to shut down on account of [not having] logs, in all my work with them people."

Even so, the loader crews had their fun. More than once in the summertime, a pranking loaderman swung his tong hookers over the train and into a mudhole, but the first chance they got, the tong hookers doused their loader boy with a bucket of ice water.

Each loader crew was attended by a locomotive crew who moved flatcars and the log loader to the piles of logs along the railroad. At day's end the two crews parked the loader and, with flatcars in tow, headed for Mauldin, where they put the log cars on a siding.

Pine logs await loading while two tong hookers (left background) maneuver pull ropes to guide a log onto a flatcar. Under the loading derrick, flanged wheels permitted it to roll along a set of tracks laid on the decks of the cars. This loader was used by Dierks in Oklahoma about 1930.

Frank J. Gibbs photo, courtesy Forest Heritage Center

Early the next morning the main line locomotive crew coupled all the cars of logs into one long train. Normally there were from thirty to forty cars, but sometimes as few as twenty or as many as seventy. If there were many, the main line engine had to be assisted by another locomotive. Setting their throttles on full power, the engineers got the long string of cars rolling, the main line engine pulling and the other locomotive pushing, both engines puffing and laying a pall of black smoke as they slowly moved the heavy train up the long incline to the Ouachita-Caddo River divide, then down to Norman. From there the main line engine pulled the train on the down grade to Glenwood and Rosboro, where the crew dumped the logs into the sawmill ponds.

Every working day, six days a week, a trainload of logs rolled south from Mauldin to the mills. With two stacks of logs on each flatcar, it took about thirty-five cars of logs a day to supply the two sawmills, with each of them cutting about a hundred thousand feet of lumber.

As the months and years passed, areas of cutover land in Montgomery County grew ever larger and more numerous. Virgin forest gave way to logging debris, tangles of brush, and a scattering of spindly undersized pines.

For Virgil Smalling, however, and Grady Gaston, and many other men and their families, cutting the virgin forest was a livelihood. As for cutover land, nobody paid much attention to that.

Courtesy Archie Dennis Taylor

Puffing smoke, a logging engine pulls loaded cars up a long grade near Mauldin, Arkansas, in 1925. This railroad was part of an extensive system built by the Caddo River Lumber Company.

6. An Awakening

Like nearly every other lumberman of the time, Rosborough and his Caddo River partners regarded cutover land as practically worthless. They had looked at virgin pine logs and counted the annual growth rings, fifteen or twenty to the inch—why, it took *forever* to make a sawlog! The U.S. Forest Service announced around 1920 that shortleaf pine would grow to eighteen inches in diameter in fifty-five to sixty-five years,[1] which, in the dry, rocky Ouachitas, meant at least seventy-five years. No lumberman could keep land for seventy-five years, paying taxes and hiring people to put out fires and catch timber thieves, until it would again be profitable to build a railroad and cut logs.[2] For lumbermen of that day, old-growth timber was still cheap and plentiful; if they couldn't find any more in the South, they could move out West where there were big trees aplenty.

Other things were more important than messing with cutover land. In the 1920s all southern lumbermen faced serious new competition. West Coast lumber was being shipped into places like Chicago, Detroit, and Kansas City to compete with southern pine. Lumbermen on the coast had to pay higher freight to transport their product east, but they could buy stumpage cheaper and mill the lumber at less cost. (They were also bragging about the West as "America's permanent lumber supply.")[3] Little mills were springing up, too, all over the South, making lumber at lower cost because they didn't have high overhead expenses.[4] All were producing for a market that was shrinking.

For lumbermen the question wasn't whether or not to cut out and get out, but only how fast to run the sawmill to cut out whatever old-growth timber remained. Some mill operators chose to go full speed, running night and day to clean up the timber as soon as possible to avoid the extra years of real estate taxes and other overhead, and to pay off bondholders ahead of time and save six-percent interest. Others decided to prolong their cut, reasoning that the price of lumber would go up as other mills cut out, so that they could gain even greater profits than those who chose to go full blast.[5] In the Ouachitas, the A. L. Clark Lumber Company at

Glenwood apparently produced at top speed, and so cut out in thirteen years. The Malvern Lumber Company owned about the same acreage in timber as Clark, but ran a smaller mill and lasted much longer. Most of the other companies operated somewhere between the extremes.

Nobody, however, really dawdled about cutting timber; every operator continued to increase his inventory of cutover land. Not only in the Ouachitas but throughout the South, cutover acreage kept expanding, so that in 1917 it was estimated that southern lumber companies owned seventy-six *million* acres of cutover timberland, an area half as big as Texas. In that year the lumbermen's leading trade organization, the Southern Pine Association, helped organize a cutover land conference at New Orleans to let members hear about ways to unload their burdens of real estate.[6]

Most of the conference speakers happened to be agricultural experts and as such, promoted agriculture. As if to keynote the whole affair, one speaker announced: "There is enough cut-over timber land in the hands of the lumbermen of the South today to feed this entire nation, if properly cleared, fertilized, cultivated and farmed. The possibilities of this land for farming . . . have no reasonable limit. It is the most fruitful soil within the limits of the continent. It will raise anything and everything."[7] He was followed by specialists who talked about how to eradicate cattle ticks, manage dairy herds, build silos, raise sheep, and grow vegetables. Many of the experts thought that cutover acreage could be converted to livestock farms. One fellow said, "get people on your land and cut it up into small farms, as many as you can, making self-sustaining and self-owned homes." The audience liked that and applauded.[8]

Possibly in response to the cutover land conference, the Bemises at the Ozan Lumber Company soon converted some of their cutover land to a cattle farm, and not long after that, T. W. Rosborough bought a peach orchard near Rosboro, a venture in fruit growing that others might repeat on Caddo River's cutover area. As it turned out, these developments were small-scale and short-lived, especially when compared with the land-disposal efforts of the lumber company having the most land to dispose of—Dierks. Not long after buying their first sawmill at De Queen in 1900, Dierks organized the Southern Land & Townsite Company to sell cutover acreage in both Arkansas and Oklahoma. In later years Dierks also planted and operated a large peach orchard, established an experimental farm in Oklahoma, and incorporated the Dierks Strawberry Farm that loaned money to farmers to raise strawberries and other truck crops around Dierks, Arkansas. Every summer, even into the mid-1920s, they hired agricultural experts who advised local farmers on how to grow fruits and vegetables for market.[9]

American Lumberman, in a feature article on Dierks published in 1920, said:

> The company's land policy is to dispose of its cut-over lands to actual settlers rather than to speculators, in tracts of 80 to 160 acres each. The land

is well adapted to growing cotton, corn, sweet potatoes, peanuts and other southern crops as well as for raising livestock. These farms are sold on easy payments, extending over a period of ten years, so that settlers can practically pay for the land from its earnings.[10]

At that time *American Lumberman* also said that Dierks, with nearly a half million acres of timberland in Arkansas and Oklahoma, had "timber supplies . . . sufficient to run its mills about fifteen years."[11]

Dierks sold thousands of acres of their best cutover land, but in the end the farm promotion was a failure. Many farmers were unable to pay for the land, so that it reverted to the lumber company or to banks that had loaned them money. The would-be agriculturists were plagued by lack of capital to develop their farms, by poor markets for their harvests, and especially by the stubbornness of the soil. Land that had produced pine trees would not necessarily produce corn or cotton, fruits or vegetables. It was the same story as in most of the southern pine region, where agricultural promotions on cutover land usually failed.[12]

In 1923, members of the Dierks family began to talk among themselves about a new approach to cutover land. The older generation, Hans and Herman, had retired and their sons and nephews were running the companies, and obviously there would be a third generation who could take charge later on. DeVere Dierks, one of the second generation officers, later wrote that the family also realized that if the Dierks operations closed after all the virgin timber was cut, they would have to abandon costly sawmills, railroads, mill towns, and other improvements. They had become aware, however, that the value of stumpage on their cutover lands was increasing. Second growth was coming up everywhere and it was growing much faster than the virgin timber, where for many decades the forest had been in a state of static balance in which trees had little chance to grow. Second-growth wood, with its widely spaced annual rings, was considered inferior to old growth, and in any case it was not profitable to cut the small second-growth trees. But wouldn't those trees later become profitable, the Dierks family asked themselves, if only they were allowed to grow?[13]

The idea of operating a lumber company on second growth wasn't at all radical, but until now it had not gained acceptance among lumbermen. As far back as 1890, Dr. Charles T. Mohr had seen shortleaf pine coming back in abandoned fields in Mississippi and had recommended that the young forest be protected so that it could replenish the timber resource.[14] Since 1912 a Louisiana lumberman, Henry Hardtner, had experimented with regrowth on his cutover land, protecting it from fires and free-ranging hogs that would destroy young trees.[15] At the cutover land conference in 1917, a Forest Service man had said there was an opportunity to have a permanent lumber industry supplied from second growth.[16] Beginning in 1920 the manager of the Great Southern Lumber Company at Bogalusa, Louisiana, had employed people to hand plant pine seedlings on the company's cutover land.[17] But in the 1920s these few individuals were odd ones, mavericks. Other lumbermen called Henry Hardtner a fool.

On cutover land in south-eastern Oklahoma during the 1920s, a farmer would deaden the remaining trees, remove undergrowth, build a rail fence, and then plow the ground before planting corn, cotton, or a truck crop. He would probably fail at farming, since in most cases, the soil was too poor.

Frank J. Gibbs photo, courtesy Forest Heritage Center

Seedling pines coming up as second growth in an abandoned field, within view of old-growth timber. Around 1925.

U.S. Forest Service photo, courtesy Ouachita National Forest

Of her childhood in Montgomery County, Arkansas, Mary Williams remembers: "Used to, you could burn the mountains off. And there would be fresh grass come up for the cattle. I usually helped Dad burn the mountains—I had no brothers, and I was the boy in our family. We would get on our horses and ride through the mountains and throw matches. . . ."

Every spring, southern farm folk set fire to the woods. As recently as the early 1920s, eighty percent of all forest fires reported in the United States occurred in the South.[24] Foresters could not practice forestry, for fires killed the young trees. To stop the burning, in the mid-1920s both the U.S. Forest Service and the Dierks companies launched a crusade to detect and report forest fires, put them out, and educate people not to set fires.

One of the earliest projects was to erect fire lookout towers. Dierks used three-legged structures that had supported floodlights at a sawmill during World War I; the tower man had to climb a hundred feet up an open ladder to his cramped platform on top. The first "towers" of the Forest Service were even more makeshift—crude wooden structures or, in one case, just a pile of rocks on which the fire lookout stood to scan the country below.[25] (By the late 1930s the makeshifts were replaced

Aware of some of these early developments in forestry, the Dierks family continued to speculate on whether there was enough timber to run their mills for a long time, assuming that old growth would be cut first and second growth cut later as it became sawlog-sized. They decided to hire a forester to inspect the timberland and tell them what they could do. To find a forester with suitable qualifications, they got in touch with Baker, Fentress & Company, the Chicago investment bankers who soon were to underwrite the Dierks bond issue for building Pine Valley and Mountain Pine. They dealt in timberland and could provide a man with experience in cruising timber and drawing up forest management plans.

That man was William L. Hall, the same individual whose survey of the public domain in the Ouachitas had led to the creation of the Arkansas National Forest in 1907. Hall had left the U.S. Forest service in 1919 to pursue a career in private forestry.[18] Those who later worked with him remember that he was of below average height, friendly and even-tempered but quiet, not a storyteller. He impressed people as business-like and energetic, a man who wanted to do his job well. When "Uncle Billy Hall" (as young foresters called him) went to work for Dierks he was past fifty years old, but he spent long days tramping through the woods and estimating timber on the vast Dierks landholding which, in the mid 1920s, amounted to 900,000 acres. Hall found the land in all conditions, from cutover badly damaged by fire, to acreage having various stages of second growth, to tracts still with the finest virgin timber.[19]

After months of field work and figuring, Hall handed the Dierks family his report. It had been twenty years since he sent his landmark report to Gifford Pinchot with recommendations that helped bring about the Arkansas National Forest. Now he played a creative role again, helping to instigate a forward-looking shift in management for another great landholding in the Ouachitas. Hall reported to Dierks that there was enough timber, old growth and the new forest of second growth, to allow Dierks to practice sustained yield forestry and *cut trees forever.*

On Hall's advice, Dierks in early 1925 began a forestry program. In that year also, with Dierks assured as a major client for his consulting business, Hall moved from Chicago to Hot Springs, Arkansas.

Trees under twelve or fourteen inches in diameter were to be left standing—a reasonable idea, for it was not profitable for big mills to make lumber from trees smaller than twelve inches. To upgrade the forest, trees damaged by disease, wind, or fire were to be cut to the lowest merchantable size. Stands of timber having too many small trees were to be thinned out. Loggers were to protect young trees as much as possible. Crews of boys were to gather the treetops and limbs left after logging and pile them away from young trees, so that if this brush caught fire, the growing pines would not be killed.[20]

Hall placed greatest emphasis on one point—fire protection. Without it, the Dierks reforestation program would fail. Hall had seen that short-leaf pines as small as eight inches in diameter could survive hot fires, but he wanted saplings even smaller to survive and grow. He knew that the southern practice of burning the woods in the spring had to be stopped.

William L. Hall, the forester who helped bring about widespread change in timberland management in the Ouachitas.

People everywhere set fires in the belief they were killing off ticks and chiggers and helping the grass to grow for their open-range cattle. Every year, for example, about one-third of the forest of southeastern Oklahoma, including much of the Dierks timberland, was burned off. Lightning, Indians, and now the rural people—all had set these ground fires that repeatedly swept through the Ouachitas. The big pines survived but small ones could not. Although fire had helped to create the open, grass-carpeted virgin forest, it could destroy second growth.

Dierks soon hired two foresters to work as fire prevention supervisors, with adequate towers, usually of steel.)

If a tower lookout spotted smoke, he telephoned its location to the head office, and occasionally went himself to fight the fire until a crew could come on horseback. Fire fighting crews often found that their methods of attack were ineffective. In time, however, they learned to stop advancing woods fires by such tactics as setting backfires from roads, creeks, or strips they cleared by hand. Their efforts were aided during the 1920s and 1930s when traveling lecturers and others with government and industry spread the gospel of fire prevention among the rural people, telling folks how fires meant loss of jobs, tax revenues, wild game, and even forage for cattle. (In error, the educators said that fire killed the grass and allowed underbrush to take over. It was true, though, that fire destroyed pine seedlings.)[26]

For a variety of reasons, people continued to burn the woods. Moonshiners set fires to hide the smoke from their stills. Some of the Dierks logging supervisors used fire to open up the woods for their operations. Sometimes Arkansas country boys quietly started fires on the national forest so that they could get jobs with the Forest Service to put out those same fires.

Glen Durrell, a forester in the Ouachitas in the 1920s, says: "I remember

one in Oklahoma and the other in Arkansas. They were to locate and build fire lookout towers, and set up a telephone system to connect the towers, the homes of fire wardens, and logging operations with the central office. They were to hire and supervise sixty-two local fire wardens, each of whom was to oversee fifteen to twenty thousand acres and educate his neighbors about damage caused by fires and the advantages of growing more timber. The foresters were also to organize fire fighting crews among those who worked in the woods, including the brush pilers, railroad section gangs, and steel gang. All of this they were to do as soon as possible.[21]

Glen Durrell, one of those two fire prevention supervisors for Dierks, remembers he had trouble convincing people to go along with the new ideas. One time he chided some of the log haulers for driving their wagons through a stand of pine seedlings. "They laughed and said, 'Those things will never make trees.' They didn't believe that trees grew." Logging superintendents continued to cut trees well below the twelve- or fourteen-inch minimum size. One of them told Durrell that Dierks would never get another cut of timber off the land, and that he was simply getting the value out for his employer.

By the late 1920s, however, the Dierks companies had made a beginning in forestry, and had stopped their program of agricultural land sales. DeVere Dierks indicated the extent of changes when he wrote in 1928 that "lands which we had sold as cut-over twenty years previous we were buying back as timberland."[22]

———

During the 1920s on the Arkansas (which in 1926 was renamed the Ouachita) National Forest, the U.S. Forest Service began to enforce rules to upgrade and reinvigorate the forest. Whenever a lumber company purchased timber from the national forest, their loggers were to cut only selected trees and then move the flammable logging debris away from young growth. The Forest Service marked the trees to be cut: first the defective ones; then enough good trees so that the lumberman could make a profit on the timber he purchased.[23]

Previously, about all the Forest Service could do for the Arkansas National Forest was to hire a few custodians to patrol hundreds of thousands of acres of roadless federal land. Those rangers tried, mostly without success, to prevent timber-stealing and woods-burning. Every year there were hundreds of fires, mostly man-caused, including some conflagrations that blackened thousands of acres. While they were unable to stop the fires, the Forest Service did get acquainted with the land and resources of the national forest, and with the people who lived in the neighborhood. The service also built trails and some primitive roads, and a network of phone lines connecting their ranger outposts.

Eventually, the Forest Service began to get larger appropriations from Congress so that they could make progress on fire control. Road construction was always the major expense with trails and phone lines second. The service also built fire lookouts and ranger dwellings, and gradually they established dominion over their area.[29]

U.S. Forest Service photo, courtesy Ouachita National Forest

Forest Service tower man C. H. Egger and his family stand in front of their tarpaper-covered dwelling atop the highest peak in the Ouachitas, 2,681-foot Rich Mountain near Mena, Arkansas, about 1924.

my first arrest of a man for setting a fire, and my chagrin when the county attorney recommended no action in the case. I didn't realize then that law enforcement comes, not when the law is written, but only when local people accept, and see the need for the law."[27]

Among the first to accept the law were timber workers and their families, for their future livelihoods depended on growing trees. Also, local residents became paid managers and protectors of the forest. Demcy Rose, a homesteader's son who became a Forest Service tower man on a peak named Buck Knob, loved his job, talked about the scenic views from his lookout, and even had pet names for landmarks. Proud of the forest, he was not to be outdone in protecting his area; no fire could burn for long before he would see and report it.[28]

With people like Demcy Rose at work, the crusade against fire began to succeed.

Moreover, in 1924 Congress passed the Clarke-McNary Act which allowed the Forest Service to cooperate with private landowners such as Dierks to control fires.[30] The Forest Service and Dierks connected their telephone systems and started reporting fires discovered on each other's lands. The Dierks fire supervisors also told their wardens to help the Forest Service "in every possible way" to prevent and suppress forest fires.

A national forest ranger named James M. Wait was sent out in 1925 to make annual "show boat" tours to rural communities in the Ouachitas and Ozarks of Arkansas to convince people that it was better to prevent woods fires. Wait traveled in a panel truck equipped with slide and movie projectors run from a gasoline-powered generator, and a camping outfit for overnight stays in the backwoods. At country schoolhouses he gave evening programs for everyone who would come. He showed movies and glass lantern slides about the destructiveness of fire and the benefits of the national forests, and livened the show with a bit of comedy. In her book *For the Trees,* Sharon Bass comments that "Wait's programs drew audiences of varying sizes—sometimes a dozen, sometimes 500 persons. The movies . . . were, in many instances, the first moving pictures seen by the mountain people."[31]

About the time Wait started giving lectures, the effects of forest protection and public education became noticeable; fires seemed to be decreasing in both size and number. Soon after Dierks and others helped to establish the State of Oklahoma Forest Commission in 1928, another lecturer was sent on the road, in a panel truck almost identical to Wait's and carrying the same message of fire prevention to rural schools in southeastern Oklahoma. In 1933 the newly organized Arkansas Forestry Commission launched still another "show boat" to carry the message around Arkansas.

———

Among other large owners of private timberland in the Ouachitas, only two soon followed Dierks into sustained yield forestry, one of those only briefly. William L. Hall worked out a forestry plan for the Strauss family who still owned more than fifty thousand acres, though their Malvern Lumber Company no longer had a logging railroad or a band saw mill. Hall also initiated a forestry program for the owners of the Wisconsin and Arkansas Lumber Company at Malvern, but they later closed their sawmills and sold their cutover land to the International Paper Company.[32]

Operators of the other big mills continued cutting as they always had. While a forester with Dierks in the 1920s, Glen Durrell visited the logging operation of the Buschow Lumber Company near Stapp, Oklahoma, and found that it employed no timber conservation practices and had no fire protection plan. Durrell remembers that it was "the ultimate in devastation. We talked about the Buschow Lumber Company as one of the bad ones, because that was a cut-out-and-get-out operation."

During that period in Arkansas, the Fort Smith Lumber Company cut out and the mill at Graysonia neared the end of its once large resource of

U.S. Forest Service photo, courtesy Ouachita National Forest

A Forest Service employee demonstrates the latest fire fighting equipment around 1910: a spray rig with horse-packed water tanks, and a shield to protect himself from the heat. These devices proved ineffective in battling widespread woods fires, and better equipment and tactics were soon developed.

virgin timber. The Caddo River Lumber Company still had nearly ten years' cut of old growth in Montgomery County, and had accumulated more timber to the north for the projected sawmill in the Fourche River watershed.

Caddo River's owners, however, had already foreclosed a part of the company's future. On December 12, 1924, they sold Caddo's cutover land in Pike County to the Dierks Lumber and Coal Company. Dierks bought practically all of Caddo River's Pike County holdings, nearly forty-five thousand acres, for about $2.75 per acre.[33] Caddo River received about $125,000 to use to buy timber in Montgomery County and farther north. Dierks would wait and cut second growth on the former Caddo River lands after cutting all the old growth earlier purchased for the mill at Dierks, Arkansas. Some of the Caddo River land had been cut over before 1910, and none of it later than 1923. Dierks might not need to touch the Caddo River land until the 1940s or later, and by that time the land would have merchantable second growth.

The Dierks family continued to buy timberland, including cutover land, and tried to manage all their land for perpetual yield. The owners of the Caddo River Lumber Company decided to forego second growth, at least in Pike County. The common view was that Caddo River's owners were acting rationally while the Dierks people were going out on a limb.

Frank J. Gibbs photo, courtesy Forest Heritage Center

Considering the Dierks forestry program with its goal of sustained yield, Glen Durrell later wrote:

> This was a decision based largely on faith in the future. The action could not have been justified at that time on an economic basis. When you put the low price of stumpage in the West and on the National Forests, the high interest rates, the relatively slow growth of timber, the costs of taxes and of administration, the lack of fire protection, the prevalence of timber theft, and the price that finished lumber would bring, all into the formula, the answer always came out that the private landowner couldn't afford to be in the tree-growing business.
>
> The only forestry going on was a very feeble attempt to prevent and control fires, and a decision by the Dierks people to cut to a diameter limit—a decision that was sometimes defeated by over-zealous logging superintendents, or by fires running through fresh logging slash and killing everything that was left.[34]

DeVere Dierks, writing in 1928, bore out Durrell, saying that the members of the Dierks family "don't yet know if reforestation will pay for itself."[35]

There had been an awakening to the possibility of sustained yield from the timberlands of the Ouachitas, and a beginning toward forest management by the region's largest private landowner, at a time of uncertainty for the lumber industry. Following lumber's lush prosperity in World War I, the 1920s had some profitable years but no outstanding ones. There was a building boom in the earlier half of the decade, but in the entire period from 1919 to 1929 the nation's output of forest products increased by only twenty-seven percent. America's old-growth forests were shrinking rapidly, and substitute materials such as brick, concrete, and steel were being more widely used.[36] The country's big agricultural expansion was over, people were moving away from the farms, and the 1920s agricultural depression had cut in half the demand for lumber in rural areas.[37] The average annual consumption of lumber per person in the United States had declined from 500 board feet or more in 1907 to 316 feet in 1920.[38] In Arkansas, the production of lumber in 1925 was only half of what it had been in the peak year of 1909.[39]

The building of new houses, which had been increasing from 1921 through 1925, began to decrease between 1926 and 1927 and kept on falling thereafter.[40] In addition to competition from the West Coast and from small mills, operators of large mills in the Ouachitas had this nationwide trend to consider. During the later 1920s, lumbermen again knew they were on the downhill portion of their industry's roller coaster of sales and prices and profits.

The main question was: how far down this time?

7. Hard Times

The down trend in building construction during the late 1920s was one of the first noticed of the various economic ills that turned into the Great Depression in 1929. The slump in residential, commercial, and industrial construction not only started sooner but became even more severe than the troubles in other parts of the economy, for in hard times, construction projects could be put off indefinitely. Between 1929 and 1933, as the nation's gross national product decreased by one-third, construction sagged by two-thirds. The lumber industry, a major supplier of construction materials, became one of the hardest-hit manufacturing industries in the United States.[1]

In the South, pine lumber production plummeted from thirteen billion board feet in 1925 to three billion at the bottom of the depression in 1932.[2] In Arkansas, lumber production dropped from a billion feet in 1925 to a little over two hundred million in 1932, and employment in Arkansas lumber mills was reduced by about sixty percent, while those who remained on the job had their wages drastically cut.[3] Among a hundred lumber companies in Arkansas that reported their income to the government annually, about seventy-five operated at a loss from 1930 to 1933.[4]

During the depression, two more of the few remaining big mills in the Ouachitas went out of business. The Buschow brothers shut down their mill and railroad at Stapp, Oklahoma, about 1932; they were not able to sell their lumber and had cut practically all the old-growth timber. Ozan-Graysonia closed their sawmill at Graysonia in 1931, although they still had some timber. Harry Keeley, who worked there at the time, says: "Before Graysonia shut down, they considered having little mills [near the standing timber] and bringing the rough lumber to the planer, but times kept getting worse and they finally quit. It got so bad they left logs in the woods. Said they were losing money every day they ran the mill.

"When the sawmill closed down, it was a year before they finished running lumber through the planer. They had a big rough [lumber storage] shed and it was full . . . five million feet, I think. Times was so bad, they couldn't sell it."

Horace Russell, who lived at Graysonia during his boyhood, recalls: "When they cut the last log, sometime in the afternoon, they tied the mill whistle down and let the steam exhaust through the whistle. It ran several hours, till nearly dark." For people at Graysonia, that prolonged, mournful shriek signaled the end for jobs, homes, friends, and neighbors—everything that some of them had known for twenty-three years during Graysonia's existence.

With Buschow and Graysonia gone, Caddo River and Dierks were the only major sawmill companies left in the Ouachitas. Some of Buschow's employees found jobs with Dierks at Pine Valley. Some from Graysonia went to work for Caddo River at a new sawmill that cut its first log in 1931—the mill that Rosborough had planned for the timber in the Fourche LaFave watershed.

Rosborough had for several years envisioned a mill in the Fourche drainage area, for more than thirty thousand acres of the Rust timber that Caddo River bought from Dierks in 1926 was on the Fourche River side of the divide. At first he wondered where he should put the sawmill because the Fourche timber was a long distance from any trunk line railroad. The problem resolved itself, however, once Charles E. Forrester of Waldron learned about Caddo River's predicament. Charlie Forrester simply wanted the new sawmill in *his* county, Scott County. Charlie was the kingpin there, owner of a hardware and mercantile business, director of the Waldron bank, owner of small sawmills and partner in a planing mill, buyer and seller of cotton, and all-around trader. He loaned money to farmers so they could make a crop; if one went broke, Forrester held the mortgage and foreclosed on the farm. He owned timber, too, and L. D. Williams and T. W. Rosborough had purchased timberland from him and expected to buy more.[5]

It is said that Forrester wanted Rosborough to put his sawmill at Waldron, some distance to the west of Caddo River's timber, but at the end of a Kansas City Southern branch line. Forrester had everyone in Waldron lined up to promote his idea—until Rosborough told them that he would have to bring in black people to work at the mill.[6] Whatever did happen, Rosborough finally decided that the mill should be in Scott County about twenty miles southeast of Waldron, and Charlie Forrester helped persuade the KCS to extend their railroad from Waldron to the mill site.

By February 1929, Rosborough owned the key parcels of land he needed for the sawmill and a mill town, 320 acres for which he had paid almost $3,700.[7] The site lay in a side valley of the Fourche River, located so that logging railroads could go up the creeks and into the timber. The KCS from Waldron could come down the level valley of the Fourche and then up Big Cedar Creek a short distance to the mill.

Charlie Forrester next persuaded the farmers along the projected twenty-two mile extension of the KCS to donate or to sell right-of-way for the tracks. Before long the right-of-way was assured and the KCS prepared to lay track.

About that time, Rosborough invited a delegation of Waldron's leading citizens, including Forrester, to come down to Glenwood for a celebration. After a sumptuous dinner and appropriate fanfare, Rosborough announced the name of his new sawmill town: It would be Forester, for Charlie Forrester, but with one "r", to suggest the town's forest setting.

Not long after Rosborough bought the Forester site, L. D. Williams drove his family up from Mauldin to look at it. There was no direct route; Williams had to go around to the west and back down the Fourche valley, and on a primitive road along the Fourche he ran into sand that pulled a tire off the car. To get to Forester from the south, Caddo River began to build a new road over the mountains. Company crews also surveyed the mill and town sites, brought in a small sawmill to cut timbers for the big mill, and moved in with mules and dirt wagons and a steam shovel to dig the log pond.

By the spring of 1930, Rosborough had construction going in earnest and new workers were being hired. One of them was Charlie Cockburn, who had been renting a farm near the Fourche, trying to raise cotton. Disheartened, he sold out but still could not pay all his debts. Cockburn had never worked on a "public job," as he put it (he meant "company job"), when he came to Forester. He helped to survey for the sawmill and later pushed wheelbarrow loads of concrete up a ramp to build the massive foundations for the mill's electric generators. When Cockburn came to Forester there was no place to live, so he set up a tent, with floor and walls of wood he salvaged from an old farmhouse and from the slab pile at the small sawmill. He covered the knotholes in his dwelling with the ends of tin cans. When winter came, Charlie, his wife, their children, and his father-in-law huddled together in the one-room tent and survived through temperatures sinking below zero.

Another newcomer was Roy Wilson. He and his wife Vada, both college graduates, were teaching school in southwestern Arkansas on depression salaries. Hearing about Forester, the Wilsons went to see Rosborough, who, as Vada Wilson says, "painted a kind of a pretty picture of it" and offered Roy a job. Roy first went to Forester alone ("a forlorn looking place," Vada says) and built houses, taught school for construction workers' children, and clerked at the company store that was set up in temporary quarters. Later Vada and their son joined him and they were able to move into a house. After the mill started up, Wilson became foreman over the operation of the rough lumber shed.

Kinnie Humphries had been at Graysonia and Rosboro. His daughter Lillian Maxey recalls that when the Humphries family moved to Forester before the mill opened, they discovered another Rosboro family were their neighbors: "Mrs. Bigger didn't let us get unloaded till she told us about the bedbugs. There were bedbugs in every house, including those nobody lived in. The bedbugs were in the new lumber. We had to put our bedposts in containers of water."

As the mill neared completion, word spread that Rosborough planned to bring black people to Forester. There were no blacks living in Scott County, and some of the farmers along the Fourche began to circulate threats. Rosborough was ready; he already had his fence around the Quarters and he had hired a white man from Glenwood to look after security. Beulah Norwood remembers: "Me and my husband was the first two peoples there. They was buildin' on the mill, tryin' to get it right, tryin' to get it runnin'. They had us fenced in. Had wide boards and they jus' fenced it in. Had gates. They had a sheriff there. We didn't have no trouble.

"I went to fishin' one day. I love to fish. A white lady was settin' there fishin'. I says, 'How you doin'? Catchin' anything?' That white lady took off a-runnin'. Throwed her pole in the water. I never did see her on that branch again."

————

Each year Hal Shaffer in Kansas City had reserved part of Caddo River's profits for the new project, but by 1930 the company's net income was declining and Forester's expenses were mounting. Shaffer became anxious, and a little stingy with money. M. T. Read, the first commissary manager at Forester, says: "Hal Shaffer was called 'the cutworm.' When they were building Forester, Rosborough had the carpenter crew to hide when Shaffer arrived." Read adds: "Rosborough's ambition was to build the mill to look nice. I think what he had in mind was building that up for Whit" (Whit was then in college).

Rosborough had told Roy and Vada Wilson about the nice homes he wanted to build, but in later reality they became modest dwellings built on the site, together with many two-room houses hauled over the mountains from Mauldin. Some of the sawmill's machinery was secondhand. The roofs of the huge dry lumber sheds came from treetops that were normally left lying in the woods. Log hauling contractors at Mauldin had to collect their quotas of these short, knotty tops from felled pines and bring them out to be sawed into six- or eight-foot sheathing boards, so that the company could save their better lumber to sell.

Construction had progressed far enough by the first of July 1931 that the new mill at Forester could cut its first log.[8] Clinton Moore, who had recently become the town's barber, was invited by the sawmill superintendent to come and watch. Says Moore: "We was all excited. We all wanted to get going. Kinda hard times there when it got started, you know. We was just all trying to stay together."

With the mill producing lumber at last, there did seem a chance of staying together, and people took stock of other needs. Some folks were still waiting for houses, and the dwellings that were occupied had no window screens, walks, fences, or other finishing touches. In the yards were old furrows where corn and cotton had grown a few years before. Everywhere were sawbriers that the farmer had failed to uproot with his plow.

But the sawmill was going, with a circular headsaw on the left side of the mill that cut small logs—poles, almost—into cants that went through a resaw, and a band saw on the right side that cut the larger logs.

The log pond was full of timber from the railroad right-of-way that was being opened into the woods. Loggers were still cutting trees so close to Forester that they walked from town to work.

———————

T. W. first sent an employee from Rosboro to be resident manager at Forester. Early in 1933 that man stepped aside for Whit Rosborough, just graduated from college, to replace him. Rosborough was glad to have his son home at last. Whit had begun college at Texas A&M., taking electrical engineering and making above average grades, but after a year he had transferred to the Massachusetts Institute of Technology, probably the toughest engineering school in the country. At MIT he pursued an erratic, almost disastrous academic career. Twice he failed more than half of his courses; twice he took year long leaves of absence. For five summers he attended summer school to repeat courses and to catch up; one course he took four times before passing. He repeated a basic electrical engineering course three times before he passed that— but passed the electrical engineering laboratory with honors on the first try. Finally, in December 1932, seven years after starting college, Whit received a bachelor of science degree from MIT in business and engineering administration.[9]

Back home, people said that at college Whit had been a playboy. He might have been, but on arriving at Forester he settled down to work. Whit had spent time in the office and the sawmill at Glenwood (probably during his leaves of absence from MIT), where his father assigned him a variety of jobs. He came to Forester knowing a little about everything around the mill, and itching to experiment. One man recalls that Whit "wanted everything perfect."[10] He designed a modification for the power plant's boilers to increase efficiency, and then put on overalls and went into the hot area behind the boilers to help install his new devices. Whit's employees remembered him for that.

Teden Cole, whose husband Beuford Cole managed the Rosboro plant, says of Whit: "He was more liberal than his father. Had more modern ideas, especially about labor, fairness to employees, and so forth. He had gone to MIT and gotten a lot of ideas there. Some of the other people up at Kansas City who were in the company thought Whit was too liberal." Perhaps so. Frank Jones, a black, says: "Color didn't mean nothin' to Whit. He didn't like for you to call him 'Mr. Rosborough,' either." Alex Nichols, another black employee at Forester remembers, "anything Whit thought that he could do to make it pleasant for the workers, he was for it." And a white man recalls, "Whit was the best man I ever worked for."[11]

For all his new ideas, Whit had his father's old-fashioned impatience with slackers. John Gwathney says: "If he ever stopped and looked at a man, that was all. He'd say 'Go to the office; your time is there.' He'd tell them they wasn't on no honeymoon. They was there to work." Another man says there was "no humor about him—strictly, strictly business."[12] People also remember Whit's nervous intensity. He worked fast ("industrious," one woman says).[13] When he walked, he almost ran.

People liked Whit Rosborough. He was friendly. He took his supper with working folk at Forester's boardinghouse. He was good looking, a slender six-footer with reddish-blond hair, a neat dresser like his father, though not quite as tall. He was athletic, amusing himself by jumping and spinning logs on the sawmill pond. He fished with the town's druggist and hunted quail and played tennis with one of the mill's sawyers. He visited for hours with Roy Wilson, the ex-schoolteacher whom he came to regard as a sort of advisor on management problems. Mostly, though, Whit and Roy talked about football.

On bird-hunting trips with George Morris, the sawyer, Whit talked about his future. His father had begun to look for timber in Oregon. Before many years, Whit confided to Morris, he and his father would be building a mill out there.

Whit was unmarried and lived in the resident manager's five-room house. A black couple, whom Halcy had chosen at Glenwood, moved to Forester to look after him. Arlean Williams, Whit's cook and housekeeper, remembers asking him what he wanted for dinner: "He was so nice to get along with. 'What you want today, Mr. Rosborough?' Whit would say 'Oh, Arlean, I don't know. Just cook.' He ate anything I fixed."

Whit Rosborough. He and his father had plans to build a mill in Oregon, but Whit was to first get some experience at Forester . . .

Courtesy Arlean Williams

Arlean's husband Jerry, who worked at the mill, took care of Whit's yard, but never played Fred Wingfield's role as chauffeur. Whit preferred to do his own driving. Before long it became known that each weekend when he drove the forty-five miles of gravel road to Glenwood, he tried to improve his time. H. T. (Red) Crawford, the Glenwood automobile dealer who sold Whit his black Chevrolet coupe, says: "He was more a perfectionist. He'd try to make that time in an hour. Each time he'd try to make it a little faster."

Arlean Williams remembers: "Daddy would call him. He'd say 'Daddy, I'll be there such-and-such a time.' Daddy would say 'Don't time yourself. Son, don't drive so fast.'

"But when he'd leave—zippp! Gone. He started off fast. He drove like a bat out of glory."

––––––––

By the time Whit came to Forester, the Caddo River Lumber Company had struggled through the two worst years of the depression, 1931 and 1932. Lumber sales had slowed to a trickle and the company was forced to cut back on production. One man recalls, however, "They managed to keep going; they furnished work . . . provided jobs when everybody else shut down."[14] Another man agrees: "Old Man Rosborough would give 'em so much work a week, enough to get by on."[15] At one point, though, all the single men at Mauldin were laid off. For a while the Rosboro mill ran only two or three days a week. The mill at Forester was put on two shifts, each working only half a day, to give more people a means of subsistence. (Ironically, at the depths of the depression the Caddo River Lumber Company may have been the largest manufacturing employer in the entire state of Arkansas, with three big sawmills having as many workers as possible on the payroll at subsistence wages. At that time Caddo River had almost certainly more than a thousand employees, and possibly more than fifteen hundred.)

People found ways to get by. Virgil Smalling, the tong hooker at Mauldin, had a family to support. He says: "The Big Compression was a bad time. We didn't get to work none hardly, but maybe a day or two a week. There was nothing run all the time . . . just what they could keep a-going. There wasn't nobody had no money then. Tried to give everybody enough work, if they could, for them to live.

"And when that [log] loader wasn't a-running, anything I could catch I would have done it. I'd log for Lyn Maxey; he was a contractor and he had seven or eight wagons. Maybe we would get to work two days.

"I'd go up to the toolhouse—there was somebody sent from that toolhouse to work every morning—and I would catch anything, if there was [a need for] an extra man. Sometimes one of them log cutters would be sick or something; all right, they would take me right along; I'd cut logs. I would be right up there and if there was a man short in the bunch, I got to go; I worked. I think maybe we got a dollar and a half a day, cutting them logs."

Floyd Kimble, whose father was a log hauler at Forester, remembers: "It got pretty slow. Dad, I think, only worked one day a week. We had five kids. They had a Red Cross that brought groceries and gave them to a justice of the peace to distribute. We was too proud. I think we got one sack of flour. That's all we ever took off of them the whole time of the depression."

Every employee was affected. M. T. Read had managed a commissary in Alabama for $250 a month, but lost his job and came to Forester as commissary manager for $81.25 a month—about $3.25 a day. L. D. Williams' son Vernon had been an engineer with the Arkansas Highway Department at $270 a month; he lost that and came to Forester as logging superintendent for $50 a month, which was raised to $75 when he got married. Archie Taylor, a locomotive engineer, had his pay reduced from $4.50 to $2.25 a day; he was one of many whose wages were cut in half. Log cutters who had been paid fifty cents a thousand board feet in the 1920s now got twenty cents. Laborers in the steel gang who had been making $2.65 a day were cut to $1.25. The largest number of workers were day laborers, paid $1.25 or even $1.00 a day. The work day was still ten hours, so they were being paid twelve and a half cents, or even ten cents, an hour.

But a job paying ten cents an hour was better than no job at all. James Davis, a black, remembers: "It was not too much of a depression. We'd leave [Forester] and play baseball, and where we'd go, everybody'd be starvin' to death."

———————

Dierks, too, cut hours and wages as the depression deepened, and in 1931 began to take more drastic measures. One by one, they closed the mills at Mountain Pine, Dierks, Broken Bow, and Wright City. Only Pine Valley remained open. Some of the employees from Mountain Pine and Dierks were able to get jobs there; others came looking for work at Mauldin and Forester. For a number of them, Caddo River provided jobs. Ella Jackson, who lived at Mauldin in the 1930s, recalls "two rows of shotgun houses, facing each other, called Dierks Town, because so many Dierks people came there—log cutters, section crew, steel gang— when Dierks was down during the depression. They built new houses. Almost all had Dierks people in them."

All of the Dierks companies were losing money. During 1931 and 1932 the Choctaw Lumber Company ran in the red for the first time in the company's history. In 1926 Choctaw sold pine lumber for an average price of $35.00 a thousand board feet; in 1932, for $18.11 a thousand— and little was sold at that price. The Pine Valley Lumber Company was a chronic money loser. The lumberyards of the Dierks Lumber and Coal Company in Nebraska, now located in a stagnating farm region, were in especially bad shape. Lumber had been in the yards so long it had termites.

Moreover, the Dierks companies were saddled with the bond issue of 1926, six and a half million dollars. Even into the depression, Dierks paid interest on the bonds, but the first payment on the principal, $650,000, was coming due in December 1932, and it became clear that Dierks could not pay. Bondholders wanted to take over the mills, tim-

Courtesy Francelle Ledford

R. J. Cates, an employee at Forester, received this book of 1¢, 2¢, and 5¢ coupons as an advance of one dollar against his next payday.

Courtesy Marie Cates Park

"I Owe My Soul . . ."

Andrew Short, who owned sawmills near Hot Springs, Arkansas, in the 1920s, gave brass tokens valued from 5¢ to $1.00 to his employees when they wanted advances against pay. The tokens were good only at Short's commissary.

Brass tokens like these were called brozine, a name that evidently came from two French words: bon, that which authorizes something; and

berland, and other assets that had been mortgaged as security. The Dierks family looked for a way to cope—and found only one. In October 1932, the Dierks Lumber and Coal Company in Arkansas, the Choctaw Lumber Company and the Pine Valley Lumber Company in Oklahoma, and the Dierks timberlands in both states were placed in receivership under the provisions of Section 77B of the federal bankruptcy law.

In the offices of the Caddo River Lumber Company across the street from the Dierks Building in Kansas City, Hal Shaffer was having to serve as both Caddo River's treasurer and to fill in for the company's president. William F. Ingham had always been preoccupied with other business interests, but early in the depression he suffered a stroke. It fell to Shaffer to pilot Caddo River through lean times.

The building of Forester drained Caddo's financial reserves, and lack of orders for lumber left the company with very little operating capital. Rosborough cut hours and wages to the bone, but from day to day there was no certainty that the company could keep going. The crisis lingered month after month through 1931, then into the winter and the spring of 1932. One of Shaffer's daughters recalls that "Father had almost a nervous breakdown . . . so worried about the company going under that he almost ended up in the hospital."[19] His other daughter says, "He worked hard to not go into bankruptcy . . . had too much pride."[20]

Shaffer felt that Caddo River needed a money cushion, a loan, but finding money in the depression was not easy. Finally, on July 1, 1932, through a Kansas City bank, Caddo River arranged to borrow a million dollars. To obtain the money, the company had to issue bonds, the same kind of six-percent-interest, mortgage-all-the-company-assets bonds that Dierks had issued in 1926.[21]

Arlean Williams, Whit's housekeeper at Forester, remembers: "We were behind him—going to Arkadelphia to see my mother—when he had the wreck. And there he was. Jerry got out of the car and says, 'Oh, baby, that's Whit—'"

On his way to Glenwood that Saturday afternoon, Whit had driven over the top of a hill and hit another car head-on. When Jerry Williams saw him lying there, he was still alive. Someone who stopped to help said his neck was broken. That night in the hospital at Hot Springs, Whit Rosborough died.

The next day Whit was brought to the Rosborough home in Glenwood—the town did not have a funeral parlor—and people began to file through the living room past the casket. Someone at first directed the blacks to the back door. Rosborough saw what was happening and intervened: "They don't have to come in at the back door. They are my son's friends."[22]

The following morning the funeral was conducted in the Rosborough living room, and in the afternoon Whit's body was taken to Prescott to be buried beside his mother.[23] He was twenty-six when he was killed on February 10, 1934, having been at Forester for little more than a year.

Through the entire episode, T. W. Rosborough retained his composure, though it was obvious that he was grieving intensely. For months afterward, the mere mention of Whit brought a hurt look to his face. He carried Whit's pocket watch as well as his own, and at times wore an old hat that was said to have been Whit's. Rosborough, however, had a strength of will—some perceived it as hard-heartedness—that enabled him to persevere in spite of personal tragedy. When Whit was killed, Rosborough was sixty-five years old, but he kept right on sawmilling.

Rosborough, then, continued to play a broad role in the lumber company and in Glenwood. He listened to and advised the black men who

signe, *a signed warrant.* French-speaking mill workers in Louisiana may have originated the term to describe the signed pay slips that they received at the end of each workday. A man could trade his "bozine" at the commissary for merchandise, or he could save them till payday and turn them in for cash.[16]

Every lumberman had to be able to provide his employees with advances, for wages were low and regular paydays always too far apart. Many sawmillers paid advances in tokens or scrip to avoid having to keep cash on hand, and to generate more income by requiring employees to trade at the commissary. The Caddo River Lumber Company used daily pay slips, brass tokens, and finally books of assorted coupons— 1¢, 5¢, 10¢—having a total value per book of $1.00, $3.00, $5.00 or more. About 1940, the company at Forester replaced coupons with credit bookkeeping at the commissary.

Did lumber workers owe their souls to the company store, like the coal miner in the song "Sixteen Tons"? A few must have, for they lived on advances and seldom got cash on payday. Many others used advances regularly but not excessively. Lumber companies also limited borrowing: a man could get an advance against wages earned but not yet received, but could not borrow against future earnings. Controlled bor-

rowing may have curbed some tendencies toward overspending, and prevented loan sharks from taking advantage of habitual borrowers.

An employee of Caddo River could get his advance in brozine or scrip and spend it at the company store—but commissary prices always were higher than in stores outside the mill towns. He could receive his advance in cash and trade with independent stores but the company charged ten percent for providing cash. Tokens or coupons could be used outside if a store would accept them, but a storekeeper often discounted "company money" ten percent because he had to bring it to the commissary to spend. Only if workers could refrain from taking advances— waiting until payday to get their full wages in cash—could they escape these costs and restrictions.[17]

While lumber companies often provided housing at very low rents, their commissaries were not only a convenience for employees but also a source of profit. The margin of profit depended on the operator; it is said that T. W. Rosborough wanted his stores to profit moderately. (Although Caddo River's records have been lost, a company store at a logging camp in southern Arkansas in 1913 netted about nine percent.)[18] Rosborough did not care where his employees traded ("Gracious damn,

came to his door, caps in hand: "Mr. Rosborough, I needs to talk to you."[24] He strolled downtown, chatted with customers at the drugstore and poolroom, stopped on the street and talked with young people about their plans for the future. Occasionally he visited the Methodist church and put a silver dollar (a large sum in those days) in the collection plate. Whenever he could, he went to sawmill baseball games of teams both white and black, at the ball park he had built for them. On Sunday afternoons Fred Wingfield drove him around the countryside where he looked at timber and stopped to see farm people. Boyd Tackett, who worked for Rosborough in the 1930s, says of his influence at Glenwood: "He wanted to be helpful to everybody. He didn't try to run everything. But everybody wanted to do what Rosborough thought best."

To his Kansas City associates and their families who were his houseguests, Rosborough seemed the true southern gentleman—tall, erect, neatly dressed, amply upholstered. Rosborough referred to Hal Shaffer as "Shay-fuh" and served grits and gravy for breakfast. Every meal was formal, in the dining room where Rosborough, in coat and tie, tapped a little bell on the table when he wanted Halcy to bring the next course. The Inghams and Shaffers also regarded Rosborough as an honest man, straightforward and fair. A well educated man. A man who was not vindicative. Also, at times, a jolly old man. And one who was a bit of a character. Though T. W. loved to eat and showed the results (though Halcy tried to regulate his eating), in other ways he was somewhat of a health addict. In bed he wore a nightcap to avoid chills; when playing bridge he kept his hat on to protect himself, as he said, from neuralgia. He drank Mountain Valley mineral water, and every January went over to Hot Springs, rented a house, and took a course of the mineral baths.

In addition to his sisters and their families, Rosborough's family circle included Halcy and Fred Wingfield, who had been with him for twenty years. A visitor to the Rosborough home found him sick in bed, and she recalls: "That little Negro woman was waiting on him hand and foot. Oh, she just loved him."[25] Moreover, Era McKeown, a Rosborough neighbor in the 1930s, says: "Halcy would tell Mr. Rosborough what she wanted to tell him; he would listen to her. She was the only person who could talk to him that way." Another observer says that Halcy, who never had children of her own, was like a mother to Rosborough.

Era McKeown remembers: "Mr. Rosborough and Fred were pals, and Fred would do anything in the world Rosborough wanted him to. Rosborough would get in that back seat with his hat on, rare back, and tell Fred to go. I think he was happiest when he and Fred would get together and go places." Fred looked after the yard but his more visible role was as caretaker and driver of the Rosborough automobiles, which usually were a four-door Chevy and a large Chrysler. (A logger remembers "Rosborough drove a big old car . . . as long as two or three fence rails, and that was back when times was hard.")[26] Fred put on coveralls to do his yard work and to wash and polish the cars, but wore a white shirt and a cap for chauffeuring. He was proud of his position and had a dignified bearing (". . . kinda prancy," says Boyd Tackett. "He walked that way; he talked that way."). Other blacks envied Fred for what they saw as his light responsibilities. Fred, like Halcy, also enjoyed considerable leeway with Rosborough, who forgave his occasional missteps. ("Freddie's been a bad boy," Rosborough told Red Crawford at Glenwood, when he asked Crawford to drive him to Forester. Fred had gone to Hot Springs on his day off, gotten drunk, and landed in jail.)

During the 1930s there was another person living in the Rosborough home. Sometime between Urcy's departure and Whit's death, Winifred Rosborough's sister, Rita Tuppen, came to Glenwood for a visit. Mrs. Tuppen had asthma and found that the southern climate helped her, so Rosborough invited her to stay in his home as a friend and companion. Rita—whose husband was in a mental institution—decided to remain in Glenwood. A slightly built woman in her fifties, gracious and educated, she took part in women's social activities and in frequent bridge games with Rosborough and their neighbors.

Courtesy Anna Watts Rosborough and Margaret Watts Rieder

it's your money," he told Ernest Jackson, a railroad worker at Mauldin. "You can spend it where you want to"). Zealous underlings, however, reminded those whom they saw trading "outside" that they should use the commissary if they valued their jobs. Those who received such reminders deeply resented them.

For all their disadvantages, the company store and company credit were less troublesome than the earlier "furnish" merchant of the rural South who would provide a farmer with supplies for the coming year on credit—with the loan secured by a mortgage on the farm. At least when a lumber worker received advances against regular paydays, he did not risk his whole means of livelihood.

T. W. Rosborough in the 1930s had no idea of retiring. Age had not softened his determination to undertake new ventures in sawmilling.

The Unfortunate Ones

John Wiley, who worked in the sawmill at Forester, holds up a finger with a deformed, broken nail. "The closest I ever come to gettin' hurt was that finger there. I was straightenin' that stuff on the slasher chain . . . and got that finger in there, someway or other. Got it in some cogs. It's stiff. It was lucky it didn't just rip it off."

An injured finger, in other words, wasn't really getting hurt; worse things happened. Virgil Smalling, braking a train at Forester, was thrown from a flatcar onto a pile of railroad rails. "That hurt my back, and it sprung my hip, and that wrist, it broke a little bone there. I was off a good while on account of that, about seven months," he remembers.

Even worse things happened. A sawyer at Graysonia decided to ride the log carriage, lost his balance, and was thrown into the band saw. A laborer at Rosboro was feeding slabs into the hog (the fuel grinder) when a snag on a slab caught his overalls and jerked him in head- first. A log hauler at Mauldin fell from his wagon and was injured in- ternally, and although a doctor came, in four days he died of unknown inju- ries. Workers were also hurt or killed by tumbling logs, falling trees, run- away trains and trucks, whirling saws and pulleys. While most lumber com- panies gave at least lip ser-

Beyond Rosborough's hearing, many people now called him "Old Man Rosborough"—he was boss and was, in fact, old. He remained the same strong-minded individual he had always been, nervous, stammering, sputtering, prone to quick decisions and outbursts of temper. Vernon Williams recalls that "if he said you are to go at a certain time—boy, you'd better be ready to go." Vernon's sister Jessie Diamond remembers: "He fired somebody and couldn't get the safe open to give the man his pay. He tore the phone off the wall." And Era McKeown says: "Mr. Rosborough was determined to have his way about everything. He did what he wanted to do." Rosborough would even overrule his trusted lieutenants, including L. D. Williams. The Williams family could tell when this happened, because L. D. came home and kicked the fence palings.

Rosborough could also be careful with money. Boyd Tackett remem- bers: "Rosborough never bought a piece of timber till he had it esti- mated. He was very, very cautious about what he'd do. He didn't throw it away—except he wasn't tight." (Contradicting what Tackett says, Vernon Williams remarks that "He was tightfisted.") Often asked for handouts, Rosborough gave nickels and dimes to children for candy, but not abun- dantly. Some of those close to him, however, remember him as generous.

Rosborough was a paternalist, an individualist, a dominant person- ality. Above all he was an optimist, willing to move forward, to take chances. During the depression when many men became discouraged, seeking security rather than taking risks, Rosborough kept looking ahead to new ventures.

Not long after his son's death, an insurance agent came to Rosborough with a check for Whit's life insurance, in the amount of fifty thousand dollars.[27] For 1934, it was a very large amount of money. It reminded Rosborough that he and Whit had talked about building a mill out West.

———

"Speed it up, Fred—"

Rosborough was in his usual place in the back seat. In front with Fred Wingfield was Vernon Williams, L. D.'s son; in back with Rosborough was Mrs. Tuppen. The four of them were in Rosborough's new 1934 Chrysler Airflow, the car that pioneered aerodynamic styling, with its rounded-off front, and swept-back fenders and rear. Vernon Williams thought the car resembled a terrapin.

This warm summer afternoon they had driven down into the Rio Grande Valley and stopped at the dusty little town of Bernalillo, where Rosborough thought he would build his sawmill if he bought the New Mexico timber. For several days they had been at a ranch in the moun- tains north of Bernalillo, and Williams and Rosborough had ridden on horseback (with Rosborough sixty-five and overweight!) through the timbered area up by Redondo Peak. The two of them had discussed such things as how much stumpage there might be; the building of truck roads and a logging railroad; and cutting the cheap fir for crossties and the ponderosa pine for lumber. A ten-mile square of timber had been offered for sale. But it appeared there were too many problems to overcome.

Now they were leaving Bernalillo, meeting pavement after fifty miles of dirt roads. Rosborough pulled out his watch.

"Gracious damn, is this as fast as this thing will go? Fred, speed it up. I want to be in Santa Fe by five-thirty. Speed it up some more."[28]

———

The New Mexico timber deal did not jell and Rosborough turned his full attention to Oregon, where he had inquired about timberland before Whit's death. During a month long trip to the Northwest, he employed an agent to buy Douglas fir stumpage. Some months later, on February 1, 1936, Rosborough acquired title to his first tract.[29] At last, he owned some magnificent Oregon timber like the fir he had seen on his honeymoon with Urcy twenty years earlier.

His agent continued to buy. The acreages were small, but while forty acres of Ouachita shortleaf pine might yield two hundred thousand board feet, a forty of virgin Douglas fir could produce nine million feet. The cost of one of these Oregon forties was high, but in truth, Rosborough was acquiring timber for as little as twenty-five cents a thousand on the stump. The Northwest was hard hit by the depression and prices were at rock bottom.

———

At 9:30 on the evening of June 22, 1936, Glenwood was almost asleep.

Toot . . . toot . . . toot . . . toot . . . toot . . . toot . . . toot. . . . Short blasts sounded without letup for a minute or more, jarring everybody awake.

"Mr. Rosborough, that's the fire whistle—"

Rosborough was already up, pulling on clothes and stumbling toward the front door. "You don't have your hat, Mr. Rosborough—"

"Gracious, we'll get the hat after the fire's out!" He hurried down the street.[30]

Rosborough saw it was in the roof of the planer and the rough lumber shed, fire breaking out along the skylights and eaves. Men were scurrying to hook up hoses—but what could they do? It looked too late. . . .

There had been a long dry spell and tonight a high wind had come from the north, bringing an electrical storm. Lightning had surely struck the shed, maybe shorted the electric light wires and thrown sparks. The fire had traveled the length of the big shed, hundreds of feet, within minutes. Now Rosborough saw fire all the way along the roof. Stacked under that roof were millions of board feet of dry lumber.

In half an hour the rough lumber shed, the planing mill, and the finished lumber shed were one monstrous inferno. Fierce heat drove back the fire fighters, and created a draft that hurled sparks and pieces of burning wood high into the wind that carried them into the town. ("Chunks of fire were falling all over everything. You could read a newspaper anywhere out there in the street.")[31] Suddenly, at the height of the conflagration, there came a rain shower. The big fire continued unabated, but the flying brands were dampened.

People as far as Hot Springs, thirty miles away, saw the light in the sky ("like the sun coming up")[32] and drove to Glenwood to learn the cause of it. Glenwood residents not fighting the fire stood and watched in fear

vice to safety (and Dierks had safety contests, even in the 1920s, to cut down on lost-time accidents), it was hard to get either workers or supervisors to pay attention, even though logging and sawmilling were filled with dangers.

Lumber employees and members of their families also died of strep and staph infections that developed into septicemia—blood poisoning. People died of pneumonia and tuberculosis. Women died in childbirth. Babies succumbed to "second summer," a bacterial diarrhea resulting in dehydration. By today's standards, medical practice before World War II was exceedingly primitive. The first effective antibiotics—sulfa drugs and penicillin—were not available until the 1940s.

The system of compensation for injury or death was primitive, too. Larger lumber companies, such as Caddo River, carried insurance to provide lump sums—a few hundred dollars for an injury, or a few thousand for a death—to unfortunate employees or their families. Payments were seldom enough to cover economic losses, and families had to rely on help from relatives or friends. Eva Diggs remembers when her father, a logger at Mauldin, got his back hurt by a falling tree, and was brought home and laid down. "Mother went to work in the hotel for one dollar a day. The guy at the hotel was good to us—

fed us leftovers. Mother would get home from work with bowls of food for the kids, four small children," she recalls.

Thus, in the 1930s and earlier, about all that anyone in lumbering could do to avoid being an "unfortunate one" was to be careful and trust to luck.

and dismay. ("I never will forget. It looked like the end of the world. It looked like the whole world was on fire. I stayed up on top of the hill, looking down over it. It was a sad thing. Everybody's jobs were burning up.")[33]

The men of Glenwood stayed up all night, watching for firebrands, putting them out, trying to keep homes from burning. Sparks fell for miles around. A barn was lost, and several houses caught fire but were saved, and the woods across the Caddo River were set ablaze. But the rain shower put out sparks at a crucial time, and Glenwood itself was spared. Also, a crew of the company's men stopped the fire along an open tramway between the planer and the dry kilns, so that the kilns and sawmill were saved. Those closest to the fire got blistered arms and backs, and several were overcome by heat, but no one was seriously hurt.

At noon the next day the fire still burned but was under control. The following day's *Arkansas Gazette* reported that the fire destroyed fourteen million feet of lumber and estimates of loss ranged as high as half a million dollars. Rosborough soon announced that the burned planer and sheds would not be rebuilt, but that the sawmill would reopen. Dry lumber would be trucked from Glenwood to Rosboro for finishing. About 125 men who had worked in the Glenwood storage sheds and planing mill had lost their jobs.[34]

A cleanup crew gathers at the wreck of a Dierks locomotive, about 1920.

Courtesy F. McD. (Don) Dierks, Jr.

8. Winding Down

The disastrous fire at Glenwood on that night in June 1936 occurred during a period of winding down for Caddo River that lasted through most of the 1930s. At the time of the fire, the company was on the verge of cutting out in Montgomery County. Within weeks, loggers began to cut the pine that surrounded and stood within view of Mauldin; those trees had been left for last. By the beginning of 1937, all the Montgomery County timber had been removed.

Caddo River about this time extended their logging railroad five miles to the southeast from Forester, up a mountainside to the Fourche-Ouachita divide to connect with one of the logging railroads from Mauldin. Over the divide they then carried to Forester whatever they could use from Mauldin—locomotives, flatcars, log loaders, railroad steel, and two-room houses. (For a few months until the tracks into Mauldin were taken up, this Caddo River logging line was the only through railroad ever operated over the high backbone of the Ouachitas. To the south it connected with the Missouri Pacific at Norman; to the north, with the Kansas City Southern at Forester.)

During 1937 the company took up Mauldin's railroads; sold the main line locomotive that had pulled log trains to Glenwood and Rosboro; and hauled more two-room houses to Forester on log wagons and trucks. Caddo River also trucked many of Mauldin's four-room homes to Forester, traveling the narrow, twisting road built over the mountains. They sold the larger buildings to a salvager who dismantled them for materials.

After Mauldin shut down, Caddo continued to operate the Glenwood and Rosboro mills on odds and ends of timber, mostly second growth. One crew with an engine and log loader picked up logs along the Missouri Pacific tracks from Norman southward almost to Gurdon. Truckers brought second-growth logs to the mills from cutover lands of A. L. Clark and Ozan-Graysonia. Thus the company was able to run the Glenwood sawmill for eighteen months after fire had destroyed the sheds and planer. At the end of 1937 Rosborough shut down the mill and put Rosboro on two shifts, still cleaning up second growth.[1]

Rosborough wanted to keep the Rosboro mill operating as long as possible, and the Bemises now provided timber, some of it from almost within view of the site of the Graysonia mill. One generation of the Bemis family, especially Rosborough's brother-in-law Will Bemis, had helped when the Rosboro mill opened in 1908. The next generation, notably Will's son James Rosborough (J. R.) Bemis, helped as the mill ran during its last year in 1938.

T. W. Rosborough now had western timber and planned to sell his interest in the Caddo River Lumber Company and build his own mill in Oregon. He began to ask some of his Arkansas people to go with him. But in the early fall of 1938, as the Rosboro mill neared shutdown and the Oregon plans took shape, Rosborough suffered another personal loss. Rita Tuppen, his sister-in-law who for several years had been his house-guest and companion, died from complications of an attack of asthma. Rosborough and Mrs. Tuppen had apparently never been romantically involved, but each had assuaged the other's loneliness. After Rita Tuppen's death, people could see Rosborough was deeply upset.

Later that fall he entered the hospital at Hot Springs for minor surgery. While he was there, Beuford Cole went to see him on business, and at the hospital was given directions to Rosborough's room.

Cole found the door closed. Inside, someone was talking . . . a woman. She seemed to be reading aloud. Cole knocked, and waited.

The door was opened by the woman, who had a book in her hand.

It was Urcy.[2]

———————

Even through the 1930s, most lumbermen considered cutover land as a burden. The depression only heightened this feeling. With money so scarce, it seemed better to sell, at whatever price, any property that would not soon be productive.

Rosborough's relatives the Bemises closed the sawmill at Graysonia in 1931, and for several years were unable to dispose of the mill and land. In 1936, however, Rosborough's nephew, J. R. Bemis, arranged for the remaining assets of the Ozan-Graysonia Lumber Company to be merged with the Ozan Lumber Company that he had reincorporated in 1929 to cut second growth. The Bemises were principal stockholders in both companies.

As the merger was being worked out, Ozan-Graysonia's directors reported to stockholders:

> In a recent inspection of land owned by the Company we found out definitely that 15,000 acres, more or less, is worthless. It is your Directors idea to abandon this land and not deed the same to the Ozan Lumber Company if the merger is consummated, because it is our opinion that the annual burden of taxes and other costs is too great to warrant this expense.[3]

Then the Bemises had a better idea—maybe the land could be sold. They got in touch with some old friends, the McMillan family in Arkadelphia who traded in timberlands, and offered them ten thousand acres of rough land, sight unseen, for twenty-five cents an acre.

The McMillans bought the land.[4] Over the next few years, as times improved, they sold it piece by piece at prices ranging from two dollars to five dollars an acre. Most of the land went to sawmill operators who by then were acquiring cutover land to hold for second growth. Finally, in the late 1940s, the McMillans sold the last of the acreage. The highest sale price had been ten dollars an acre.

H. W. McMillan, one of the family members involved in these transactions, says, "We found out later that Ozan would have taken ten cents an acre if we had offered it to them." But the McMillans could be satisfied; they had turned a very nice profit. And the Bemises were satisfied; they had gotten some money in lean times when they needed it. The Ozan Lumber Company still had fifty thousand acres of Ozan-Graysonia's cutover land. In 1937, J. R. Bemis proceeded to build a medium-sized sawmill at the town of Delight, a few miles south of Graysonia, using equipment salvaged from the old Graysonia mill.

Not long after the Bemises sold their "rough" land, Rosborough asked C. H. Williams, who had been superintendent at Mauldin when the town shut down, to try to sell off what remained. Williams approached Bill Wingfield of Mount Ida and asked him if he wanted a ranch. Wingfield says that Williams told him: "Pick out any amount of land here in Mauldin. I'll sell you any acreage at four dollars an acre. Pick out the best house and I'll sell it to you for a hundred and fifty dollars, with a good well and everything. I'll sell you that building where the [hardwood] sawmill was for a hundred and fifty dollars."

Wingfield says, "It was hard times then and I didn't have the money."

Williams also tried Dixie Gaston, who had worked for the company as a section foreman on the railroads. He offered Gaston two of the best houses and "all of old Mauldin" for a thousand dollars. Gaston didn't have the money either, but did buy a three-room house from Mauldin's Stri-ped Town for ninety-five dollars. The price included delivery to Norman on a flatcar.

Williams talked to Robert Lyons, who had been a log cutter for Caddo River. The company was letting Lyons and his family live rent-free on an eighty-acre tract of cutover land near Mount Ida, and now Williams told Lyons the price of the land could be as little as $2.50 an acre. Lyons says this was his reply: "Mr. Williams, I can't pay for it. I can't get no money to buy nothing with. I ain't got it, and got no way of getting it."

Nellie Lyons, Robert's wife, recalls: "We could have got all that land but we didn't have money to buy with and we was scared to go into debt. We just couldn't see ahead."

And Robert Lyons adds: "We lived up there [at Mauldin] in their company houses when we worked for them, and after that job was over, that left a lot of us people . . . that left us out of work. After they sold out, and left out of this country, it was nearly impossible to get a job anywhere because there wasn't but a bunch of little bitty sawmills back in the hills. They didn't use no men, hardly. [Caddo River] said 'You boys move on some of this land we got here, and fix you up a little homestead and make a living if you can.'"

Several families did move onto rent-free "Caddo River leases," as they called the parcels of cutover land on which they settled. Robert Lyons traded a fattened hog for four thousand feet of rough oak lumber, and with that he built a two-room house on Caddo River's eighty acres of cutover. He and Nellie then began to piece together a living. Together they cut pine logs ("She's a good hand with a crosscut saw") for a dollar a thousand ("Times were getting a little better then"). Together they cut and sold stovewood for a dollar a rick, and picked and sold blackberries and huckleberries for ten cents a gallon. They sharecropped. They gardened and then canned their produce. In the fall they went to Oklahoma to pick cotton and gather pecans. Their children helped and everybody's earnings went toward food and clothing for the family. Nellie says: "Oh, we've sure had a tough time but we always had something on the table. We've managed to have food. We didn't go hungry."

Robert and Nellie Lyons lived on the company's eighty acres for seven years after the closing of Mauldin. In 1943 they had to relocate again, for the U.S. Forest Service by that time owned the land. The eighty was a portion of some cutover acreage that the Forest Service had bought from Caddo River in 1939—one small part of land purchases during the 1930s that more than doubled the area of the Ouachita National Forest.

To better understand this important change in land ownership, it is necessary to review some earlier happenings.

Although the Ouachita National Forest was established in 1907, not until the 1930s did the national forest became firmly integrated into the local economy. During its early years there were many boundary changes, a series of additions but mostly eliminations. Boundaries were extended in some areas to include other public land that was unfit for agriculture, and pulled in at others to eliminate cultivable lands. Acts of Congress in 1906 and 1912 required the Forest Service to identify all land within national forest boundaries that was suitable for agriculture, and to make this land available for homestead entry.[5]

These congressional stipulations resulted from a great political controversy that embroiled the U.S. Forest Service in the agency's early years. By 1900 or soon after, individual owners controlled practically all of the original public domain that was suitable for farming, but there were still aspiring farmers who sought public land. There had to be more soil *somewhere,* they cried, land that the land-hungry could acquire and cultivate to produce food for a burgeoning population. One seemingly easy solution was for Congress to arrange for releasing lands that the Forest Service had "locked up."[6]

So, during those years up to about 1920 that constituted the tail end of the homesteading era in the Ouachitas, the employees of the Arkansas National Forest spent much of their time classifying land as agricultural or nonagricultural, inspecting homestead claims, and redrawing their maps for boundary changes. Lands that were found to have agricultural value were listed and opened to homestead entry.[7]

Some people did not want the Forest Service to own any land at all. In 1910 the Committee on Public Lands of the U.S. House of Representatives held hearings on a bill whose purpose was "to exclude from the

Arkansas National Forest all lands within the County of Montgomery and restore same to public domain." Its backers wanted land available for homesteads and also for claims under the Timber and Stone Act. They saw the Forest Service as the dominant landowner in Montgomery County, although that point was blunted when the hearings revealed that six large private landowners (Paul Rust and others) owned half as much land in the county (56,700 acres) as did the Forest Service (120,000 acres).[8] The bill to eliminate the national forest in Montgomery County was not approved, but two years later some of the same private interests persuaded the local congressman to introduce another bill that would have abolished the entire national forest.

The national forest was not abolished, but it did shrink considerably during the years before 1920. The original withdrawals of land for the national forest in 1907 and 1908 totaled 1,663,300 acres; this was the gross area that included both federal and private lands within national forest boundaries. By 1919 the boundaries had been pulled in so that the gross area within them was 958,290 acres, of which about 625,000 acres were federal lands.[9]

Even as the national forest was being reduced in size to make a larger area available for homesteads, Forest Service field employees sensed a different trend. William E. Wootten, classifying agricultural and non-agricultural land on the national forest, reported in 1917 that on the rougher lands that had been homesteaded, "50% . . . have been abandoned as homes, and many former homesteads are now held by timber speculators. However, the present demand for these lands is not from people who wish to engage in timber speculation, but from people who are willing to use this land for home-building purposes under most adverse conditions."[10]

Wootten added that "the Forest is a 'graveyard' where hundreds and hundreds of deserted 160-acre tracts, filed upon or passed to patent before the creation of the National Forest, stand as monuments to the non-agricultural character of thousands and thousands of acres of lands within the exterior boundaries of the Arkansas National Forest."[11] Wootten said there had been "a popular demand for such land for farm purposes based on misdirected ambition."[12]

Two years earlier, another Forest Service man had offered the opinion that "it is apparent that the coming of good roads and the automobile into this region is certain to raise the standard of living, bring news of better opportunities elsewhere, and result in the abandonment of lean acres not meeting the requirements of reasonable comfort."[13]

"News of better opportunities elsewhere" began to take effect in the Ouachitas soon after 1920. Farm families saw and wanted such things as automobiles and sewing machines, but could not afford them. The price of cotton, the cash crop, was depressed, and on many farms the output was down because of poor soil. By that time, however, people could get jobs with the lumber companies, or in agriculture out West, or even with the Forest Service. People stopped trying to homestead. Those who lived on the poorest land moved away.

By the 1930s it was obvious that the economic future of the Ouachitas was not in cotton or corn. Hill farming was bankrupt. The virgin forest was nearly gone but the second growth was coming on. As the depression continued to cast its pall, local leaders came to realize that the only immediate economic development they could expect on worn-out and cutover lands in their counties was that which could be provided by the Forest Service. For the first time, many of these leaders wanted *more* national forest.

During the depression the federal government poured money into national forest improvements in the Ouachitas, especially through the Civilian Conservation Corps (CCC), which was designed to give jobs to unemployed young men between the ages of eighteen and twenty-five. From 1933 until the coming of World War II, the "CCC boys" greatly expanded the forest road system. They strung phone lines, erected fire towers, and built ranger stations, warehouses, and repair shops. They developed campgrounds, picnic areas, and swimming lakes. The CCC crews waged the continuing battle against wildfire in the woods. As never before, the Forest Service had plenty of manpower to carry out long desired projects and programs.

The CCC also helped with fire protection on Ouachitas timberlands outside the national forest. Glen Durrell, working for the State of Oklahoma Forest Commission in the 1930s, helped to organize CCC camps in the Ouachitas of southeastern Oklahoma. The first priority was to build roads that would make the country accessible for fire fighting crews. The CCC also fought fire, and put up lookout towers, ranger dwellings, and phone lines. Durrell says, "It is generally agreed among foresters that the CCC program advanced fire control work by about twenty years." [14]

Here and there on the national forest, the CCC planted pine seedlings in old fields and clearings. The total area planted was less than a thousand acres, a very small part of the entire forest, so that probably the largest value of these plantations was their visibility. [15] Folks could watch and see from year to year that the trees were growing, that today's young tress would be tomorrow's prime source of wood products.

The Forest Service had authority under the Weeks Law of 1911 to buy woodlands to protect the headwaters of navigable streams, and under the Clarke-McNary Act of 1924 to purchase land for timber production. [16] Under both laws the service could acquire cutover tracts and worn-out farms. The supervisor of the Ouachita National Forest began to recommend—and county leaders to lobby for—specific areas to be purchased. Higher level administrators in the Forest Service invariably approved these recommendations to enlarge the national forest, and made purchase money available from funds appropriated by Congress. All over the eastern United States in the 1930s, the national forests were being expanded as the government bought up submarginal land.

One of the first "purchase areas" created for the Ouachita National Forest was a westward extension into the Ouachita Mountains of Oklahoma. The first big block of land to be acquired was fifty-three thousand acres from the Buschow Lumber Company. The Buschow brothers were close to cutting out and the Forest Service was the only available buyer

for their cutover land. In December 1930, they transferred the first and largest part of it, 48,257.15 acres, to the Forest Service for $67,560.01.[17]

The price was $1.40 an acre, which today seems ridiculously cheap. But times were tough and people had no money. A year after the Buschow purchase, the Forest Service was being offered more land than there was money to buy, and the service had to cancel and return one-fourth of the 160 options on tracts that had been obtained from would-be sellers. Options had been taken at $1.30 to $5.00 an acre. By 1933 the service was having to quote these same would-be sellers still lower prices, from $1.10 to $3.75 an acre, in line with depressed values for land in surrounding areas. At that time the service's regional forester stated: "Considering the vast acreage of cutover land, which will not support agriculture and from which returns sufficient even to pay taxes cannot be anticipated for a long term of years, it is my belief that the offers currently being made by the Forest Service represent as much or more than any other buyer would pay for the lands."[18] Actually, at that time there were no buyers other than the Forest Service.

With the knowledge and approval of Dierks, the Forest Service drew the boundaries of the Oklahoma purchase area to include much of the timberland belonging to the Dierks mill at Pine Valley. William L. Hall had looked at the land there and informed Dierks that it could not produce enough second-growth timber to sustain the mill, so Dierks had

Civilian Conservation Corps enrollees doing "hard work in the large rock," as an observer said, to build a road over Oklahoma's Kiamichi Mountain in 1934. Furnished with little power equipment, CCC crews did much of their road construction by hand. With a large pool of labor, the CCC helped develop the first extensive system of all-weather roads to penetrate the back country of the Ouachitas.

decided to operate the mill continuously to remove the virgin pine and then shut down. Dierks sold sixty-one thousand acres of Pine Valley's cutover land to the Forest Service.[19]

Within the Oklahoma purchase area encompassing 291,489 acres, the Forest Service bought 154,000 acres during the decade from 1930 to 1940, at an average price of $1.62 per acre.[20] In Arkansas the service acquired a much larger area, buying hundreds of failed homesteads; buying twelve thousand acres in Scott County from Charlie Forrester after he cut it over with his small mills; another twelve thousand acres from former sawmiller William Blake Barton; and cutover land from other lumber companies, including Caddo River.

During the 1930s the Caddo River Lumber Company sold cutover land to the Forest Service through a dozen different transactions.[21] The earliest took place in 1931 and involved only about fifty-five hundred acres at the northeast end of their Montgomery County holdings, at a price of $2.47 an acre.[22] In 1932, however, Caddo River floated their million-dollar bond issue, and that, along with the continuing grind of the depression, surely affected their outlook. Next they sold sixteen thousand acres to the Forest Service at $2.60 per acre, and concerning that sale a service officer wrote:

> A considerable stand of merchantable timber has been left, comprising the 10, 12 and 14 inch trees which the company then expected to make the basis of a second cut after 10 or 15 years. This conservative policy has now been abandoned by the company because the immediate returns per acre were proving insufficient to meet the necessary bond payments and at the same time yield a satisfactory operating profit. The trustee for the bond holders was very largely responsible for this change in policy.[23]

The trustee for Caddo River's bondholders was a Kansas City bank, and apparently its officers were conservative financiers who cared nothing about conservation forestry. It appears that Caddo River's owners thought the same way, for in the spring of 1933 they again approached the Forest Service about selling land. Now, less than two years after starting up their mill at Forester, they had decided to sell its eighty-four thousand acres of timberland, retaining only the right to cut the old-growth timber.

Negotiations took more than a year. Forest Service people inspected the land and did their paperwork. By April 1934 the regional forester was writing his chief that "this land . . . will to a very high degree promote the consolidation of those parts of the Ouachita National Forest in which they lie."[24]

Caddo River would deliver the eighty-four thousand acres to the Forest Service as cutover land in installments of about fifty-six hundred acres a year as they would finish cutting the timber during a period of fifteen years. For this cutover land, Caddo River wanted $2.00 an acre. The Forest Service appraised its value at $1.97 per acre, but because the service would not gain immediate possession (that is, on the average they would not get the land until seven and a half years in the future), they discounted the price to $1.40 per acre, to be paid to Caddo River as soon as the sale documents could be completed. And then, because funds were short or because somebody saw a chance to tighten the screws, officials in the Forest Service set a price limit for dealing with Caddo River at $1.25 per acre.

Caddo River's Hal Shaffer and his companions at the bargaining table must have been jarred by this latest price cut. The forest supervisor was in Kansas City for negotiations, and soon reported to his boss, the regional forester: "They are keen traders and plenty tough, but I believe their hopes have been blasted to where they will deal within the price limitation."[25] On June 1, 1934, an option for sale of the eighty-four thousand acres was executed at $1.25 an acre.

One month previously, Shaffer had written the forest supervisor to inquire about selling still another large block of cutover land. He had heard that the voters of Montgomery County had petitioned the Forest Service for a boundary enlargement to encompass Caddo River's cutover territory around Mauldin. Could Caddo River sell this land to the government, even though it was presently outside the national forest?[26]

The answer was yes. The national forest boundary was duly enlarged, and Caddo River in 1935 offered to sell the Forest Service sixty-nine thousand acres of Mauldin's cutover land. Caddo River asked for $2.50 per acre. The final price was $2.00.

Some Montgomery County residents did not like the idea of the Forest Service acquiring so much local land. They complained that the petition asking for boundary enlargement had been slipped through without everybody knowing its consequences. Now agricultural land would be locked up; people would be put out of their homes; the county would lose population and its tax base. In the presence of this opposition, the Forest Service proceeded cautiously. As the forest supervisor explained in a letter to his regional forester in May 1935:

> When ever a family is found living on or cultivating a piece of ground or part of the tract looks reasonably suitable for agriculture we examine it, but leave it out of the report. Certain individuals . . . are very anxious to find grounds to start resistance and I do not intend to give anybody a chance to say that we are depopulating the county or spoiling anybody's home.[27]

Because of the government's necessary delays for appraisals and title searches, the Forester and Mauldin land sales were not concluded until 1936 and 1937. Shaffer had wanted the proceeds to help pay off Caddo River's bondholders, but by the time he received the money, times were better and he had already used the company's profits to buy back the bonds, redeeming the last ones in May 1936.[28] Originally the bonds were to be retired in ten years. Shaffer, anxious to get Caddo River out of debt, had done it in four.

With the sale of the Forester and Mauldin lands, Caddo River's owners had disposed of most of the company's real estate. In addition to other small acreages at various times, in 1938 they sold the Forest Service one thousand acres including the site of Mauldin for $1.90 per acre, and in 1939, the last forty-eight hundred acres of Montgomery County cutover

On solid tires, this chain-driven log truck carried a skimpy payload. Its leaky radiator forced the driver to carry a bucket for frequent refills. The truck was used at a mill south of Mena, Arkansas, in 1919.

land for $1.80 an acre.[29] (Apparently this last sale included the eighty-acre "lease," mentioned earlier, on which the Lyons family lived.) They had sold some small parcels to individuals, and still owned some timber and the mill and residential areas at Rosboro, Glenwood, and Forester. The owners of Caddo River had sold to the Forest Service approximately 190,000 acres of land for prices ranging from $1.25 to $2.60 per acre.

Why did they do it? By the 1930s they must have known there was a chance, at least, to operate on second growth. They were not in the kind of financial trouble encountered by Dierks. Caddo River never went into receivership; in fact, the company made a small profit even in the depths of the depression. Was it Hal Shaffer's fear of debt and bankruptcy? Had he decided to sell off land to maintain the company's good credit rating with their Kansas City bank?[30]

Fiscal conservatism must have played a part in the owners' decision to sell. More important, however, was that no one saw a future in cutting second-growth timber in Arkansas. Will Ingham, the leading stockholder, was in his sixties, and immobilized by a stroke. Each of Ingham's two sons had worked for Caddo River in Arkansas and neither of them wanted to stay. T. W. Rosborough and Hal Shaffer were not interested, either. About 1935, they acquired Ingham's interest in Caddo River (at which time Rosborough became the company's president), but they too were intent on liquidating. Shaffer was approaching sixty, and his son and sons-in-law were not attracted to lumbering. Rosborough might have taken over the company with his son, but even before Whit's death, Rosborough evidently had agreed with Ingham and Shaffer to sell the

cutover lands and eventually close out the business. Rosborough had seen Whit's future, and his own, with big timber out West, not with what he regarded as inferior second growth in the Ouachitas. In his communications with the Forest Service, Rosborough tried as hard as anyone to be rid of Caddo River's cutover lands.

––––––

On the land that was being cut over to supply the Forester mill, Forest Service men were now present to see that the terms of the sale were carried out. Caddo River's loggers were to cut only the trees ten inches or more in diameter. They were to cut trees so that seedlings and saplings would not be damaged, and were to help prevent and suppress fires. After cutting the timber, Caddo River would transfer the land to the Forest Service at the rate of about fifty-six hundred acres a year over a fifteen-year period from May 1935 to May 1949, when it was expected that the last of the virgin timber on the eighty-four thousand acres would be removed.[35]

During the 1930s the Forest Service purchased nearly 800,000 acres of land. One-fourth came from the Caddo River Lumber Company, the largest single seller. From the original 640,000 acres of public domain in 1908 which had been reduced to 625,000 acres of federal land within the national forest boundaries by 1919, the purchases in the 1930s had more

A heavily loaded dual-wheel truck rolls across a temporary bridge on Dierks land in Oklahoma about 1936. Additional wheels made it possible to double the load.

Cat-Truck Logging

By happy circumstance, at the same time the last of the virgin timber that could be profitably logged by railroad was being cut, it became possible to log the smaller second growth by truck.

The motor truck was first used for hauling logs in 1913, and in 1918 the Caddo River Lumber Company purchased two log trucks.[31] After that, the company logged country

close to Glenwood and Rosboro by truck while bringing logs from Montgomery County by railroad. In those years, however, roads had not been developed and the trucks themselves lacked strength and power. Loggers could take wagons and mules farther into the woods than any truck could go, and bring out bigger payloads.

Within a few years crawler tractors became widely used for pulling road graders, and they were followed in the 1930s by bulldozers. As more powerful dozers were developed, it became possible to build truck roads into the woods for one-fifth the cost of building logging railroads.[32] At the same time, log trucks were being greatly improved. Dierks, for example, helped a truck manufacturer develop a heavier dual-wheeled truck that came into use during the mid-1930s. By 1940, log trucks everywhere were equipped with dual wheels to haul heavier loads.

The caterpillar tractor, or "cat," and the dual-wheeled log truck were a potent combination. It required at least four thousand board feet per acre to log profitably by railroad, but only five hundred board feet to log by truck.[33] A mill operator could log tracts of timber as small as ten or twenty acres, as far as twenty miles away from the mill, and now make a profit.[34] Logging by truck

than doubled the national forest's public land. Counting another eighty thousand acres acquired in land exchanges, the Ouachita National Forest at the end of the 1930s encompassed nearly one and a half million acres.[36]

Unlike Caddo River, Dierks sold timberland during the 1930s only when it was not needed for future use by their mills. Even as Dierks went into receivership, the family saw a fighting chance to hang on to the timber empire that they and their forebears had developed. In cases where a company's management was considered competent, the bankruptcy law allowed what was called a "friendly" receivership instead of a complete takeover by outsiders. The federal court in Kansas City appointed Herbert Dierks, president of the three Dierks lumber companies that were in receivership, and Walter A. Graff, a representative of the bondholders, as trustees to operate the companies. The court also ordered them to prepare a plan of reorganization that would make the Dierks operations more efficient and would indicate how debts could be paid.

The reorganization plan was approved by the court and its implementation was begun in 1936. The three lumber companies—Choctaw, Pine Valley, and Dierks Lumber and Coal—became one corporation, the Dierks Lumber and Coal Company. Since the three companies had practically identical lists of stockholders, officers, and directors, as well as interwoven and interdependent operations, the merger at least eliminated some duplicate bookkeeping. Already, in 1934, the ownership of the Dierks timberlands had been consolidated. Formerly the Dierks lands in Arkansas were held by the Dierks Lumber and Coal Company and those in Oklahoma by various members of the Dierks family. Now they were owned by a trust established for the benefit of the family, with three relatives serving as trustees.

Through the depression years the Dierks family held down personal expenses and here and there developed a little income, disposing of cut-over land to the Forest Service, and selling oak stumpage to small mills that made staves for whiskey barrels after the repeal of Prohibition in 1933. But their main salvation was a considerable capacity to manufacture lumber. After 1932, two or three of the Dierks sawmills could be run at least part-time, and by 1936 when reorganization took place, the economy had edged upward so that all five of the mills could be in operation. That year turned out to be a good one for lumber, as years went in the 1930s; even Pine Valley showed its first profit since the mill opened in 1927. The Dierks mills began to generate a large stream of income which rapidly reduced the debt. By late 1938 all of the bondholders had been paid off. Fred H. Dierks gathered up the cancelled bond certificates and took them down to his basement where he burned them in the furnace.

Soon after the bonds were retired, the Dierks company directors—all of whom were family members—resolved that thereafter, the company could not borrow more than two million dollars.

In January 1939, a year after the Glenwood mill sawed its last log, T. W.'s sawmill at Rosboro cut out and closed down. A crew of men removed items that could be used in Rosborough's new sawmill in Oregon, including several pumps, two electric generators, and other machinery. Rosborough sold the remainder, the sawmill building, and the lumber sheds to salvage dealers. (Two months after shutting down, and after Rosborough had pulled out the equipment that he wanted, the sawmill burned to the ground.[37] One wag said that the fire would have been an insurance fire—except that they'd let the policy lapse.) Salvagers dismantled or moved most of the buildings of Rosboro. The company arranged for some of the smaller houses to be hauled on trucks to Forester. Rosborough's old home and a few others remained in place. Lyn Maxey, who had been a log hauling contractor at Mauldin, bought the mill and town sites for a cattle ranch.

Rosborough was going to Oregon to build another mill, and he was taking thirty-nine of his Arkansas employees—and their families—with him. He sold his home in Glenwood. He sold Caddo River's last twelve hundred acres of timber to his nephew, J. R. Bemis.[38] The Glenwood newspaper reported that Rosborough was naming his Oregon mill the Rosboro Lumber Company, "in honor of the town of Rosboro, Arkansas, his first love." On the eve of departure, Rosborough entertained a large number of friends with a farewell party.[39]

A few days later, near the end of March 1939, Rosborough left Glenwood. As usual, Fred was at the wheel, with Halcy now beside him. But instead of heading towards Oregon, they went east. Rosborough directed them to drive first to Huntsville, in northern Alabama. He was going to get married again.

Years before, Rosborough's favorite niece, Martha, had introduced him to her husband's unmarried schoolteacher sister, Anna Watts. During the winter, Martha and her husband Tom succeeded in bringing Anna and T. W. together again, and the result was that suddenly Rosborough proposed marriage. At forty-eight, "Miss Anna" was attractive and pleasant, and an intelligent conversationalist. She would be a good companion to T. W.

So Rosborough married Anna in Alabama, and the newlyweds proceeded to Oregon with Fred and Halcy. Seventy years old, Rosborough was beginning what would be a happy marriage. He was also embarking on what would become the most crisis-laden, but rewarding, sawmill venture in his life.

While Rosborough would be building his mill in Oregon, his nephew, J. R. Bemis, would establish a smaller sawmill on the very site of his uncle's old mill at Rosboro, where he would profitably produce lumber from second growth. The Caddo River Lumber Company, though, would no longer be at either Rosboro or Glenwood. Moreover, T. W. Rosborough would be selling his interest in Caddo River to Hal Shaffer, who had become president of the company upon Rosborough's departure for Oregon.

also made it possible to selectively cut only mature trees on a tract managed for sustained yield.

Caddo River and Dierks, the last two operators of logging railroads in the Ouachitas, relied more and more on logging by truck, and in 1940 Caddo River shut down the logging rail system at Forester. Dierks continued to operate main line railroads out of Mountain Pine and Wright City to bring logs from the far reaches of their extensive timberlands. When Mountain Pine's railroad closed in 1971 and Wright City's in 1972, these were probably the last log-hauling railroads to operate in the eastern United States.

Shaffer would continue to operate Caddo River, which after years of retrenchment had become much smaller. The company consisted of one remaining mill, at Forester. There, the mill and woods workers and their families, many of them veterans of Caddo River's earlier days, were still experiencing the lingering effects of the Great Depression. They had learned to cope with economic hardship, however, and it was even with some pride that they called their little town a Depression Town.

9. Forester

Like all its neighbors, the Rodgers home was dark green with white trim. It had no porches, only front and back steps with little gabled roofs projecting over them, and the crawl space underneath the house was open to the breezes.

Inside, a small, linoleum-floored living room seemed to be dominated by the sofa along one wall that faced a wood-burning heater. Beyond the living room, the family dining room contained an icebox (whose melt-water dripped through a hole in the floor), and a table, chairs, and sideboard in a limited area. Off the dining room, Voisey Rodgers' kitchen had a wooden counter, some shelves, and a kerosene cook stove, with broom, mop, washtubs, and other odd-sized items pushed into corners. Water for cooking and dishwashing came from a hydrant outside.

Also adjoining the living room were two small bedrooms, with clothes hanging in corners behind curtains. Off one bedroom was a space without fixtures or plumbing but called the bathroom. Voisey gave her children baths in a No. 3 galvanized tub in the kitchen, and in cold weather she set the bathtub close to the living room heater. She washed clothes outside, using three tubs (one with a rub board for washing, two for rinse) on a bench in the backyard, and heating water in an iron wash pot over an open fire.

The entire interior of the house was finished with narrow beaded boards having the beads visible as parallel lines running around walls and across ceilings. The company had not painted inside, so that the prevailing color was of new lumber gradually darkening from smoke and finger smudges.

In color scheme and construction, the Rodgers house and all the others of the neighborhood were essentially identical. The Rodgers home measured twenty-four by thirty-two feet, providing less than eight hundred square feet of living space. But the building was new and sturdy and could be kept warm with the living room heater, even though the floors got cold. (Someone said that Caddo River's carpenters put sawdust in the walls for insulation.) And the Rodgers family had five rooms; they lived in one of the larger, nicer homes in Forester. Voisey's husband, Loy, managed a business that was owned by several investors in Waldron, the Fuller-Judy Chevrolet Company. He drew seventy-five dollars in salary every month, a guaranteed three dollars a day, so his family was better-off than many of the mill people.

Fuller-Judy Chevrolet, in a sheet metal building next door to the Rodgers home, was a typical small-town car dealership: a showroom with plate glass windows in front, a parts department and repair shop in back, a grease rack and Esso gas pumps outside. The automobile showroom, spacious and centrally located, also served as Forester's polling place on election days. Fuller-Judy stood at the main intersection of town.

Directly across the street was another concession that Rosborough had granted to an outsider, Carter's Drugstore. Vernon Carter rented the building from Caddo River and carried a line of drugs and tobacco, and ran a soda fountain with ice cream and soft drinks. Even for the 1930s, the drugstore looked old-fashioned, with its front porch, broad wooden steps leading up to the door, aging secondhand fixtures, and a wood stove in the center aisle.

Catty-cornered across from Fuller-Judy stood Caddo River's commissary, a plain warehouse of a building having a corrugated iron roof. Halfway along its front was the entrance, flanked by two display windows (ladies' clothing on the left, men's on the right) and a pair of loafers' benches. Inside, a large potbellied coal stove rested in a square box of sand on the bare wood floor. At the back was an office for the store manager, bookkeeper, and timekeeper. To the right were yard goods, clothing, and shoes. To the left, candy (just inside the front door), groceries, meats, and hardware. Out back were an ice house, and a feed house at the end of the KCS railroad tracks.

Along the same street as the commissary and drugstore were the lumber company's office (for the resident manager, office manager, and other clerical help), the company doctor's office, the post office, and a children's play area with slide and swings. Behind the playground was a barbershop (two chairs; one barber) with a back room having a shower where people could take baths on paying the barber (men could also shower or use a tub at the sawmill's boiler room).

Behind the commissary and opposite the KCS's yellow depot was Forester's two-story hotel, having a lobby, dining room, and about eight guest rooms downstairs, and twenty more upstairs. The dining room contained two long tables with picnic benches, a third table with chairs for ladies and other special guests, and an icebox; the kitchen was equipped with a large wood-burning range. Downstairs also were the ladies' and men's bathrooms, and rooms for Mrs. Vise, the hotel manager, and her three daughters. The lobby, with its coal heater, served as a sitting area for everyone. The guest rooms were not heated.

Two blocks west of Fuller-Judy's garage stood Forester's white-painted church facing the center of town, and the school buildings. Forming three sides of a rectangle were six two-room houses, their partitions re-

Courtesy Albert A. Maupin, Jr.

moved to make six classrooms for nine grades ("Mr. Rosborough said they should not be crowded," one resident recalls).[1] Each building was heated by a coal stove.

The community described here—business area, church and school, and three- and five-room houses—formed a compact neighborhood about three blocks wide by five long. In the early 1930s all of it was new. And it was Spartan—outside hydrants, privies, wood or coal stoves, bare wood interiors. Simplicity. Uniformity, too. Not only the houses, but all the other buildings except Fuller-Judy, the depot, and the church were stained dark green. This was Green Town.

Just outside town on the road toward Waldron, a white house stood by itself, the largest house at Forester, with wallpapered rooms and cedar-lined closets, the home of L. D. Williams. L. D. and his wife shared eight rooms with their daughter and her three children, as well as a housekeeper. With his son Vernon who lived in Green Town, L. D. remained in charge of timber and logging, while Forester's resident manager looked after the mill and town.

The resident manager's home was an expanded version of the five-room houses in Green Town. As if to remind the manager of his responsibilities, his house was set close to the sawmill, at the top of a slope along the edge of Green Town that overlooked the log pond and the mill. From his

Forester's Green Town in 1937 includes vegetable gardens, outhouses, and a row of four-room houses recently moved from Mauldin.

Courtesy Henry Overby and Bertie Hight Overby

back windows the manager could see the entire plant, sprawled along the Cedar Creek bottomland.

In appearance the Forester mill was not unusual, except that the rough lumber shed seemed to stretch far into the distance. It was a gigantic building, eighty feet wide and a thousand in length, reportedly the largest lumber storage shed in the South. Its roof reached more than fifty feet above the ground and dominated any view in that direction. Inside the building an overhead crane spanned the eighty-foot width and traveled along tracks the length of the shed. The crane operator could pick up four-by-four-foot packages of lumber and deposit them anywhere in the cavernous storage area, one package on top of another until they were stacked six or seven high, reaching a height of as much as thirty feet. When full, the rough shed held millions of board feet of dry lumber.

The structure blocked the view of another residential area to the north, Forester's black quarters. Lined up in straight rows, homes there were stained a dark red color with white trim. Some houses had four rooms but most had two or three. Robert Canady recalls: "They hauled my home from Glenwood up there with the furniture in it. I had a little old two-room house." The Quarters also had a little white church, a one-room red schoolhouse, a boardinghouse called the Hotel, and a recreation building that, as usual, was known as the Barrel House.

Southeast of the sawmill and across Cedar Creek was still another housing area for many of the whites who worked in the woods. Log cutters, section hands, and steel gang laborers lived there in Cannon Town, which had been named for Frank Cannon, foreman of the steel gang. (Cannon got drunk one Christmas and made a scene at the church and was fired, but his name stuck.) Most of the homes were two-room houses brought from Mauldin and set in pairs, one at right angles to the

Millions of board feet of lumber could be stored in this vast building, measuring eighty feet wide by a thousand long, that stood at Forester in 1937. The photographer was in the cab of a bridge crane that could travel the length of the building to deposit or pick up four-by-four-foot "packages" of lumber. At the far end where the floor was lower, lumber was stacked thirty feet high.

other to form an "L" with an open hallway between them. These unpainted dwellings were aligned along dirt streets, with every so often a drilled well and hand pump.

Forester's people were basically democratic in spirit and nearly everyone got along well, but between those who lived in Green Town and Cannon Town there was a noticeable difference. As austere as it was, Green Town was Forester's Silk Stocking Hill to people who lived across the creek. And from the Green Town side, Cannon Town was . . . well, the place where the woods people lived. There were many people in Cannon Town (and a few in Green Town, too) who remained apart from the church and social activities whose organizers were usually from the higher income families in Green Town.

Whatever the differences among people in Forester, all of them moved to the same rhythms of the workday. At five in the morning the mill whistle blew three times to wake people up. At six it blew twice—last call—and at seven it blew once to put folks to work. At noon the whistle sounded for lunch (which in Forester was still called "dinner"). At one o'clock the whistle blew for the afternoon stint, and at six for the end of production. Men walked home with bundles of kindling from the mill, or with scraps from the planer to build things. They gathered at the Loafers Bench (Gossip Bench; Buzzards Roost) by the commissary, or in the barbershop, and talked about how many logs each had cut that day; how many "heavies" that scaled more than one hundred board feet each had cut; how many feet of lumber they had cut at the mill. And whether there would be any money left over after buying groceries.

In the hot, dry summers the dirt streets turned to dust. The company had planted Chinese elms in the yards but as yet there was not any shade. Families sat outside their houses at night, waiting till things cooled so they could go inside to bed. The company posted warnings about water shortage and urged people in Green Town to conserve water so there would be enough in the town's storage tank for fighting fires. (But at night, people quietly watered their gardens. Food production still meant more than fire protection.)

During the wet winter months the dirt streets turned to sticky mud. The wind blew and whistled under the houses—and into the houses of Cannon Town that weren't as tightly built. All year long, smoke and cinders from the mill's stacks and refuse burner settled on houses, on yards, on Monday's wash. The direction of the wind determined which neighborhood would receive the fallout. The prevailing wind was from the south, so that the Quarters got most of it.

The ice man made his deliveries with a wagon and a team of mules. The scavenger made his rounds with an open two-wheeled cart pulled by one old mule, collecting trash, garbage, and the contents of privies, hauling it a mile north of town and dumping it in a wooded area, empty tin cans, excrement and all. Meanwhile, at the drugstore, Vern Carter the druggist mixed turpentine and mercuric chloride to fill a popular demand for something that would kill bedbugs, and sold his concoction for thirty-five cents a pint. (Carter recalls that a woman came in and said she wanted "a dime's worth of that bedbug medicine. I don't want to get rid of 'em. I'm just tryin' to keep 'em down a little bit.")

People scrambled for a living. After Jeff and Gertie Barnett came to Forester in 1931, Jeff was able to work only part-time as a log cutter. Says Gertie: "I made a garden in my backyard and sold the garden stuff to people that did not make gardens, and the colored people. And we raised our meat. We had our own fattening hogs. Canned our vegetables. And picked blackberries, and canned them. And we bought peaches; when they would bring peaches in there to sell we could can them. And I sold milk and butter to the colored people and some of the white people that did not have cows. Just first one thing and then another. I done all my own work, all my washing and my sewing. So we made it all right."

The Barnetts and several other families kept hogs in pens at the edge

U.S. Forest Service photo, courtesy Ouachita National Forest

Sunshine and smoke create dramatic contrasts at the Caddo River Lumber Company's plant at Forester, Arkansas, in 1937. Smokestacks rise from the sawmill's power house; the mill itself is hidden just beyond. In the foreground, a pond provides storage for logs and, with the elevated tank at left, a source of water for fire protection.

of town, and had meat. But Albert Maupin, whose father was the office manager, remembers that in their large family, meat meant an occasional serving of baloney, or fried salt pork instead of bacon, or a chicken from the pen in the backyard. "There weren't many fancy cuts, around there," Maupin says. "Mostly it was vegetarian. On Sunday people might eat a little bit of meat. But during the week it was cornbread, potatoes . . . green beans out of the garden. Dried beans, too—worlds and worlds of dried beans. That's where the protein came from, the combination of corn meal. . . ."

Even the children helped make ends meet. In the Maupin household, young Al saw that the chickens got the table scraps and a supplement of green stuff—weeds that he pulled in the back alley. At Forester's hotel, Mrs. Vise's three daughters all had their assigned chores. The youngest, Betty Jo Isenman, remembers "the almost endless amount of hard work . . . long hours and primitive facilities, compared with today's standards. Dishwashing was done by manually filling tubs with hot water. I can recall standing on a bench with arms deep in suds." Betty Jo was eleven when she started helping at the hotel.

There was plenty of work to do, but not enough for pay. For many months Caddo River operated the Forester mill on "short shifts," one crew working in the morning and another in the afternoon. During this time the company closed the mill at Glenwood and its employees came to Forester for half-day work. Always the company tried to provide a subsistence. Alex Nichols, a black who lived at Forester, recalls: "They didn't charge us no rent. We cut our own wood—no fuel bill. I worked on the green chain from seven to twelve and made seventy cents for half a day, in 1932."

Moreover, in 1933 the company brought in twenty-five black workers who had been at a sawmill owned by Will Ingham's brother Sid at Eutaw, Alabama. Both the men and their wives rode from Alabama to Arkansas in the back of a trailer truck. On arriving in Forester they were given a week's free board and the men were given credit to buy work clothes at the commissary. The Alabama mill had cut out and they had been jobless and practically destitute.

Remembering the condition of blacks in the 1930s, Alex Nichols' brother Charley says: "A lot of 'em were coming and going, looking for jobs. Jobs was hard to find. Nothing but Army, and CC camps. . . ." And Lenard Cockburn, a white, recalls: "I have seen Negroes, especially, buy a nickel's worth of meat, or a quarter of a cabbage . . . almost no money; very little refrigeration."

Even so, Forester with its industrial payroll had more money circulating than many towns in western Arkansas. Schoolteachers liked the town because the lumber company helped pay their salaries, in cash. Elsewhere in Arkansas, hard pressed school districts lacked money to pay their teachers.

Forester was also a magnet for local entrepreneurs. Cecil Elliott, a farmer in the Fourche valley, sold fresh beef and pork to the commissary and peddled turnip greens around town from his Model T truck. Charlie Carter, who farmed on Cedar Creek, sold strawberries, blackberries, corn, and peanuts. Charlie Cockburn sold sweet potatoes to the commissary for a dollar a bushel. The lumber company tolerated these produce-sellers as long as they did not compete with the commissary. L. D. Williams, however, personally ordered more than one apple-peddler out of town.

Earl Herrin contracted with the lumber company to buy cutoffs from the planing mill for fifty cents a truckload, which he sold as firewood for a dollar a load, delivered. On a larger scale, Charlie Forrester's bank at Waldron handled Caddo River's payroll, and checking and savings accounts for some of Forester's employees. Waldron stockholders shared in the profits of the Fuller-Judy Chevrolet Company, where occasionally they sold a new car, even during the depression. (One, at least, went to a black mill worker. Alex Nichols recalls that by June 1934 he had saved enough money to buy a new Chevrolet at Fuller-Judy for $727.00.)

Vernon Carter's contract with Rosborough had been worded to keep his

Blacks operate an edger in the Forester sawmill during 1937.

drugstore from selling the same lines of merchandise as the commissary. On his arrival at Forester, however, Carter learned the commissary was not interested in selling radios. He immediately stocked up with radios, mostly low-priced models including ones that could be run from batteries. People wanted entertainment, and by the end of his first year, Carter had sold $9,500 worth of Philco radios in Forester and the surrounding area to both whites and blacks. "I never had a written contract," Carter says. "I would repossess if the customer didn't pay. Out of all I sold, I don't think I lost but one set."

One enterprising local man was able to buy, as scrap metal, some slot machines that had been confiscated and broken up in Missouri. From a clock company that produced their internal mechanisms, he obtained replacement parts, and with a mechanic, he restored the machines. He installed his one-armed bandits at business places around Scott County, including the drugstore and the Barrel House at Forester.

Unfortunately, the sheriff soon confiscated the slot machines and put them again in the junkyard, but the slot-machine man as well as others continued to make money by moonshining and bootlegging. Charlie Cockburn remembers: "One of the bootleggers from down in the

Forester druggist Vernon Carter, at left, and his boat paddler show off a string of panfish caught at the Fourche River. Says Carter: "It never was a week went by that I didn't go fishin', whether it was cold, or what it was. It's a wonder my wife ever put up with me."

Outdoor Living

The people of Forester, cooped up in their little houses during the depression and surrounded by woods and streams and other open spaces, spent a lot of time outdoors.

They hunted rabbits, quail, coon, fox, and deer, and fished with worms, flies, and gigs. They took hikes to the fire tower and camped along Fourche River. They made moonshine up the creek (one or two did) and skinny-dipped in the creek ("Somebody kept watch to see if anybody was comin'—and boy, when they did, we'd hit the bushes—").[2] They rode bicycles, tricycles, horses, and ponies. They played outdoor games: marbles, croquet, softball, baseball, and basketball. They indulged in the gentler yard sports of gardening, partying, and just sitting.

Since these happy pastimes were available and affordable for almost everybody, Forester folks made it through the hard times pretty well.

Courtesy Vernon E. Carter, Sr. and Vernon E. Carter, Jr.

Fourche valley went down behind the Colored Quarters. Blacks knocked a board out of the fence, came out, and got whiskey. Whiskey was brought in from every direction." Not that the trade was confined to blacks. Alcohol was peddled and consumed in the white neighborhoods, too.

Everybody listened to the radio, tuning in on the popular comedy programs of the 1930s such as "Amos and Andy" and "Fibber McGee and Molly." And of course, "Lum and Abner," for that pair were almost hometown boys, having come from Polk County just to the south. The radio brought news and comments by Walter Winchell, the aspiring young talents on "Major Bowes' Amateur Hour," and the suspenseful episodes of "The Shadow." Most popular of all were the country music shows. Family and friends would gather, one of them would go and water the ground wire for better reception, and then the radio would be turned

Forester's citizens often took walks on Sundays after church and dinner. Dressed in their Sunday best, strollers would amble along the logging railroads, or on the road around the sawmill where this fellow scratches a grateful pig.

Courtesy Albert A. Maupin, Jr.

on. After it warmed up, everyone would sit and listen to "Grand Ole Opry" blaring and then fading and then blaring again through the static on a summer's night.

Summertime was outdoor time. In the evenings people sat in their yards listening to the radio or talking as they watched their kids playing under the corner streetlight. On Sunday afternoons they went to baseball games; after Whit Rosborough's death the company helped employees build a ball park with roofed bleachers (and a board fence whose materials came from the then unnecessary fence around the Colored Quarters). On warm days both children and grownups—at least among the whites— cooled off in the Pump Hole on Cedar Creek behind the Quarters, where the company had built dressing stalls and fastened a diving board to a rock ledge, and somebody had hung a swing rope from a leaning tree. Both whites and blacks fished along Cedar Creek, and some of the whites fished and swam at the Fourche River. The Fourche, however, lay several

Courtesy Vernon E. Carter, Sr. and Vernon E. Carter, Jr.

Swimmers immerse themselves in Cedar Creek, the coolest place at Forester in the summertime. The pool was called the Pump Hole, for the mill had a water intake there. During severe droughts, sawmilling took precedence over swimming and the Pump Hole got pumped away.

miles outside town and not many people were able to get there.

After his son's death, Rosborough carried out one of Whit's own wishes by giving Forester a community building. It had a large meeting room with a framed portrait of Whit, a stage with dressing rooms, and a small kitchen in back. Upstairs was a Masonic hall for members only. The structure's interior was unpainted and the kitchen had only a cold water faucet and hot plates, but the building was used frequently for school programs, teenagers' parties, weekday bridge sessions for the women, and Saturday night domino, checker, and card games for the men.

Being isolated, Forester's people were obliged to entertain themselves. In the church auditorium, school children gave plays to audiences of parents and friends. At the Loafers Bench, men swapped stories. In the lobby of the hotel, Mrs. Vise and her boarders spent evenings joking and teasing and playing cards and dominoes. (Moreover, on April Fools' Day she dished out pieces of her special butterscotch pie to those who wouldn't get mad when they discovered theirs were filled with sawdust.) It was a way of life not to everyone's taste. One girl from southern Arkansas who came to visit her sister at Forester remembers: "Forester was the end of the world. A big day in Forester was going to the post office to get the mail, and to the drugstore to get a Coke."[3]

For children, Forester was a good place, a protective environment. Here they could safely roam the town, build playhouses in the woods, inspect the goldfish in Dr. Thornton's pool, watch the men pushing logs at the sawmill pond (and wish somebody would fall off a log), and play

The Forester Junior High School basketball team of 1936 and their coach. There was no gymnasium and the team practiced out-side—most of the time in overalls, the 1930s equiva-lent of blue jeans.

on flatcars and in the caboose on the railroad sidings. Frances Rodgers Dalton recalls her childhood: "We would go down to the sawmill. They were not quite as particular back then about letting people go through and see what was going on. We had to be careful where we were; they would tell each one of us where we were supposed to be. 'Course it would scare us, to hear all the noise." Later, as ten-year-olds, Frances and her girlfriends ventured into the mill at night. Mr. Goard, the night watch-man, admonished them for being there, but let them stay a while and slide down the sawdust piles.

Without money to buy toys, children made baseball gloves from dis-carded canvas work gloves, and baseballs from wool yarn they unraveled from worn-out socks and wound around a jack ball or a marble and then sewed.[4] Small children, boys and girls alike, often played with toy auto-mobiles. (Their parents did not have real ones, but toys cost only pen-nies.) Frances Dalton remembers that when it rained, she and her friends played under houses in Green Town, making roads in the dust for their little toy cars.

Vada Wilson, who helped with the community's annual Christmas programs during the depression, says: "The company would give us money to buy every child a gift and a committee of us would go to Fort Smith, and we could go to the wholesale houses and buy gifts for the children. So every child got some kind of special gift and also there'd be candy and oranges and nuts." On the night of the gift giving, the church was crowded with children and parents. Frances Dalton recalls: "They would call out all the kids' names, and you would go up there [to the Christmas tree] and get your package. There was so many of the kids that . . . that was just about all the Christmas they had."

There were 180 children in the whites' school at Forester during the 1930s, distributed among the nine grades. Many of these youngsters dropped out of school after the eighth or ninth grade (if not sooner) and went to work. The few who went on to high school had to travel twenty-two miles to Waldron. In the early years they went in private cars—sometimes getting flat tires or getting stuck, or having to wait or detour when floods covered the low water bridge on the Fourche. ("The roads were not good; the parents would walk the floors and the streets when they were late getting back.")[5] Later they rode an unheated bus ("You carried a quilt to keep warm") with board seats ("When we hit a bump, we hit the ceiling").[6] As the economy improved in the late 1930s, there was a better school bus and about thirty pupils from Forester were enrolled in grades ten through twelve at Waldron.

The high school students became exposed to a larger world than at home, but as commuters they could not take part in many extra-curricular activities (and some students from Waldron contemptuously called them "sawmill kids"). At Forester they were isolated; the possibilities for dating were limited and most socializing took place within the small group at home. Some teenagers felt constricted while others seemed not to mind. The high schoolers put on three-act plays, held ice cream or candy parties, went on picnics and weiner roasts, and hiked together along the railroad tracks or up to the fire tower north of town. Most teen activities, even the swimming parties, were organized through the Sunday school at Forester's church.

In fact, the church was central to the social as well as religious life of the entire town. In the 1930s Forester's Methodists had a Missionary Society, a Men's Brotherhood, a Boy Scout troop (sponsored by the Sunday school), a Young People's Union, and a Hi-League.[7] The Baptists probably maintained about as many of their own organized groups.

As was often the case in company-owned sawmill towns, a Methodist and a Baptist church, with separate membership rolls and sets of officers, shared one building. A Baptist preacher conducted services one Sunday and a Methodist the next, while the Sunday school used nondenominational literature. Members of both churches attended services every Sunday. Nearly everyone in Forester must have been a church member; at one point the Methodists listed 331 members and the Baptists had surely an even greater number. The denominational makeup of the church tended to follow economic levels at the mill, with the higher paid employees often being Methodist and those not in the managerial ranks more often Baptist. There were also lower income people who felt uncomfortable in the church as it was, and so did not join, or at least did not attend services.

Not counting the Christmas tree program, the best attended church

Courtesy Vernon E. Carter, Sr. and Vernon E. Carter, Jr.

For children, Forester lacked the advantages of urban areas but also was spared the hazards. People who lived there remember the town as a good place for kids.

services all year were probably the outdoor meetings of the annual union revival. A tradition in the Ouachitas, as elsewhere in rural America, these revivals or protracted meetings were conducted each summer for two weeks or longer under a brush arbor at the edge of town. From one year to the next, the Baptists and the Methodists took turns in providing the preacher and the song leader. In August 1937, Forester's Methodist preacher wrote that "The entire city of Forester is being stirred with an old time Holy Ghost revival, so much so that many have expressed themselves as never having seen its equal. Some have reported that the very atmosphere in all the departments of the plant has been changed. It is the principal topic of conversation. Brother Baker, and Brother Lawrence are both Spirit filled and specially equipped men, and are bringing us great messages in sermon and song as is evidenced by 53 conversions."[8]

Meanwhile in the Colored Quarters, the black people lived their own lives. In the 1930s approximately three hundred and fifty blacks lived in the Quarters, and about one hundred of the men worked at the mill. Theirs was an isolated community, with an eight-grade school having one teacher, and a little church that sheltered the Forester Temple (Baptists) and the New Salem Methodists. Preachers from out of town took turns coming to preside at services.

For a while the Baptists and Methodists each had a choir. Every three or four months on Fifth Sunday, the black Baptist choirs of Forester and several towns to the south gathered for a singing convention, and about every second year it came Forester's turn to be the host church. The cooling shed at the dry kilns, across the road from the Quarters, was emptied of lumber and rows of seats were arranged across the wide interior. On convention day the visiting choirs converged on Forester, along with hundreds of whites from all over Scott County. The cooling shed filled with singers and listeners. Groups from the different churches took turns singing, each trying to outdo the others and win the banner for best choir. All afternoon they performed, singing spirituals that gave voice to deep emotions, belting out gospel songs embellished with accent and lively rhythm. Eva Mae Little, a black woman who became a choir singer in the church at Forester, recalls "as many whites there as there was colored. Some of these white people, they would just get on in there with us, and just sing right along with us."

The black people staged another big event, on June 19—"Juneteenth," Emancipation Day, the blacks' own holiday (and a holiday for whites, too, for without blacks the sawmill could not operate). Alex Nichols recalls: "The old man [Rosborough] would give us a cow, and a hog, and we'd barbecue them." For a day and a night, men watched over the meat as it slowly cooked. When it was done, whites bought much of it by the pound, or in sandwiches. Sated with barbecue, everyone adjourned to the ball park to see the Forester Braves, the black baseball team, play the winner of an earlier game between the Rosboro Black Yankees and the Caddo Stars of Glenwood.

Singing and barbecue got blacks and whites together, but the goings-on at the Barrel House were limited to blacks only, though whites sometimes hung around outside. Like those of Glenwood, Rosboro, Graysonia, and other sawmill towns, Forester's Barrel House was a place where blacks could openly indulge in pastimes that the company did not allow in white neighborhoods, at least not in public. The large central room, called the Hall, had a dance floor and a pool table, and a counter where the manager served short orders, home brew, and wildcat whiskey. At one end of the same building, with a separate entrance, was the Gambling Shack where men shot craps across a green felt table (with dice so small they could not be loaded), and played dominoes and poker and Georgia shin. There, too, some of the ladies sat all day and played po-keno, a bingo game with numbers being called from a shuffled deck of cards.

Of the Barrel House, one black man says, "You could do anything you was big enough to do, 'long as you didn't kill nobody."[9] About six o'clock on Saturday evening, Glen Roberts, the ice man, delivered two or three hundred pounds of ice there, and remembers "they'd be wheeling away, all dancing, all about half drunk." Another white visitor recalls: "If you ever seen anybody that acted like they enjoyed life, them niggers did at the Barrel House. Three or four groups . . . somebody in each group

. . . each one of them wanting to talk loud enough to be heard over the others." [10]

It was too much fun for some whites not to notice and be a little envious, for after all, not even dancing was allowed in the whites' community hall. Over the years, the Barrel House resounded to the sad, strong voices of blacks singing blues, to pickup combos playing jazz, even to a fiddler sawing out square dance tunes. L. J. Thompson says: "Old Man Buster used to play the violin, and I used to second him with a guitar once in a while, and an old French harp. Buster [would] git that little cigar up there, twist that mouth around and say 'Give me a light.' Yeah, he'd light it up, and that pint of white lightnin' sittin' there between his feet. And you'd get him started at it, and *whoop!*—all night long."

In the freewheeling atmosphere of the Barrel House, alcohol sometimes became the catalyst for violence. Heavy drinking lowered inhibitions, and frustrations boiled over as aggression. Often the apparent (if not real) cause of trouble was rivalry over women. L. J. Thompson says: "Most of them fights came from the women's side of the thing. You'd dance with the wrong woman or something or other, you might get nipped. . . ."

Everybody in town knew, or heard, that black men carried pistols, and black women (or some of them) kept razors hidden in their clothing. Stories of fights made the rounds: a black woman had cut off a man's ear; a man at the Barrel House had gotten a woman in a bear hug and sliced her buttocks with a razor; Shoe-Booty was drunk and started to shoot someone, but the other fellow shot him first. (In twenty years at Forester there would be half a dozen murders committed, all by blacks knifing or shooting other blacks.) It seemed to suffice if those involved in capital offenses were apprehended; those in lesser scraps were ignored. ("As long as they didn't bother the whites, they were pretty well left alone," says a white man who lived at Forester.) [11] Whites told their children to stay away from the Barrel House, and assumed that since blacks were fighting blacks, it was their own fault and therefore their community's problem. (Not until later years would anyone carry out research to find the underlying social and cultural reasons for black-on-black violence, and consider how to prevent it.) [12]

L. J. Thompson recalls that all of the fights at Forester involved "probably not over five percent. Most black people, when they got high, they wanted to dance, and have fun. . . ."

To keep law and order in sawmill towns, lumber companies often employed their own town marshalls. Caddo River's marshal at Forester was Daniel S. Bray, a former country schoolteacher and county sheriff, a tall, skinny, rawboned man resembling Abraham Lincoln. Bray was widely respected; at Forester during the depression he and his wife drove out to impoverished farm homes and left fruit, candy, and comic books for the children. Daniel Bray, however, was getting old. He trembled from a nervous disorder, and sometimes talked to himself, with gestures, as he walked down the street.

By 1940 Forester's Green Town had a look of permanence, with fenced yards, shade trees, cow sheds, and chicken coops. In the background are the mill's smokestacks and water tower, and (at left) a portion of the immense rough lumber shed. White smoke rises from the sawmill's refuse burner. Beyond lie the peaceful Ouachitas hills whose timber sustained the town.

Fortunately, Bray had no overwhelming problems. Somebody from outside town broke into the commissary one time, and into the post office twice, but crimes in Forester tended to be more internal in nature: a poker game behind the toolhouse (which Bray ignored if he knew about it), or drunkenness and wife-beating (which called for discipline by the company's managers). Or the time that a mean boy tried his .22 on the Hight family's cow and fatally wounded her. Or when boys captured and killed some of the town's cats, skinned and dressed them, and sold them to blacks as possums. (After the trick was discovered, blacks insisted that any dressed animal offered to them as possum—or rabbit, either—had to have one foot attached, with the fur on.)

Bray did have a few bigger cases. Henry Overby, who was a log cutter living in Forester's hotel, remembers when two men from out of town

Courtesy Albert A. Maupin, Jr.

brought a couple of "wild girls" from Waldron and had them register at the hotel. Arriving home from work, Overby found Mrs. Vise, the hotel manager, worrying about what her new guests were up to. He told her that one of the men was at the drugstore, advertising the girls. Hearing that, Mrs. Vise went to get Mr. Bray. He came and started to march the girls out—and a local tough met him at the gate.

Bray jerked out a blackjack and shook it in the man's face. "You get out of my way."

"Old man, don't you know you couldn't hit me with that?"

Bray pulled out his .45 pistol. "I could hit you with this. Now, you get away from here right now." The man moved. [13]

Daniel Bray was regarded as being totally fearless and somewhat trigger-happy. A good marksman, especially with a pistol, he often pulled a gun when making an arrest. At times he pulled the trigger, too; one of the men who ran the Barrel House retained some of Bray's shotgun

pellets under the skin of his backside. Bray's most powerful weapon, however, was the backing of the lumber company. A man could lose his job and his home if he fooled around with Mr. Bray. It was said that Bray could walk up to any kind of fracas, even without his pistol, and disarm the combatants.

Law enforcement guidelines for a sawmill town's marshal as set forth by the lumber company were a bit fuzzy. Whites were supposed to be virtuous (at least in public), while blacks were allowed to have fun (up to a point), and always, lumber production was to proceed without interference. Actually these instructions were not hard to administer. Bray stopped fights when he could get there in time, and safeguarded the public morals. He kept bootleggers in check—though like the woman who wanted only a small portion of the druggist's bedbug medicine, he didn't try to get rid of them, just kept them down a little. For years, Charlie Copeland made and sold home brew in the Quarters and was apparently never bothered by Bray (though Charlie's churchgoing wife Katie in a fit of righteous wrath once smashed his brewing crock). Local residents sold hard liquor, both moonshine and bottled-in-bond, out of their homes and cars on both sides of town.

But if there were any instances of drunkenness on the job, or if he heard of any unusual amounts of liquor being brought into the Quarters, Bray cracked down. He raided bootleggers' stashes and confiscated whiskey and beer (disposing of it by giving it to trusted friends, and keeping some of the beer for himself if it were Blue Ribbon).[14] And, as everybody would remember, Bray shot and killed Harrison Defoor, a Fourche valley farmer, following a car chase out of Forester when he discovered Defoor selling wildcat in the Quarters.

Bray was always busy on Halloween. All evening, troops of boys roamed the town, dodging the marshal and making mischief. They soaped windows and turned over outhouses. They strung fire hoses up and down the street (the company reprimanded Bray for letting that happen). They turned wagons upside down in front of the drugstore and the commissary. But as Floyd Kimble recalls: "Bray finally caught us. He told us 'I'm going to join you, do everything that you all do.' That took all the fun out of it. A big group of boys had put a toilet out in the middle of the street." Another Halloween, Bray deputized the boys themselves to watch the town and patrol certain areas so he'd know where they were.

After Halloween's night of turmoil, any grown-up could collar some boys and ask them to wash a soaped window, or put something back that had been moved, and they did it without argument. One resident says, "There was never any trouble getting it back."[15]

Bray had another idea for managing boys. At his suggestion the company employed many of the town's youths during summer vacation to cut weeds, clean drainage ditches, dig holes for pit privies, repair bridges, and clean up and groom the outfield at the ball park. Bray was put in charge, and in the mornings he kept separate crews of whites and blacks at work. Then, as one of those boys, Joe Angel, remembers: "In the afternoon you would go to the ball park and you would play ball. [The blacks] had a team. The whites had a team. You would choose up sides and you would have whites and blacks on the same team. You would play each other, and there would be different age groups. This would go on all afternoon."

Bray loved baseball. He also conducted a Sunday school class in the woods at the edge of town for some of the boys who were shy about going to church. To show them the fate of the unrighteous, he took some of his charges to the Quarters to see the body of a black who had been killed in a fight. Angel says: "He was a giant of a man . . . he had huge muscles. He was laid out, and all I can remember is the gash on his arms." (One of the white girls sneaked in, too: "A black man, all cut up, was lying on a kitchen table. Oh, how awful. . . . Daddy about had a fit when he heard I'd been down there.") [16]

———

J. D. Thornton, the company doctor, treated injuries that resulted from fights. Lenard Cockburn recalls being in Thornton's office when a black man came in pleading "Doctor, oh, Doctor, I need to see you, bad." The man had a kitchen knife run through a muscle of his arm. Thornton distracted the man's attention a moment with "You do have some problems, don't you" and jerked the knife out of his arm. After the man had settled down, says Cockburn, "Old Doc painted his arm with antiseptic, bandaged it, and sent him on his merry way."

Like the company's doctor at Mauldin, Thornton practiced a lot of first aid but sent serious cases to Hot Springs. He did deliver babies, and took pride in his record of having lost none of the mothers or newborn. Thornton, a middle-aged, bulky man, was a typical country doctor of his day, not highly trained ("He wasn't all that qualified. And he knew he wasn't"), but conscientious ("I never knew him to refuse to go anytime day or night"). [17] He was well liked. He believed in simple remedies ("Dr. Thornton advised a child with worms to chew a plug of Man's Work Chewing Tobacco"). [18] And he wasn't much for the niceties. Once a young woman went to see him for a sore throat and learned he was outside milking his cow. Presently he came in and painted her throat—without washing his hands. [19] ("Kinda old-fashioned—sloppy, too," says Era McKeown, "but got the job done.")

Dr. Thornton practiced in a little building in front of his home. Albert Maupin recalls that he and the two older Thornton boys "used to hang around, lots of times, just to watch him treat these people. Cuts, bruises, boils, or whatever, we just taken it all in. Part of our education; it was a public place." To cuts and scrapes, Thornton applied a black, fishy-smelling salve named Icthyol, supposedly antibiotic. On boils he packed a clay-like substance called Anti-Phlogistine, which, when it hardened, he peeled off to pull out the festered core, allowing the boil to drain and heal. An easygoing man, Thornton moved at an unhurried pace. If called on at milking time to deliver a baby, he first would finish milking. "His clock ran pretty slow," says Maupin.

Thornton had come to the town before the mill opened. He had prac-

everyone in town had come out in the streets. Forester's sawmill was burning.

Only minutes before, the night watchman had discovered the fire on the ground floor of the mill, spreading through grease and oil drippings under the carriages, with sparks popping. He hurried to the power plant; the operator blew the whistle. Already flames shot up through the mill, igniting wood dust, spreading explosively.

Fire fighters found the mill a mass of flames, beyond saving—sparks were falling on the lumber sheds! Men brought ladders, climbed up and strung out along the roofs, stomped sparks, put out spot fires; others came running to help. They pulled fire hoses and wetted walls and roofs closest to the sawmill until intense heat drove them back. Would this be another fire like Glenwood's—but this time in a lumber shed a thousand feet long?

"More water—Keep them pumps goin'!" But the fire pumps needed electric power, and the power plant stood only yards away from the sawmill. Searing heat warped and curled the sheet iron on the boiler room wall, and the timbered wall of the fuel house caught fire. Operators in the power house anxiously watched pressure gauges, dragged boiler fuel from the burning fuel house, shielded their faces from the heat. . . .

For two long hours the battle continued. Finally the fire was contained, under control. The sawmill was gone, and some of the boiler room wall, and much of the fuel house, but the rest of the plant was intact. Men kept vigil on the lumber shed roofs all night to guard against stray sparks.

The sawmill would be rebuilt, but many of the mill crew and all of the woods people would be out of work for months. Log cutters, log haulers, laborers, sawyers—both whites and blacks had to find temporary employment at other mills around western Arkansas. Others started clearing the fire's wreckage; still others began working for L. D. Williams, hacking railroad ties for twenty-five cents a tie. For those without work or on short wages, the company waived house rents.

Les Williams, a section crew foreman, was out of his job, and had a wife and three children. Les and his wife Lora decided to stay in Forester, cut stove wood with a crosscut saw, and sell it for a dollar a rick to farmers along the Fourche. Lora says: "We didn't have much a lot of times—potatoes, and beans, and bread—but we never did go hungry. And we fed ourselves through that, without getting any tips off the government, or buying on credit. We wondered some what we was going to do next. But we didn't worry, much."

Ten months before the Forester mill burned, Rosborough had closed the sawmill at Glenwood and sold the building and machinery to a salvage company.[27] After the fire at Forester, the Glenwood mill was still there and Rosborough bought it back. He summoned the contractor who had built the Forester mill, an elderly millwright from Mississippi named Harry Mitchell, and told him to move the Glenwood mill to Forester. Under Mitchell's direction, a crew dismantled the mill, marking each piece. Before long, they had it reassembled at Forester. They

Courtesy Dorothy Sage Newkirk

Courtesy Vanita Kimble Britton

Country and Western

Country music scholar Bill Malone says that the 1930s were "a time of expansion and transition for country music, away from its folk roots, into mass media (radio, records, movies, concerts)." During that time, he says, the romantic image of the cowboy became firmly established.[20]

Even an isolated mill town such as Forester could be affected by these changes. Before the coming of the "cowboy" image, guitar player Harry Standerfer could comfortably pose in overalls with his companions next to a Model A car. Standerfer remembers: "We had the Forester Band, went all around the country. . . . We played for dances, mostly square dancing, some round dances. When we'd go to a farmhouse to play, the old farmer was the one who called the set." The band continued to play until World War II, one of numberless fiddle-and-guitar bands that were part of the rural culture of southern whites.

During the band's existence, however, nearly everyone in Forester and the outlying log camps acquired a radio—battery-powered, if need be—and many listened to mass-media country music such as "Grand Ole Opry" and "Bob Wills and His Texas Playboys" and other programs. After Forester's movie theater opened in 1937, people could actually view the singing cowboys, the first one being Gene Autry, who came from Texas and Oklahoma. "Autry," Bill Malone says, "had the widest exposure of any country singer in the thirties, and with his depiction of the cowboy he provided country music with an image that was much more appealing than that of the allegedly backward hillbilly." [21]

By 1940, when the Turner family's band stood on the steps of Forester's Caddo Theater for their portrait, the theater was featuring not only Gene Autry but also Roy Rogers and other cowboy stars, and the local musicians had donned cowboy hats. Only the clowns in the group still wore overalls.

put machinery in place (including equipment from the Rosboro sawmill that had cut out in January 1939) and by mid-April, six months after the fire, the mill crew started up their "new" sawmill. The one that burned had been equipped with a band saw and a circular saw; the mill that replaced it had two band saws.

With the mill making lumber again, people resumed their normal lives. For a while they continued to talk about what might have caused the fire, whether it was spontaneous combustion, or maybe an electrical problem. Or possibly a spark from the refuse burner; there had been a strong wind that night. No one knew for sure, and the mystery remained unsolved. [28]

––––––––––

Before the mill burned and after it was rebuilt, Forester temporarily gained in population. People came from Mauldin, Glenwood, and Rosboro after those operations closed. From Mauldin, the company transferred more than a dozen four-room houses into Green Town, and many two- and three-room dwellings into Cannon Town and the Colored Quarters. Mauldin still had many leftover houses, two-room portables and three-room shotguns, and the company set those in a field across the creek from Green Town. B. H. Angel, a log hauler, was living there already, and his uncle Dan Angel, another hauling contractor, was to move there shortly, so L. D. Williams named the place Angel Town. Before long, the new neighborhood included about twenty-five families of log cutters, log haulers, and railroad workers.

Even as newcomers moved in, about twelve other families from Forester, selected by T. W. Rosborough, accompanied him to Oregon in 1939. George Morris, the sawyer who had been a friend of Whit's, says that he was asked to go because Whit had wanted it that way. "After Whit got killed, Mr. Rosborough carried out every plan that boy had made. And I guess that he had talked to his dad about me a-comin' out with him."

Vernon Williams, Forester's logging superintendent, also went to Oregon with Rosborough, and his younger brother Max took his place at Forester. L. D. Williams, less active now, had become senior advisor on timber and logging, while Will McKeown was resident manager over the town and mill. With Rosborough gone, Hal Shaffer in Kansas City was in charge overall as Caddo River's president.

Max Williams remembers: "Hal Shaffer, Papa, McKeown, and I were the operating committee. They asked me one night in a meeting, 'Can you log this mill with trucks?' I said, 'I'll save you five to eight dollars a thousand.'" The committee members then agreed that the logging railroads would be replaced with a fleet of logging trucks.

Since the mid-1930s, several contractors had brought logs to the mill on trucks, and at many locations, Caddo River had built roads with bulldozers and then used trucks instead of wagons to haul logs to the railroad spurs. Now, in 1940, the company arranged with log haulers to replace their mules and wagons with new trucks. Caddo River would do

Two Angel Town children sit for a snapshot. Their neighborhood was made up mostly of two-room portable houses, many set side by side in pairs with an open hallway between. Never painted, and with years of prior use in camps on the logging railroads, these houses always wore a weather-beaten look.

the financing; the contractors could buy their trucks by having the company deduct one-third of their payments for hauling logs, until the trucks and trailers were paid for.

The company then sold four locomotives to other railroads. The rest of the railroad equipment and material was disposed of as scrap: the Number 2 engine (originally purchased in 1911), the repair shop, carloads of rails, a gondola carload of railroad spikes, and other iron and steel. Workmen turned flatcars upside down, removed wheels and axles, burned wooden decks, and cut up the steel frames. Everything was shipped out on the KCS. Witnesses said the scrap had been sold to "an old Jew," and it was rumored that he sold it to the Germans who were at war in Europe, or to the Japanese. "Later they shot it back at us," some said.

Log haulers who had lived in railroad camps came to live in Cannon Town and Angel Town and parked their new log trucks beside their homes. At this time, Forester's population probably reached its maximum. According to the census taken during the year the railroads were abandoned, Forester counted 1,306 residents. Waldron, the county seat, had 1,298.

By 1940, however, people had begun to see things differently. Although Forester had been a refuge during the depression, there were now other places that looked better. Archie Taylor, for one, recalls that he moved to Forester in 1931 as a locomotive engineer, but left six years later when Caddo River's seven operating locomotives had been reduced to two. "I left to provide myself with a better job before I got too old," he says. He and his wife sold most of their belongings and headed west in a 1932 Chevrolet with two small children and savings of two hundred dollars. Taylor found a job in California with the Southern Pacific Railroad.

Frank Jones, a black, says, "Everybody was lookin' for greener pastures." He left Forester in 1937 and went to Chicago, but returned in two years, then went back to Chicago in 1940. Says he: "I liked Forester. Only thing I didn't like about it was the pay."

In earlier years Caddo River had hired the sons of employees, and required that mill workers live in Forester; men who lived outside town could not get jobs. Luke Stinson, who farmed in the Fourche valley during the 1930s, says, "Us old country boys wore out the road walkin' back and forth to Forester looking for jobs." Paul Frost, another farmer on the Fourche, recalls that he saw "employees with cars, buying groceries when we were starvin'." At last, though, the company started hiring out-of-towners. Frost went to work at Forester about 1940. Stinson got a steady job there in 1942.

About the end of 1940, young men at Forester began to be called into military service, and the company for the first time hired six women to work in the planing mill.

When Harry Mitchell finished rebuilding the sawmill at Forester in 1939, Rosborough employed him to design and build his new plant at Springfield, Oregon. Rosborough, however, had his own ideas about building a sawmill, and when it was two-thirds complete he and Mitchell argued and Mitchell left abruptly. Another overseer was hired and in June 1940, several months behind schedule, the nearly completed mill cut its first lumber. The mill proved to be out of alignment. The lumber was too thick or too thin—unsaleable. Mitchell had also designed a mill that could not handle the long, heavy western logs.

To build his mill, Rosborough had obtained a $500,000 loan from the government-backed Reconstruction Finance Corporation (RFC).[29] Now without funds—he had even borrowed on his life insurance to buy timberland—he managed to borrow another $575,000 from the RFC to rebuild the sawmill.[30] He persuaded his employees to take a cut in wages. To meet payrolls, he borrowed on unpaid invoices for whatever lumber he was able to sell.

Rosborough hung on and continued to revamp his mill, and it began to produce better lumber in greater quantity. But then came another problem unlike any he had ever experienced. All of Oregon's other mills were unionized, and the hourly wage employees of Rosboro Lumber Company proceeded to go union, too. Rosborough the autocrat now had to face representatives of the working people.

Among the union's leaders were some of the very men T. W. had brought from Arkansas. George Morris, the sawyer who had been Whit's friend, was on the negotiating committee. Morris remembers meeting with Rosborough: "He was sittin' there behind his desk. And I could tell he was gettin' kindly mad. 'Cause he was just kinda swellin' up. And he sat there till that union man got through talkin'. And he come down on the desk with his fist—'Eye gracious damn! Hell's fire! I raised those boys on two bits an hour! Wanting *eighty* cents an hour?'"

But Rosborough had to agree to their terms. Not long after, Miss Anna wrote her nephew about T. W.'s labor worries: "He says he wouldn't be so entirely unable to adjust if he were forty years younger. . . ."[31]

———

In the fall of 1941, the Dierks mill at Pine Valley, Oklahoma, cut out. Fourteen years after the mill had opened, its timber was gone. Dierks had cut everything in the upper Kiamichi valley, and even had built a

During defense mobilization early in World War II, black women in Forester knitted sweaters, caps, and other clothing for the armed forces. A separate knitting club for white women was also organized by the company doctor's wife, Inez Thornton.

Courtesy Inez Phillips Thornton

truck road over Kiamichi Mountain in order to cut timber that earlier had been reserved for the mill at Wright City.

First the Pine Valley sawmill shut down, and after some months the planing mill did also. When the planer closed, a power plant operator tied down the whistle, as had been done ten years earlier at Graysonia. A Pine Valley resident recalls: "When that whistle blew the last time, it was so *lonesome*. It just blew and blew and blew. It was so sad."[32]

People moved away and Dierks dismantled and salvaged. The big electric generator, the three tall smokestacks, and a number of shotgun houses were hauled to Mountain Pine. Other houses were taken to other Dierks mill towns. Nearly all the buildings were moved or torn down.

When Pine Valley closed, the remaining four Dierks mills (Mountain Pine, Dierks, Broken Bow, and Wright City) and Caddo River's mill at Forester, became the last remaining major sawmills in the Ouachitas.

––––––––

For two years a war had been raging in Europe, a war brought by radio into every home. For a year there had been a peacetime draft. As the country mobilized for defense, the lumber industry began filling orders for military needs.

On Sunday afternoon, December 7, 1941, the people of Forester learned of the bombing at Pearl Harbor. To them the blow was a double one—a Forester boy, Dan Reagan, had been killed aboard the battleship *Oklahoma*.

Before enlisting in the Navy, Reagan had been one of Daniel Bray's baseball players. Now the old man sat down and began to write a poem:

> "Pearl Harbor," yes we remember,
> We add the Oklahoma too,
> To these we link Dan Reagan,
> 'Till we fight this war clear through.[33]

10. Last Years

In the aftermath of Pearl Harbor, one hundred and forty of Forester's men entered military service. Many other townspeople joined the migration of both whites and blacks from the South to defense plants in the North and on the West Coast. James Davis recalls: "A lot of people left during the war . . . [to go to] California, or Michigan, where the boom was. The town didn't build back up. You couldn't get people to stay. That big money drawed a lot of 'em away."[1]

The largest number of whites went to San Diego to work in aircraft plants and shipyards, following several families who had moved there before the outbreak of war. Lester and Morna Miller, for example, settled near San Diego in 1942, and they in turn assisted many who arrived later. California defense industries offered more jobs, easier work, and better pay than in Arkansas, but housing was scarce. Morna Miller says: "Forester was like a family. If somebody came from Forester, your old neighbor or friend, why, you just made room for him until he could find a place and get a job and get settled.

"People from the Arkansas area had a reputation for being good workers. It was easy for Arkansas people already at work in California to recommend and secure jobs for their friends. I never knew of an unemployed Forester person." By war's end there were twenty-five families from Forester in the San Diego area, many of them in National City, the suburb where the Millers lived.

Soon after Pearl Harbor, T. W. Rosborough visited Forester and talked with mill workers whom he wanted to join him in Oregon. After more than two years of construction, dismantling, and reconstruction, his sawmill was ready for full production. Several men from the Forester mill decided to follow Rosborough back to the West Coast.

With so many employees leaving, the mill managers at Forester had to scramble to find replacements. Charlie Cockburn remembers: "During World War II, the mill *had* to have help. They hired people who weren't qualified." Forester now had vacant houses; employees lived along the Fourche valley and shared rides to the mill.

Forester was experiencing the same trouble as the rest of the southern pine industry where, in the first six months of 1942, three of every ten men left their jobs. To stop this manpower drain, the federal government's War Manpower Commission in September of that year classified the major forest industries as essential to the defense effort. The War Production Board later arranged for draft deferments for loggers and sawmillers.[2]

Max Williams, Forester's logging superintendent, recalls that his able-bodied men were being drafted: "They started to taking our loggers. I got a-hold of the War Production Board in Little Rock. They never took another one. We had two to volunteer." And Williams says: "The sawmill ran twenty hours a day during World War II—two ten-hour shifts. The mill was cutting three million feet a month. The military took everything we produced." Forester made lumber for Army camps in Arkansas and Oklahoma, and its planing mill produced ammunition boxes.

There was plenty of work but wages remained low in comparison with those elsewhere. Even longtime employees continued to leave. Wayne Pettijohn, the assistant shipping clerk and a Forester employee since 1931, left in 1943 to join the Firestone Rubber Company in Louisiana. Jimmy Mitchell, a sawmill worker and one of the blacks who had come from Alabama in 1933, left in 1943 for a shipyard job at Wilmington, California. Luther Turner, a saw filer with a log cutting crew since 1933, left in 1944 for a shipyard in Houston. John Gwathney, a log cutter since 1933, went to cut logs in Oregon. Gwathney recalls: "The biggest check I ever drawed [for two six-day weeks at Forester in 1942] for cutting logs was $124. The first check I drawed when I came to Oregon was $374."

Forester endured wartime shortages of many kinds. Basic commodities such as cloth, sugar, and gasoline were rationed. Deliveries of ice were stopped for a while. The rubber rain slickers that loggers wore were unavailable. New logging trucks were impossible to find until Hal Shaffer located some in Kansas City. Three different times, Max Williams put his son Charles on a train to meet Shaffer, receive a truck, and drive it back to Forester. The boy was only fourteen, but there was no one else who could go and bring home the trucks.

Daniel Bray, now near seventy, tried to keep up a semblance of old times by patching together a wartime version of the white men's baseball team. Colvin Irons recalls: "During the war I was playin'. It was not the best team. I was really too old to play. Bray was short on ball players; he was trainin' 'em. . . ." Bray also spent much time writing letters to his former ball players, and to all the other Forester boys who had grown up and were in the service. Henry Overby remembers: "He corresponded with every one through World War II. They'd tell Mr. Bray things they wouldn't tell their mamas."

When Germany surrendered on May 8, 1945, Will McKeown shut down the entire plant for an hour and the sawmill and planing mill employees gathered in the green lumber sorting shed for prayers. Forester's schoolchildren were taken to the town's flagpole near the commissary for a patriotic service. Bill Wilson, then five years old, remembers

In the aftermath of Pearl Harbor, one hundred and forty of Forester's young men entered military service.

that "the mill whistle blew, and kept blowing." He recalls that at the flagpole "somebody ran an extension cord out into the yard, set up a record player, and played a record of 'When Johnny Comes Marching Home.' Mr. McKeown, who was known for his long prayers, prayed an unusually long one that day."

———

On July 17, 1945, a month before Japan surrendered, Shaffer sold Caddo River to the Dierks Lumber and Coal Company. Dierks acquired the Forester mill and town with about two thousand acres of land, and the remaining four years of timber cutting rights on twenty-two thousand acres of land sold by Caddo River to the Forest Service during the 1930s. When Shaffer and the Dierks officers signed the sale papers, the Caddo River Lumber Company ceased to exist as a corporation, after thirty-nine years of life following the company's founding in 1906.

Hal Shaffer was sixty-five and wanted to retire. For several years, he had also been buying back the Caddo River stock owned by L. D. Williams to make sure that his friend L. D. would be well compensated for the shares that Williams had acquired many years before. (Shaffer subsequently sold the company to Dierks for a low price.) After Shaffer sold Caddo River, Williams, past seventy years old, moved away from Forester and into retirement.

At the time of the sale, the Dierks newsletter for employees carried a significant but little noticed statement concerning the Forester mill. "Present plans are to continue operations during the War Emergency and as long thereafter as timber is available. The sale of the property involves the transfer of title of a small amount of timber lands. Future cutting will depend, to a considerable extent, upon the availability of Government-owned timber."[3]

Most of the mill's supervisors were men of long experience who had been at Forester since the 1930s, and Dierks made no changes in personnel. The only difference at first was that Dierks officials from Kansas City and from the company's other mills visited Forester frequently and asked questions. Caddo River's people had lived under a simpler organization having only Rosborough or Hal Shaffer at the top. Now they worked for a company having several second generation members of the Dierks family in the top positions; young third generation members being promoted into management; and persons who were not family members in charge of various aspects of manufacturing. With these layers of management and divisions of responsibility, Dierks was a larger, more modern corporation than Caddo River. The old one-on-one relationships with a paternal figure were past. As everywhere else in the lumber industry, the strong, pioneering individuals who had once dominated successful enterprises were being replaced by professional managers as corporate employees.

One of the first changes made by Dierks at Forester was to eliminate the refuse burning pile. From then on, wood waste was ground up for boiler fuel or converted into marketable products, as Dierks had done for years at their other mills. Henry Soderling, who worked in the planing mill at Forester, says: "Caddo River didn't have a sale for short lumber, but Dierks did. Anything twelve inches long and an inch and an eighth wide, they could use it. They run one-by-ones, four feet long, for mop handles." Small pieces of wood were worked up into parts for toys, pieces for porch furniture—any number of items—and shipped out by the carload.

Roy Douglas, who was the dry kiln foreman at Forester, remembers that "after Dierks ran the plant a year, the manager called in the foremen and said, 'This mill has made us more money than any of the other plants,' and announced that a box factory would be built." The box factory was equipped to make fruit and vegetable crates from small pieces of wood, including hardwood for which there was no other market. Dierks also tooled up to produce Trim-Pak—the pieces of wood for a door or window, all cut to proper length and wrapped together in a package. Next to the big sawmill they built a "billet mill" to cut two-by-fours and other lumber from eight-foot lengths of small trees. In the sawmill, they frequently cut hardwood for lumber, flooring, and crating. The company also bought pine fenceposts that local people had cut and peeled, treated them with a preservative, and shipped them to buyers in the Midwest. Now there were more people working at Forester than ever before, though many of them lived outside town.

Many of the workers were women. At one time in the late 1940s, ten women wrapped Trim-Pak, while thirty-five worked in the box factory. Women bundled hardwood flooring, ran cutoff saws, or made surveyors stakes. One woman found herself moving and stacking four- and six-inch boards as they came out of a planer. Another, Letha Jameson, says: "I helped load boxcars—one day, two-by-twelves, twelve feet long—with a preacher named George Epperson. I was stout as a man." Mrs. Jameson worked next in the planing mill—where one day she saw a man get his arm caught and pulled into a resaw. She grabbed him and jerked him back as hard as she could, freeing him from the saw.[4] She says: "I done practically everything the men done, but the men was getting a dollar an hour, and I was just getting seventy-five cents. But after I pulled that man out of that saw, they raised me up to a dollar."

The sawmill built by Rosborough's nephew on the site of the big mill at Rosboro was designed to cut small second growth logs. In this aerial view, logs are piled at the left, and at bottom center where they were pulled up the incline into the mill. Another inclined conveyor carried refuse from the sawmill to an open burning pile (top right). Rough lumber was loaded on flatcars and shipped to another plant at Delight, Arkansas, for drying and finishing.

Courtesy Mr. and Mrs. James Rosborough Bemis

One day not long after the end of the war, T. W. Rosborough visited the sawmill that his nephew, J. R. Bemis, had built on the site of the big mill at Rosboro. Strolling past piles of small second-growth logs on the yard outside the mill, he met an employee, Clint Thornton, and sat down to chat. Thornton recalls: "Rosborough looked at a tiny log and told me, 'They get more for that than I got for that good stuff.' Little old poles, goin' up there [into the mill]. He just sat there and shook his head.

"Rosborough said, 'I could have stayed on here and kept going. I thought I had to have a log that. . . .'

"He learnt that he couldn't just cut the big timber."

Rosborough's Oregon mill, however, had successfully cut big trees. It had run three shifts all through the war. In four years, Rosborough had paid all his debts and become a millionaire. But he had developed heart trouble, and in 1946 he sold his majority interest in the Rosboro Lumber Company to Beuford Cole, Vernon Williams, and other minority stockholders and came home to Texarkana. "In the later years," Rosborough said at that time, "a man's heart is with the friends of his youth and his kinfolk."[5]

In Texarkana he built a fine home for Miss Anna and himself, with an adjoining apartment for Halcy and Fred. By the time this was finished, he was feeling better, and becoming increasingly restless. Perhaps his nephew's successful mill at Rosboro served to inspire him. In any case, he decided to build another sawmill.

Rosborough was nearly eighty years old and walking slowly, but he remained tall and erect, and felt still better as he contemplated his new project. He organized the Ark-La-Tex Lumber Company, named for three states in which he had sawmilled in the past, and began to put up a mill on the outskirts of Texarkana. With Fred Wingfield he toured the countryside in a jeep, looking for the best timber. Here and there he located a small tract and bought it. "I'm building the prettiest sawmill," he told an acquaintance, "and I need the prettiest tract of timber to run it on."[6]

Again T. W. came to Forester to recruit employees. Several, attracted by the chance to be part of a new enterprise, decided to join him. Rosborough told Will McKeown that he could be the general manager at Ark-La-Tex. McKeown discussed the proposal with the old man but did not give him an immediate answer. Era McKeown recalls that her husband then went to Texarkana and "spent a weekend with Rosborough— and he was upset by what he saw."

McKeown saw that Rosborough's long career in sawmilling was nearing its end.

———

After the war, Forester again had full-fledged men's baseball teams, both white and black. As always, they were sponsored by the company, and played ball teams from Dierks mill towns, and from other small towns in western Arkansas. The blacks played against black teams mostly, but because there were few black communities nearby, the blacks also played

Courtesy Era Baxter McKeown

white teams. Forester's black and white teams occasionally played each other on the home field.

The whites had a good win-loss record but the blacks are better remembered because of their style. When the black team played at Forester, there was always a full house; spectators, both black and white, overflowed the stands and stood along the baselines.

James Maxon, a baldheaded black man who ran the casino at the Barrel House, served as master of ceremonies. Lifting his megaphone, Maxon with booming voice started a showman's line of patter, remembered as something like: "You are now privilege' to see the Forester Braves, a first class team, the greates' team in America—"[9] He went on to introduce the players while wives and girlfriends shouted acknowledgment. It seemed every player was known by nickname: Bean, at first base; Dudely, in left field; Old Folks, at shortstop; Junior, the pitcher; Scab, the catcher. Maxon introduced the players on the visiting team, and as the game got underway he announced the batters (amid loud response from the crowd in the black stands) and rendered a play-by-play commentary, sometimes riding the umpire; Maxon was a little partisan.

Vendors worked the crowd, selling peanuts, popcorn, lemonade, and soft drinks. A few spectators may have indulged in stronger drink, for as Lenard Cockburn says: "Occasionally there would be trouble. Somebody would get mad about something, somebody would pop off, and boy,

Together But Apart

White people recall that blacks at Forester "knew where the line was," meaning the unwritten rules and customs that spelled racial segregation.

Part of it was physical division: separate housing, churches, schools; separate windows, marked White and Colored, at Forester's post office; separate seating areas at the movie theater; separate seating on the bus to Waldron; and separate dining. Whites went to the Quarters and purchased and drank home brew in the kitchens of blacks, but blacks were not to sit down and eat with whites.

Another part of the code was that blacks were expected to play a subordinate role. At the post office and the commissary, whites were served first. ("Some of those colored people were really nice people. They'd stand back till all the white people were taken care of. They'd never crowd you.")[7] Whites played practical jokes on blacks (once some men at Forester frightened a black by laying a dead snake around his neck)[8] but blacks were

Courtesy Bertha Sanders

they'd go to Fist City. When that stuff started, the ball game would stop, and guys would go up and pull these guys apart, and somebody would sit and hold this one, and somebody would hold that one, and then the ball game would proceed."

As for the black team's style of playing, Cockburn says: "Anything they'd do, if somebody'd laugh about it, they'd do more of it. They was all relaxed and just havin' fun. Everything they did was comical. Oh, they made lots of boo-boos, but it didn't bother 'em a bit." The players talked to one another and to the crowd in the stands. Scab would catch while sitting in a rocking chair—and he could throw to second base while remaining seated. Bean did tricks with his baseball cap ("You could not tell whether he caught the ball with his hat or if he caught it with his glove").[10] There was another show in the stands, where the black girls, all in their Sunday dresses, could barely sit still in their excitement. If their team scored, up to the top of the stands they climbed. And if one of their boys hit a home run, the girls streamed down onto the field, and danced, and kissed the lucky batter.

The best-remembered black ball player of all was a tall, loose-jointed fellow named Reese Tatum who arrived one summer halfway through the baseball season. He played third base and sometimes pitched. The lumber company gave Reese a job in the rough shed, in which, as one black man describes it, the new ball player "was just sweepin' up . . . just piddlin' around. If a guy could play baseball, the company would give him a job—and not a hard job."[11]

Reese had been playing ball in the North with a team of black comedians called the Ethiopian Clowns, and apparently his feet had gone bad.[12] He appeared on the field at Forester in what had been his uniform with the Clowns, a grass skirt. Soon the amused crowd saw their rangy third baseman catch a grounder with his foot, making the ball roll up his bare leg into his skirt where he grabbed frantically to retrieve it.[13]

He could pitch, too ("When he pitched, it was three ups and three downs; they couldn't hit that smoke ball").[14] He also could catch (". . . layin' down behind the batter, on his stomach, catchin', just showin' off. I've seen a faster man play. I've never seen a man handle the ball like he did").[15] He could steal bases, after clowning a bit to distract attention. His great natural ability—and certainly his eye-catching appearance—were helped by his incredibly long arms. He was six-feet-three but had a seven-foot wingspan ("His hands came down below his knees. He could throw a ball straight from center field to home plate").[16] James Maxon thought that long-armed Reese walked like a goose with its wings dropped low, and Maxon started calling him Goose; anyone who played with the Forester Braves had to have a nickname.[17]

After about eight weeks at Forester, Goose left as suddenly as he had come. Some people heard that he had been born in south Arkansas at El Dorado, and that he, or his parents, had lived and worked at Glenwood. Later they would hear of him again, not as a baseball player but in his new role as Clown Prince of Basketball, Goose Tatum of the Harlem Globetrotters.[18]

Will McKeown had hired a new sawyer for the mill and within a week found him drunk on the street and fired him. L. J. Thompson recalls what happened soon after: "Old Man McKeown and Bill Whisenhunt [the town marshal who followed Daniel Bray], they had a meeting out there at the mill one day, called everybody out there on the mill yard, and [McKeown] got up on that platform out there and told 'em, he said, 'I know every man that's sellin' whiskey and beer out there in them Quarters.' And he said, 'Now, as long as you sell it among yourselves, nobody's goin' bother you. But if you start sellin' to these white people, you're goin' to jail.'

"So they wanted to know why. And he said to 'em, he said, 'You know, when a white man gets to drinkin', he's like an Indian. He gets drunk, and then he'll turn around and tell you that he can whip you; he wants to fight somebody. And if you won't fight him, then he'll go home and whip his wife.' Yeah, that's just what he said about it."

In spite of McKeown's threat of punishment, the town's commerce in alcohol probably did not change much. Scott County was legally dry, but locals, including Forester residents both black and white, trafficked in whiskey and beer as a means of drawing off some of the mill's payroll. Some people drank too much and got into fights or beat their wives. At such times Forester seemed to be the stereotype sawmill town, rough and tough.

But the drinkers were constrained; everyone who worked for the lumber company had to be *able* to work. Anyone who could not, or who

never *to play such tricks on whites. In the Forester mill, Bill Taylor recalls: "The colored people had some good jobs. We had one who was a {lumber} grader. But I don't remember any one really having an extra-skilled job, machine setup or something like that, that takes special training." Neither did blacks ever fill supervisory positions.*

Formal contacts between blacks and whites were often marked by extreme courtesy; blacks at Forester invited whites to their church and made a fuss over them when they arrived, escorting them to front row seats. In addition, everyday relationships between the races were probably more easygoing than in many places farther south. Blacks and whites at the mill often worked side by side, usually at the same day-labor tasks, and received the same wages. Charley Nichols, a black, even says that at Forester "there was no white and no black, just people." James Davis, another black man, says: "Whites and blacks mixed at Forester—the white people and black people got along up there. They worked together, they played together, they drank together. . . . "

But overall, through those decades when the virgin pine of the Ouachitas was being cut, the old relationship between the races prevailed. Only in the 1950s, when the last big pines were coming down,

*did a new relationship be-
gin, as a tide of social
change began to sweep
across the nation.*

did not like the work, eventually left town. A core of residents always remained, who shared mutually positive feelings about their community.[19] Many of them had lived in Forester through trying times, depression and war. Now all of that was past, and they could begin to do things for themselves and their town.

They rejoiced when Forester was connected to the REA's electric power line; no longer would their lights go off at ten o'clock. Community leaders also incorporated Forester so that the town could receive a rebate or turnback on state gasoline taxes paid on the company's logging trucks. With these funds, Forester's mayor and aldermen launched civic improvements: a fishing pond, a picnic area, and asphalt pavement on the principal streets.

Forester's people wanted activity and growth. They organized a Lions Club, took the lead in establishing the Fourche Valley Chamber of Commerce, and made Forester a member of the Arkansas Municipal League. They flocked to any public meeting—fifty or even a hundred people to local PTA programs. A Sunday school wing and other improvements were added to the church, and a new school was built having six large classrooms, indoor restrooms, and a library.[20] Encouraged by what they had been able to do, citizens started referring to their community building as "the City Hall," and talked of having political power. If a candidate for office could carry Forester and her outlying communities in the east end of Scott County, they said, he could carry the whole county.

*In 1948 Forester welcomed
a new six-room heated
school to replace the six
small, drafty buildings
in use since the opening of
the mill.*

Courtesy Era Baxter McKeown

After the war, Forester's city council sponsored a summer recreation program for children, with outdoor games five days a week at the school playground. Here, four boys square off at croquet before a gallery of spectators.

Town leaders diligently promoted civic projects, but always the dominant figure was William Andrew McKeown, the company's resident manager ("Mr. McKeown was the school board, the city council. He could fire you and kick you out of your house on the same day").[21] Will McKeown was actually a soft-spoken man who counseled teenagers to seek higher education, and often stopped to talk with the town's children. Deeply religious, he was a pillar of Forester's church. McKeown got mad on seeing a man drunk in public—a sawyer, at that—but it was more in his nature to pour oil on troubled waters and promote harmony in his church and community.

McKeown's wife benefited by her husband's position, but Era McKeown was basically a forthright, energetic woman who became a driving force in the PTA and other community works. Having a college degree in music, she also became the town's leading figure in musical affairs. She spurred her piano pupils and church choir to perform ambitious works. She saw that many of the church services offered special music, including lengthy pieces by Handel and other classical composers. John Evans, a Baptist minister at Forester, recalls "right good music for that small a church. Mrs. McKeown was good; she never did put on a slovenly program."

Ranking socially below the McKeowns were mill supervisors or foremen who doubled as town leaders, aldermen, or church deacons. Next were the townspeople, many of whom were content to take life as it came. But others imbued with the work ethic sought to better themselves and provide greater opportunities for their children.

Getting ahead was not easy. Ed Angel, a log truck driver, and his wife Edna had ten children, and the youngsters had to help support the family. But the parents saw that every one of them went to school. When the creek was high, Ed took them across from their home in Angel Town in his truck so they would not miss classes. "They didn't miss a day," says Vada Wilson, one of their teachers.

Eva Mae Little, a black woman, cooked and kept house for families in Green Town. Mrs. Little says: "I was just a *handy* woman in Forester. Any time they called me—different ones, they would call me—I'd just tear out and go to work."

John Little, Eva Mae's husband, worked at the mill. She says: "John was older than I, and he really known how to *save* money. After we got married, we started with money in Waldron Bank, at ten dollars, whenever . . . and fifteen dollars, and twenty-five dollars. When we put twenty-five dollars in the bank, we thought we put a heap of money in there."

Laverne Hawkins, whose father was a night watchman at the mill, remembers her mother taking in laundry to buy her a piano, and her piano teacher, Era McKeown, urging her to go to college. Laverne went, and helped pay her way by working in the college library. Mrs. McKeown helped her get the job.

Bill Taylor, whose father drove a log truck, shined shoes at the barbershop to pay for his first bicycle. He also delivered ice and groceries, fixed flats, greased trucks, hauled firewood, and mowed alleys. At fifteen, he got his first job in the mill.

Remembering Forester's people, Naomi Phillips, who lived there when she was young, says that the town "had some of the cream of the crop. People got to be close . . . they all worked at the same place. If one had trouble, everybody heard about it and helped."

Era McKeown recalls: "It was just a little ambitious town. They wanted to do well; they wanted to do things. There was a spirit of love among the people of Forester. A spirit of cooperation. People were interested in each other . . . interested in helping each other. I'd never lived in a town like it before."

After World War II, some of the people at Forester wanted to be more independent; they didn't want the company (or people higher up in the company) directing their lives. Those having fundamentalist or Pentecostal beliefs broke away from the town's Baptist-Methodist church. There, as Lora Williams recalls, "They just didn't care anything about the Pentecost people. They didn't want you to have a guitar or anything like that in their church.

"An Assembly of God minister from Waldron asked the company if he could have a revival at Forester, out by the ball park. [The company agreed] and ran lights out and gave some lumber. The revival lasted six weeks. Brother Hale baptized fifty-eight during the six-weeks revival."

The company observed the results of the revival (which took place one summer about 1950) and saw a means of providing for people who did

Courtesy Bertha Sanders

A gospel singing group connected with Forester's Assembly of God church entertains during a loggers' safety rally at the town's community hall in 1951.

not attend the community church. They gave Brother Hale a job at the planing mill, two small buildings, and permission to establish a church at Forester. The buildings had been toolhouses, and Hale's congregation scraped away dirt and grease as they patched the two structures together for a church ("We just taken scraps, nearly, and made it").[22] Forester's Assembly of God became known as the working man's church whose members and leaders lived in Cannon Town or Angel Town.[23]

A more serious challenge to the company came around 1950, when employees started a drive to form a labor union. Many union backers were Fourche Valley people who worked in the new departments at the planing mill—Trim-Pak, and the box factory. They had not worked at Forester during the depression, so did not carry memories of the company providing jobs in lean times. Some had belonged to unions in defense plants during the war, and knew that they promoted better wages and working conditions. Also, since these employees lived outside Forester, they could campaign for a union without fear of being evicted from company-owned housing.

Bill Wilson, the younger son of Roy and Vada Wilson, remembers that the union was also desired by the log cutters. "When we'd have a prolonged rainy season they couldn't get [into the woods] and they didn't get paid and they just literally didn't have any food. I've been [in a home] where they'd have flour and honey for the entire meal. They'd just mix some flour and honey together and serve it around the table. I know that a lot of them fished and poached game to make it, have enough to eat. And they were the ones that were agitating for the union."

The entire southern lumber industry, including both Caddo River and Dierks, had always been vehemently anti-union. In 1912, mill owners squelched a union movement that had spread through mills in the Deep South, and unions got nowhere in the South for more than twenty years thereafter.[24] In 1935, however, the National Labor Relations Act gave employees the legal right to organize. Some lumber companies soon formed their own "company" or "dummy" unions, with trusted employees in key posts, to avoid having to deal with the independents. The Caddo River Lumber Company in 1937 organized such a union, the Federated Employees Association (a replica of the Bradley County Employees Association formed earlier that year by the Bradley Lumber Company at Warren, Arkansas).[25] Henry Overby, in the shipping department at Forester at the time, recalls that his supervisor told him to join the Employees Association. "The purpose of that union was to help the company sell their lumber. The company set it up so they could label their lumber 'union made.' I was treasurer of that union. I don't remember them doing much of anything."

Until World War II, lumber companies had a backlog of men wanting jobs. Nobody argued about lumber's low wages. New employees were often bankrupt farmers, and logging and sawmilling were the only means available for making a living. Many men found that the lumber industry was much like being on the farm. In the past they had bought on credit at the "furnishing" store whose owner provided for their needs until they sold their cotton; now they traded on credit at the commissary whose owner saw them through till payday. At times they had lived as tenants on farms; now they lived as tenants of the company. They had viewed the landlord, maybe, as a father figure; now they saw the lumber boss in the same light. They had hunted, fished, and socialized in their own community when on the farm; now they lived in much the same environment while at the mill. With little money, and no knowledge that anything better might exist elsewhere, many of these people remained tied to lumbering, but they were content with what they had. If they heard about labor unions, they distrusted them because they were run by outsiders. Whites especially distrusted biracial unions, for among laboring men, blacks competed with whites for jobs.[26]

Mill owners also worked under restrictions that influenced their thinking about labor. Lumbering was boom-and-bust, very competitive; mill operators sometimes had to sell lumber below cost to cut their losses. From the 1920s on, all the southern mills faced serious competition from the West Coast. Highly mechanized, cutting huge logs, the mills on the coast were twice as efficient as those in the South. (In one survey for the period from 1926 through 1935, West Coast mills produced a thousand board feet of lumber with eight man-hours of labor; in southern mills, it took seventeen man-hours.)[27] Western mills paid their workers twice as much as southern mills and still remained competitive. (In 1943, the average hourly wage in western mills was $1.04; in southern mills, forty-eight cents.)[28] Wages were a large part of the total cost of manufacturing lumber. (In 1939, wages averaged sixteen percent of the total cost of manufactured products for all industries, but twenty-eight percent for lumber.)[29] And beginning in the 1920s, larger southern mills faced new competition from thousands of small mills that were able to produce lumber with minimal overhead costs. In this environment, the large mill operators wanted to hold wages down.

Ruth Allen, author of a history of lumber workers in east Texas, comments, "Historically the pattern was set early; high wages paid to a few skilled workers such as sawyers to prevent their migrating to the Western firms and very low wages paid to a large basic group classified as unskilled laborers." In 1900, she says, wages in lumber were about the same as those in other industries, but around 1910 wages in the lumber industry began to fall behind, and lumber workers moved slowly downward on the economic scale.[30] (In Arkansas from 1923 to 1935, lumber mill wages ranged from 74.2 to 93.5 percent of average weekly wages of all industrial wage earners.)[31] A few southern lumbermen thought it was wrong to pay low wages. One said that low pay encouraged sawmillers to use "cheap Negroes" instead of modernizing their mills to reduce costs.[32] Another said that wages were so low and hours so long that even men of ability could not rise above their surroundings.[33] For a long time, however, there was little change. Only after World War II stimulated the entire American economy did there seem any real chance for ordinary workers in the lumber industry to claim a bigger piece of the money pie.[34]

In the spring of 1946, the CIO launched "Operation Dixie" to organize unions in the South, especially in textiles and lumbering. Though the campaign lagged as time passed (the CIO's biracial organization was accused of being Communist, among other things), a mill as large as Forester's was worth a sustained effort to organize.[35] Also, by the late 1940s the CIO had established local unions at all the other Dierks mills and wanted one at Forester for better leverage in negotiating with the company. Union people realized that when their other mills went on strike, Dierks could put their nonunion plant at Forester on overtime to fill the company's current orders for lumber.

Union organizers came to Forester and held meetings at night in the ball park (without lights, so attendees would not be recognized and punished).[36] Will McKeown and other Dierks officials spread the word that if the mill went union there would be no overtime work (many would recall later that they said the mill would be shut down). McKeown reminded employees that they were already being paid the same wage scale as unionized employees in other Dierks mills. Pro-union men talked up the union among their fellow workers in the mill, and McKeown fired some of the more outspoken ones for creating what he saw as a disturbance.[37] Feelings ran high; union supporters marched at night and threw eggs at the homes of management.[38] Finally there was an election—and the union lost.

The CIO persisted. In 1951 another union election was held and the

International Woodworkers Association of the CIO was voted in, 151 to 150, for both the mill and the woods crews.[39] Forester, though, was not to be a closed shop; state law provided that employees were not required to join the union. Only about eighty-five became union members.

Sherman Hawkins, who was a member, says: "The union strove for job classification—one man assigned to one job—[better] working conditions, and fringe benefits. Working conditions means a lot to a person's health." But Roy Douglas, who was the dry kiln supervisor, says: "I had to have men that could go anywhere—stacking sticks, pulling [lumber from] the kilns. The union wouldn't let them do it. They said 'No, he works here.' They just almost govern your crew." Vernon Hawkins, Sherman's brother and another union member, says, "That union put a stop to that one man doin' a two-man job." Frictions continued. McKeown refused to meet with the union about grievances, and refused to let the union meet in the community hall. Later he changed his mind and let them in.

Among both union and nonunion people, there was an underlying dissatisfaction with Dierks. Vada Wilson recalls her husband's feelings: "Roy never was as happy with the Dierks organization as he was with Caddo River. The men who owned the thing were not as considerate of the employees as Caddo River. They'd be more critical, and maybe not as helpful as the owners of Caddo River had been." Harley Ferguson, who grew up near Forester, says: "Caddo River Lumber Company got along with the public much better than Dierks did. Doc Thornton doctored a lot of people in the rural area at no charge, [but] didn't call on many people in the rural area after Dierks came on the scene." Ferguson says further that Dierks stopped the sawmill's shop foreman from doing small jobs—braze-welding broken wash pots—free of charge for local farmers as he had done in the past. Sherman Hawkins says that Forester's work force, in having a union, "were searchin' for a refuge. Dierks Lumber and Coal Company, they drove 'em." And Vernon Hawkins says: "Talk about a sweatshop, that was it. But there wasn't nothin' else in Scott County."

Caddo River was probably more lenient, but the dissatisfaction may have stemmed partly from a changing economy. Now there were jobs available with easier work and higher pay than at Forester, and people were aware of it. But higher paying jobs were only available outside the southern lumber industry, and away from the rural Ouachitas where most of the working people of Forester preferred to live.

From the other side of the labor controversy at Forester, Fred M. Dierks says, "It was kind of a hard proposition to get everybody to improve their efficiency up there."

———

In addition to having to work with the union, the company had an increasing problem in getting timber for the Forester mill. In 1949 Dierks cut the last of Caddo River's reserved timber on the Ouachita National Forest. After that, they had to bid on tracts of government timber as the Forest Service put them up for sale. Then the Forest Service was placed under a new requirement. Fred Dierks recalls: "The small

Courtesy Bertha Sanders

Higher wages after World War II allowed even a working man and his family to own a new Chevrolet DeLuxe.

mills in the area politicked a deal through where they got set-aside sales, where we couldn't bid on, say, half of the sales coming up with the Forest Service. They could bid on our sales but we couldn't bid on theirs. So when that went into being, the amount of timber we were getting for the mill was substantially reduced—the stuff that we were needing for Forester."

Dierks adds: "We were expecting to rely on the northeasterly corner of the Dierks [Arkansas, sawmill's] block of timber to keep Forester going in between the times, maybe, that the government wouldn't put up enough sales or we might not bid high enough to get a sale."

The Dierks company tried to get support from Congress to guarantee a supply of national forest timber for Forester, but they were unsuccessful. In the building boom of the postwar years, the demand for Forest Service timber became intense. Dierks and a number of smaller firms—all of them able to log distant tracts with trucks—engaged in a contest to bid the prices of national forest stumpage to new highs. Lynn Barker, who lived at Forester at the time, says: "I can remember when a big sale would come up. Employees would wonder if Dierks would get it. And they didn't every time. Somebody else did."

A Modest Prosperity

During the depression the people of Forester could purchase little except life's necessities, but after World War II they had more money and could enjoy things that had earlier been considered luxuries. They visited the local beauty parlor. They bought new Chevrolets. From Sam Hickey of Mount Ida, they purchased household appliances.

Actually, the higher quality national forest timber so earnestly sought by all the mills was some of the last virgin pine in the Ouachitas.

Rumors flew: The mill was going to close down for lack of timber. Employees listened and then looked for jobs elsewhere. One was Tellious Thompson, a black man who sought "more outreach" by working at one job during the day in the sawmill and another at night in the planer. He recalls: "I was already lookin' for somewhere to go. My brother-in-law came down there from Portland [Oregon] and he was talkin' about work was plentiful. So I packed up and loaded my stuff on the truck and headed for the West Coast. I left to better myself." In doing so, Thompson became one more participant in the mass migration of blacks and whites out of the South during the 1940s and 1950s. From 1940 (a year when Forester's population was at its maximum) to 1950 (the year when Thompson left), this out-migration reduced Forester's population from 1,306 to 818.

Early in 1952, however, Forester's people became encouraged. Even though the union had been voted in, Dierks proceeded to strengthen the sawmill with new timbers, add equipment to make hardwood flooring, and install other machinery to remanufacture pine lumber. In February, the Dierks employees newsletter stated that "these and other improvements which are being planned will give the Forester mill a new lease on life, providing continuous employment for many years to come."[40]

In succeeding months, other events tended to reinforce Forester's sense of identity and well-being. The last section of the twenty-two-mile highway to Waldron was paved. Townspeople became excited, too, when an old friend and former Caddo River employee from Glenwood, Boyd Tackett, announced as a candidate for governor. Throughout the primary campaign they kept track of his progress, and when he swooped into Forester one day in his helicopter and alighted at the town's main intersection, they crowded around to wish him well.

Not long after Tackett's visit, however, Will McKeown was called to talk on the phone with Fred H. Dierks in Kansas City. Dierks told him that the Forester mill must be closed as soon as possible.

————

McKeown somberly gave his employees the shocking news.[41] Within days, log haulers brought their last loads to the mill. As those logs went up the conveyor into the sawmill, a crew of men retrieved submerged "sinkers" to clean out the pond, and towed them over to the haul-up conveyor.

Melvin McConnell, who set blocks on one of the sawmill's carriages, remembers cutting those sinker logs—"the prettiest lumber you ever saw, but it smelt awful. Then we got down to the last one. That was the saddest day of my sawmilling career."

On the afternoon of September 3, 1952, the last boards came off the headsaw, traveled along conveyors through the edger and the trimmer, and moved along the green chain, until finally, at 2:20 p.m., there was no more lumber to work. Forester's mill had cut out.[42] Will McKeown called the mill crew together, made a farewell speech, wished the men good luck, and closed with a fervent "God bless you all." Many of his listeners were choked with emotion.

In the next issue of the Dierks newsletter was a statement: "While the mill is located in the National Forest, most of the areas in the vicinity have been cut over and the remaining timber is too small for milling. The procurable timber supply is inadequate to afford economic operation of a plant this size." [43] Some, however, felt that shutting down the mill was Dierks' way of shutting out the union that had been voted in the year before. They recalled McKeown and the Dierks officers saying during the union's organizing campaign that "If it goes union, we'll shut her down in a year or two." [44]

The presence of the union may have been one reason for closing the mill, but the overriding reason was lack of timber. The Forester mill had been planned and built to cut virgin pine for about twenty years, and it cut for twenty-one before timber became too scarce and too expensive.

Fred M. Dierks says: "We thought that perhaps the Forest Service might put up enough timber [for sale] to keep it going if we remodeled it—rejuvenated into maybe a small operation or something.

"We'd get a batch of timber and go along pretty good and then when we were out—why, it just took the hide off. Also we were getting to the point where we [had] trimmed up [or cut] a lot of the timber up on the northeast corner of the Dierks [Arkansas, mill's] block for Forester, and we didn't want to eat into it any more. We just said, okay, this is as far as we are going to go, to plan additional [cutting of] timber off another viable mill. So we just had to close it down." Dierks adds that the Forester mill lost money continuously for about six months before shutting down. [45]

Imodel Franklin, Will McKeown's secretary at the time the mill closed, says, "I know that the last timber sale they got, they paid ninety dollars a thousand—and that was extremely high at that time."

On April 20, 1952, less than five months before the mill he had built at Forester shut down, T. W. Rosborough died at the age of eighty-three. He had come to the Ouachitas in 1906 to build a sawmill and cut the virgin shortleaf pine, and had stayed as a mill operator for over thirty years. He went west when seventy years old to cut Douglas fir, barely escaped bankruptcy, and became a millionaire. He came back home to Texarkana, and when near eighty, began to build another sawmill. Ill health forced him to sell it at a large loss before it had cut a single log.

But not long before he died, Rosborough had bought a tract of timber in the mountains of New Mexico, and talked of building another mill. . . .

Though Forester's sawmill closed in early September, the planing mill remained in operation till past New Years, processing millions of feet of rough lumber from the big storage shed. People were leaving town, first the loggers and the sawmill crew, then the employees from the rough shed, the planer, the shipping department. Dave Cooks, a black who

residents' ability to pay. Hickey made friends with others in the black community by throwing a beer party for them at the home of one of the local bootleggers. Says Hickey: "If they liked you, there wasn't nothin' they wouldn't do for you. I sold the blacks around forty thousand dollars worth of goods and never lost a penny."
At about ten p.m., Hickey would start back to Mount Ida. During each visit to Forester, he put a few more people on the way to greater material comfort, a happy state from which they—as Hickey realized—would not willingly retreat.

worked in the planer, says, "When that mill cut out, we come flyin' out of there like birds—people went everywhere." Clinton Moore, the town barber, says: "I knew I had to get out and get another job. I just knew I had to get going [in] some other direction."

Era McKeown remembers: "As their jobs would end at the mill, they'd move out. It was just a sad time. You were telling somebody good-bye every day." Schoolchildren and teachers moved away, so that by Christmas there were two teachers left with the remaining pupils from eight grades. When the black school closed, Vada Wilson taught the last five or six of those children in her home until they also departed.

At the mill, the remaining work gradually diminished to one last task, loading lumber into boxcars. Roy Wilson, a foreman and sixty-one years old, helped load cars and liked the physical exertion. "Barber" Moore, out of work, also signed on to fill boxcars—and found he was in trouble. An elderly black lumber handler watched Moore, and then came over and showed him the right movements, how to give a board the right shove so that it would just skim into place. Says Moore: "Well, he took two weeks learning me how to do that, but after I learned that I didn't have so many blisters on my hand."

There had been almost 350 employees at Forester, in the woods and in the mill. About forty-five men were given jobs at other Dierks mills; half were blacks, mainly lumber handlers.[46] Other employees at Forester had to find work elsewhere. For many of them it was not easy. Log haulers, who had purchased their trucks on credit, could not find employment after the mill closed, and so lost the trucks with which they made their living.

Families were moving to places as far away as California and Oregon, taking a few pieces of furniture in their pickup trucks after selling the rest. Imodel Franklin, McKeown's secretary, remained working at Forester after the mill closed, and says: "What impressed me the most was how people from the area came down, like vultures, to get what they could in distress sales. After [those who were leaving] priced their furniture, [people from the area] would try to jew them down, knowing they would have to leave."

People came and dug up shrubbery and flowers that residents had planted and cared for over the years. Dr. Thornton, preparing to move to the Dierks mill at Mountain Pine and unable to take all his flowers, saw in his fish pond a tub of water lilies. He lifted it out and carried the tub down to the log pond at the sawmill to leave it in the water there.

Eva Mae Little remembers the last weeks that she and her husband John spent in the Quarters: "We'd go to Waldron and visit up there, and go to Hot Springs and visit on weekends. We'd just get out and go, because we'd get lonesome. There wasn't nobody there. Just we two sittin' down in there. And it was *dark*. Every house was dark."

McKeown kept asking the Littles to stay another week and help with the closing. Finally John Little called for a moving van so he and Eva Mae could go to the home they had purchased in south Arkansas. "And they came, and they started loadin,' and I was the happiest woman you ever seen in your life. I said, 'Y'all can't get this furniture out of this house fast enough for me. Lemme get back to civilization.'"

As townspeople left, salvagers arrived. Dierks kept some mill hardware and machinery, and moved a number of houses to Mountain Pine, Dierks, and De Queen, but sold everything else. Lumbermen and others from Arkansas, Louisiana, and Texas bought sawmill machinery, planers, electrical equipment. A company in Tulsa bought the boilers and smokestacks, which they dismantled, cleaned, and painted for resale. The overhead crane from the rough lumber shed went to a purchaser on the West Coast. A salvager bought the sawmill building for its wood framing; another dismantled the dry kilns for their brick. Will McKeown purchased the church building to use its lumber in the McKeowns' new home at Waldron.

House movers came, knocked over fences and cut down trees to get at vacant dwellings, eased the buildings onto their flatbed trucks, and hauled them out to places around western Arkansas and eastern Oklahoma. A twelve-by-thirty-six-foot shotgun house cost $250 delivered within twenty-five miles of Forester. Other small houses cost $100 a room, delivered. The eight-room L. D. Williams home, Forester's largest, cost a local resident $1500 transported to his property in the Fourche valley. Garages sold for a few dollars; privies went for a dollar each. Five-gallon cans of green stain, left over from the last painting of Green Town, were sold at ten dollars a can. As the winter of 1953 passed into spring, Forester became an open, vacant area littered with refuse from departed families and dismantled buildings. Abandoned dogs and cats roamed the empty streets.

By summer, all of the houses were gone. The commissary and drugstore remained, now empty, as did the hotel where a watchman and his family lived, and the lumber company office. Imodel Franklin still drove to Forester to handle correspondence and answer the phone. It was not enough to stay busy. She brought a little radio to the office, and sat there alone making embroidery.

The last major project to close out Forester was to dismantle the vast, empty lumber storage sheds. The finished lumber shed and the thousand-foot-long rough lumber shed remained unsold until a wrecking company from Little Rock finally bought them at a reduced price.

For three months a crew of ten or twelve men worked to tear down the two buildings. Day after day, they ripped off more and more of the roof—the short boards that had been cut from treetops, back in the depression—and let it fall to the ground. They ripped and tore off the siding that covered the walls. They pulled out windows, which they saved only if it were easy; otherwise, they let those fall too. All they were really after was the heavy framing lumber, and the twenty-inch timbers that had supported the crane in the rough shed.

Then everything was down and the salvaged material hauled away. There remained only long, rectangular heaps of splintered, broken

Movers haul a three-room house away from Green Town in the fall of 1952. Houses were sold at bargain prices and within a few months all were gone.

Courtesy Era Baxter McKeown

boards where the two sheds had stood. It looked as if a tornado had passed through.

Forester was the last of its kind, the last cut-out-and-get-out sawmill town in the eastern United States.

Epilogue

After the salvagers left, the Forester townsite became a cattle pasture, and it remained so for twenty years until a new owner of the land, Weyerhaeuser Company, planted the area in seedling pines. Forester had symbolized the end of the old cut-out-and-get-out era of lumbering, and now the same ground nurtured a tree plantation, evidence of changed thinking about timber. In fact, both the land and the people of the Ouachitas saw fundamental changes in the first three decades after the mill at Forester closed.

The last large-scale cutting of Ouachitas virgin pine probably occurred on Dierks timberland during the early 1960s. Even twenty years later, loggers would occasionally find an old-growth tree, or a patch of them, but the original forest was gone. By the 1980s most of the second growth also had attained sawlog size and had been cut. Both the Forest Service and the major timber companies had managed their land for several decades to produce a continuing supply of raw material.

Timberland that had always remained low-priced began to rise in value around 1940, and continued to do so as new buyers recognized the land's potential for producing merchantable trees. Dierks had purchased cutover land since the 1920s, as had International Paper Company, whose holdings in the Ouachitas included land that had once belonged to the A. J. Neimeyer, Ozan-Graysonia, and Wisconsin and Arkansas lumber companies. More recently, in a sort of reversal of the industry's historic east-to-west migration, national timber companies whose principal holdings were in the West came to the Ouachitas. In 1964, the Potlatch Corporation bought the Ozan Lumber Company, including its timberland, from the Bemis family. In 1968 the Georgia-Pacific Corporation purchased the remaining lands belonging to the Malvern Lumber Company from the Strauss heirs. About this time also, an Arkansas based firm, the Deltic Farm & Timber Company, bought timberland in the eastern Ouachitas once owned by the Neimeyer, Fourche River, and Fort Smith lumber companies.

In 1969, one of the giants in the wood-products industry, Weyer-

The Big Timber

haeuser Company, bought the last and largest of the family-owned timber firms, Dierks Forests, Inc. (the Dierks Lumber and Coal Company renamed by the family in 1954 to give due recognition to the company's basic asset). By buying Dierks, Weyerhaeuser acquired nearly 1.8 million acres of timberland, what had been the largest family-controlled landholding in the United States. About half of the land was in Arkansas and half in Oklahoma. Nearly nine-tenths of it lay within the Ouachitas.

For over forty years Dierks had managed this land for a sustained yield of sawlogs, and the total volume and value of the timber had increased. Many of the trees, however, were lower value pine and hardwood—better for the pulp mill than the sawmill. Also, many had become more valuable for plywood than lumber. (In the 1960s new manufacturing technology made it possible to use southern pine for plywood.)

To fully utilize their raw material, Dierks would have had to greatly expand manufacturing capacity, especially in pulp or paper, and in products such as plywood. Since the 1940s Dierks had added plants to produce woodfiber insulation board and preservative-treated products to better utilize timber, and a modest-sized paper mill to utilize waste from their sawmills. Except for borrowing to build the paper mill, Dierks financed all of the plant expansion (and timberland purchases, too) with profits from operations. But large ventures into paper and plywood would have required hundreds of millions of dollars, more money than a family-held corporation could raise. (Short-term borrowing would have endangered the company's financial stability; a long-term bond issue by a family business would have found no investors; a large sale of stock could have enabled outsiders to take over the company.) In addition, many of the Dierks family remembered the company's troubles during the depression and did not want to borrow money at all.[1]

Dierks always had been run by members of the family, and by the late 1960s those in charge were several grandsons and a great-grandson of the original Dierks brothers. There were several hundred family heirs and many non-family stockholders besides. Relatives were scattered, had diverse interests, and none of them owned any sizeable portion of the company's stock. Dividends on stock were too small to make it attractive for income, and in a limited market it was difficult to sell Dierks shares for a price reflecting their real value.

Weyerhaeuser offered the Dierks stockholders a price they could not turn down: $317 million in cash and Weyerhaeuser preferred stock.[2] When concluded in September 1969, the acquisition was the largest in the forest products industry up to that time. The depreciated value of all the Dierks manufacturing facilities—three sawmills, paper mill, treating plant, and woodfiber plant, and a gypsum wallboard plant, two railroads, and several smaller facilities—totaled about $50 million. Most of the purchase price, then, was for timberland at about $150 per acre.

Weyerhaeuser saw the timberland as the prime asset. Dierks had practiced what is known as *uneven*-age management of the forest, cutting selected trees of varying ages, leaving others to grow and scatter seed in the openings created by removal of some of the trees. Weyerhaeuser felt that this system had two drawbacks: low value hardwoods blocked off sunlight from young pine seedlings, so that hardwoods survived and pines did not; and many of the pines that did survive were less than optimal quality. Weyerhaeuser believed that the South's favorable soil, warm climate, and adequate rainfall would make it possible to grow mature, marketable trees in as little as half the time needed on their lands in the Pacific Northwest. And, within each timber growing cycle, Dierks lands could be made to produce up to five times as much usable wood as that being grown by Dierks.

Seeing an opportunity to produce much more raw material, Weyerhaeuser in 1970 began a long-term program of highly intensive, *even*-age forest management, removing all trees from sizeable parcels of land (subsequently limited by company policy to 350 acres), clearing away the refuse that remained on the ground, and planting loblolly pine seedlings whose parent trees had been selected for fast growth and good form. About thirty years later, after several thinnings and fertilizings, and continuous protection from fire, insects, disease, and hardwood competition, these trees would be harvested in one operation. The cleared ground would then be planted again with a new crop of seedlings.

Even-age management was also begun by other timber firms and the U.S. Forest Service. The Ouachita National Forest, at 1.6 million acres the second largest landholding in the region and the largest national forest in the South, includes much land, usually rough mountain terrain, that is not suited for intensive even-age forestry. Moreover, the Forest Service is required by law to provide a variety of benefits for the general public, not only timber but also watershed protection, livestock forage, recreational opportunities, and wildlife habitat. Therefore the Forest Service practices even-age management on the best timber growing areas and less intensive management on the less productive areas.

Since the 1950s the nation's population and their demands on natural resources have grown enormously, and land use and management in the Ouachitas have become more intensive everywhere. Timber companies and the Forest Service have greatly extended their networks of forest access roads; the Army Corps of Engineers have built nearly a dozen multipurpose reservoirs; rural residents have turned to large-scale poultry raising; outsiders have moved in to retire or to begin new careers; recreationists have come to enjoy the hills and lakes. Through the 1970s, the Ouachitas were part of an Ozark-Ouachita rural growth area stretching from St. Louis to Dallas and encompassing the Ozarks, the lower Arkansas valley, the Ouachita Mountains, and northeast Texas.[3]

With increasing urbanization, affluence, and personal mobility, greater numbers of both residents and nonresidents use the Ouachitas for recreation. People hunt, fish, and sightsee on lands that also produce timber. Since the 1970s, as they have seen even-age forest management become widespread, they have perceived the clear-cuts and pine plantations as an abridgement of their old freedom to view and roam a wilderness forest, and some have protested vigorously. In response, timber companies and the Forest Service have made some changes in management

one of those big logs."

The largest pine log known to have been cut on the Ouachita National Forest was forty-four inches in diameter.[7] The largest known to have come from Dierks timberland scaled 1,325 board feet; it was cut in Oklahoma in 1930.[8] The largest pine log at Forester scaled a little over nine hundred feet.[9]

The champion hardwood logs were more massive than the pine. The largest one at Forester, a sixteen-foot oak log cut in 1952, scaled 1,225 feet.[10] It had to be broken into quarters with dynamite before it could be moved into the mill. The largest hardwood log known to have come from the Ouachitas was cut by Dierks in Oklahoma in 1926; it was five feet in diameter and scaled 1,764 feet.[11] The biggest hardwoods grew in rich bottomlands near streams.

The quality of the lumber from old growth pine was early recognized. In 1912 the Forest Service reported: "Shortleaf pine in Arkansas is generally considered of a higher grade than the same species grown in other regions. It is a favorite material for sash, doors, and ceilings."[12] For more than fifty years, a group of companies including Dierks and Caddo River promoted their pine lumber under the registered trade name of Arkansas Soft Pine, worthy of a premium price. The companies adhered to standards of quality, stamped their practices, and companies such as Weyerhaeuser have emphasized that all of their land, including acreage not under even-age management, remains open for a variety of recreational pursuits. (The U.S. Congress has separately established, on the Ouachita National Forest, several wilderness areas in which no timber cutting can take place.) As clear-cutting continues, however, controversies over timber management and recreation are likely to continue. The fact that there are such disagreements suggests how public priorities have changed. Before 1950, timber workers, and the general population as well, were mainly concerned with making a living. By the 1970s and 1980s, quality of life issues such as recreational or esthetic preferences had become important.

Since 1900, land ownership in the Ouachitas has slowly moved toward a stable pattern according to the uses that owners have found economically possible. Today the region's best farmland remains with farmers, much of the better timberland is owned by forest products companies, and much of the rougher terrain is administered by the Forest Service. Many old farms have reverted to woodland, while in other areas the woods have been cleared for pasture. Not all the land is being used wisely, but most of it is being managed for longer term benefits than the single cutting of timber or the few years of cotton and corn that were sought in the past. Land is much more highly valued in the marketplace; timberland in the 1980s was priced from $225 to more than $400 an acre, plus the value of any standing timber on the land. Pine stumpage prices ranged from $150 to $300 a thousand board feet. Just to prepare the ground and set out pine seedlings, timber companies and the Forest Service were paying over $100 an acre.[4]

Lumbermen were slow to change during the half century when they were cutting the virgin pine, but since the 1950s the industry has changed at an accelerating pace. Following a nationwide trend among corporations having "company towns," Dierks sold their company-owned homes to the families who lived in them; Weyerhaeuser later closed the last of the old Dierks commissaries. (By that time the people of Mountain Pine, for example, were able to drive to Hot Springs for shopping.) Labor unions became an accepted fact in the larger mills, and while wages were still low when compared with those in the North and West, employees lived more comfortably, and without the pervasive influence of an employer in their personal lives.

Sawmilling and logging have also been transformed. Today at Weyerhaeuser's Mountain Pine mill, for instance, logs are trucked in as tree lengths. At the mill these long logs are first cut into sections according to the highest valued use for each portion of the tree. Parts that are suitably free of knots and other defects are routed to the sawmill, plywood plant, or wood treating plant; defective parts are converted into wood chips for the paper mill. There is no waste; all of the wood goes into one product or another, and the bark is used for boiler fuel.

Inside the Mountain Pine mill, one can still see the heavy wood framework of the original building, and the basic steps in making lumber—sawing, drying, planing—have not changed. But today many of the

Courtesy A. V. Pirtle

Men unload logs and sort and pile lumber at one of the last portable sawmills to operate on the Ouachita National Forest, near Mena, Arkansas, about 1947. "Peckerwood" mills like this soon disappeared as timber became higher priced. One drawback with these smallest mills was their inability to make profitable use of wood refuse, such as scraps and sawdust in the foreground.

operations are automatic or remotely controlled. No longer do doggers or a blocksetter ride the carriage at the headsaw; their work is accomplished by power equipment controlled by the sawyer. No longer do men sort and stack boards by hand along the green chain; these tasks are automated and controlled by a computer. Even the smaller mills in the Ouachitas—few, now, compared with how many there were in the past—have become mechanized. Moreover, they convert their waste wood into chips for paper mills, or sell it as fuel.

Weyerhaeuser doubled or tripled the output of all three Dierks sawmills, added three plywood plants, enlarged the Dierks paper mill located in Arkansas, and built a very large paper mill in Oklahoma. By the 1980s their manufacturing capacity was about even with the output of marketable wood from their timberlands at that time. For plant expansion and for timberland conversion to even-age plantations, Weyerhaeuser had spent approximately one billion dollars.[5]

Perhaps the most significant underlying feature of far-reaching technological changes in both lumbering and forestry is the now widespread use of computers. All of the major land managers in the Ouachitas, both private companies and the Forest Service, have installed computers to store and manipulate great masses of data, which include inventories of standing timber, instructions for process control, and information for financial accounting. Joe Angel, whose father once hauled logs for the Caddo River Lumber Company with four mules and an eight-wheel wagon, became Weyerhaeuser's management informaton (computer) systems manager in the company's regional office at Hot Springs. Reflecting on one small part of the computer's role, Angel says: "The old sawmill bookkeeper's main concern was keeping track of employees' use of credit [at the company store]. That has disappeared, and now computers are programmed to figure earnings in terms of various union and nonunion wage and salary scales . . . attendance . . . the whole range of deductions for insurance, retirement. . . ."

In retrospect, the people who cut the virgin pine were in a state of transition from the pioneer era (homesteading; subsistence farming) toward the world of the late twentieth century (computers; insurance deductions). Although farm families usually had little trouble in adjusting to work and life with a lumber company, the sawmill environment was industrial rather than agricultural. Families had to adapt to regular hours of work; men had to accept the tedium of routine, specialized tasks; everyone had to learn the pitfalls as well as the pleasures of being in a money fueled economy with regular paydays. Life seemed a little easier than back in the country, though, and the children had better schools. Later, when these families migrated to Houston or San Diego or some other city or town, they adjusted more easily than had they gone straight from the farm.

Thus the Ouachitas timber people became part of a familiar trend in American history: the nationwide migration from agriculture to industry and from rural to urban areas. Agricultural Americans have often moved from the once dominant job category of "farmer" to that of "laborer" doing manual but non-farm work. More recently, many of their children and grandchildren have joined a national movement from "laborer" to "clerk" or "professional," with the latter two categories covering many kinds of careers based on processing of information: secretary, bookkeeper, keypunch operator, lawyer, engineer, teacher, and others.[6]

Nearly all of these Ouachitas people were money poor when they left the sawmills. In the decades since, nearly all have attained greater material comfort if not great wealth, and many of their children have progressed even farther. From Forester, for example, sons and daughters have become doctors, engineers, and teachers. One is a trial lawyer; another, a college athletic director. One is an owner of a Mercedes-Benz dealership; another, a director of nuclear research. One is a marketing manager for Safeway; another, a plant manager for Weyerhaeuser. Others pursue varied professions and vocations; among them are homemakers, farmers, and timber workers.

Blacks who formerly worked in sawmills are less well off. ("The most I ever made at any job was $1.35 an hour.")[15] Though many enjoy some degree of comfort, many others live below the poverty line. Probably there were only two black people from the sawmills who gained real wealth or fame. Goose Tatum, who worked briefly at Forester, became a basketball star. Louis Jordan, who worked in the mill at Glenwood about 1930, went on to New York to play his alto saxophone, lead a combo, compose novelty songs, and make hit records such as "Is You Is or Is You Ain't My Baby."[16] Tatum and Jordan made it on their own considerable talents. For most people the route to success was through the schoolhouse, but blacks did not have the same access to education as whites. And to most, it hardly seemed worthwhile to get an education, in times when even educated blacks found only menial work or became low paid schoolteachers. In the 1950s, opportunities for education and better jobs began to open up for black people, but that was too late for many mill-

Courtesy Frank Diggs and Eva Corley Diggs

Among the hundreds of logs along a Dierks railroad near Mountain Pine, Arkansas, in the 1930s, none are exceptionally large. A number of them have fire scars, and "red heart" which appears before the onset of decay. These logs are typical of most of the old-growth pine of the Ouachitas.

workers, and for many of their children who had grown up in mill towns.

If working people made so little material progress in the lumber industry, was it because they were exploited as "cheap labor" by the mill owners? Some historians maintain that both the natural and human resources of the South were deliberately exploited by outside forces which included the northern capitalists who owned sawmills and timber. Indeed, from around 1900 there are documented accounts of black woods workers in Mississippi and white mill families in Texas who existed in squalor and peonage, forever in debt to their employers.[17]

From the evidence at hand, the timber industry in the Ouachitas was never that bad. Most owners of the big mills were northern capitalists, and they did waste timber, and they paid low wages for long days of hard work. But the waste of wood and the harshness of life resulted more from the economics of lumber and from the times in general than from the desires of mill owners. As described earlier, lumbering was feast or famine, and very competitive. Also, until after the 1930s there was a pervasive imbalance in the nation's wage-price structure that tended to favor employers. Ordinary workers in many industries were low paid and unable to buy many of the world's goods.[18] Employees in the natural resource industries—lumbering, farming, and mining—were even lower paid than those in manufacturing industries which at that time were largely concentrated in the North.

This sixteen-foot oak log scaled 1,225 board feet and was the largest ever cut at the Forester mill. It came from the bottomlands of the Ouachita River.

Courtesy Bertha Sanders

Courtesy William A. Hensley, Sr.

William Hensley, Sr., the man on the right in this scene near Hatfield, Arkansas, in 1914, traveled not more than twenty miles a day as a log hauler—but Hensley's son in later years traveled thousands of miles each day as an airline pilot. In comparable generational leaps, other sons of Ouachitas mule skinners have become bankers, engineers, a law professor, and a computer systems manager.

Eventually the waste of timber stopped when it became profitable to make use of the parts of the tree that had been wasted. Conditions for working people began to improve after New Deal legislation permitted labor to organize and guaranteed a minimum wage, and when the urgent demands of World War II reinvigorated the nation's economy. In the Ouachitas these changes had a positive effect upon the region's timber workers. They, like many other working people of the United States, for the first time had a chance to move into the middle class.

Many of the people from logging camps and sawmill towns recall hard times, but very few complain of unfair treatment by their employers. Often they talk of their hardships as challenges that were overcome, and remember that those were the times when they were young and healthy, with friends and neighbors who cared and shared. Invariably, when they talk of those years, their negative recollections are mixed with positive ones. As Jeraldine Meredith says: "I wouldn't want to go back to the Forester days; they weren't the good old days. I've split wood and carried in wood. Got up and built fires, on a cold floor. I've done a lot of cannin' on a wood stove. No fun." Then she says, "But if we got a little somethin', we appreciated it."

Bill Taylor recalls his youth at Forester: "They [the lumber bosses] gave me the opportunity to be what I have been. They were good to me, but it wasn't easy to get there; you had to work a lot harder than you do now."

Alex Nichols, who lived at Rosboro and Forester, talks about the sawmill experience as it was for black people: "It was a school for us. We learn't there. We had a place to stay. It was a springboard. . . ."

Talking with these people, one can sense the traits and values typical of people in the rural South: hospitality, religious convictions, a strong work ethic. They take pride in having worked without complaining. As Virgil Smalling says: "Back in them days, if a man worked, he *had* to work. If he didn't do the work, they was another man that could do it. Now, the way it is now, if a fellow strikes something he don't want to do, why, he can blow around right smart. We didn't blow around about none of it. We done what we was told. We went into it."

Those who have shared with us their memories of logging and sawmilling in the Ouachitas have not only provided glimpses of their own lives; they have enlarged our understanding of a region's history.

With such understanding, we can even recount the stories, the historic backgrounds of scattered physical artifacts that remain from cutting the virgin forest. The water lilies that still bloom on Forester's mill pond remind us of the town's closing days, of the company's Dr. Thornton, and many other facts of Forester's existence. Reading the motto "Always Fair to My Fellow Man" on T. W. Rosborough's gravestone, we realize that it does reflect (if imperfectly) the man's essential nature. Though an autocrat, Rosborough was in some ways ahead of his time: He protected black people, and he provided a kind of corporate social security for his employees during the Great Depression.

At times we are struck by the turns of fate. In a wooded area at Forester lies the concrete foundation of the new school building that so symbolized the townspeople's optimism and—when it closed four years later—their dashed hopes.

At other times, on seeing houses from defunct mill towns that provide homes today for people in other communities, we sense the continuity of life. (Forester's former Barrel House became a weekend cottage on a lake in Oklahoma.)

Questions arise that cannot be answered. A headstone in the cemetery at Havana, Arkansas, is inscribed URCY MAY ROSBOROUGH. Why, after another marriage following her divorce from Rosborough, did she take that surname to her grave?

To one unaware, these scattered relics mean little; they are just houses, or gravestones. Some of the remains of the sawmills themselves may provoke passing curiosity. The crumbling walls and foundations of the mill at Graysonia, in a dense jungle of trees and vines, might seem to a traveller to be ruins of a culture lost beyond memory.

But that is not true. The big-sawmill era was with us only yesterday. Events of those times, the sights and sounds and colors of sawmilling in its heyday, have merely been displaced by a rising tide of more recent progress.

A great deal has happened in very little time. In less than a hundred years, the place named Forester has been forest, farm, town, pasture, and pine forest again. Within the lifetimes of men and women still living as these words are written, virtually the entire story of sawmills cutting the great virgin forest of the Ouachitas has taken place.

Photo by author

Like monuments from a past age, concrete walls and footings of the Dierks mill at Pine Valley, Oklahoma, stand in a pasture within view of the distant ridge of Kiamichi Mountain.

Notes

Prologue

1. Ralph Clement Bryant, *Lumber: Its Manufacture and Distribution* (New York: John Wiley & Sons, 1922) xv, 3–4.

2. Southern Pine Association (SPA), *Economic Conditions in Southern Pine Industry* (New Orleans: SPA, 1931) 1.

3. William B. Greeley, *Forests and Men* (Garden City, NY: Doubleday, 1951) 40–41.

4. Bryant, *Lumber* xv; Nelson Courtlandt Brown, *Lumber: Manufacture, Conditioning, Grading, Distribution, and Use* (New York: John Wiley & Sons, 1947) 1–3; Milton D. Rafferty, *The Ozarks: Land and Life* (Norman: University of Oklahoma Press, 1980) 173–84; Nollie W. Hickman, *Mississippi Harvest: Lumbering in the Longleaf Pine Belt 1840–1915* (University, MS: University of Mississippi, 1962) 68–100; SPA 1.

Chapter 1. New Century

1. "Mitchell Cogburn," *The Looking Glass* Aug. 1976: 3–4; "Andrew McBride," *The Looking Glass* Feb. 1978: 4–5.

2. Carey Croneis, *Geology of the Arkansas Paleozoic Area* (Little Rock: Arkansas Geological Survey, 1930) 13–18; William D. Thornbury, *Regional Geomorphology of the United States* (New York: John Wiley & Sons, 1965) 277–86. Some sources indicate that "Ouachita" is derived from the name of a tribe of Caddo Indians; others say that it comes from a Choctaw Indian word meaning "hunting ground."

3. There is little written history of the Ouachitas, so this sketch is based on fragments from county histories and other sources. The origins of the region's settlers are considered by Aileen McWilliam in *The Looking Glass* July 1979: 16; and by Shirley Abbott in her book *Womenfolks: Growing Up Down South* (New Haven: Ticknor & Fields, 1983).

4. The foregoing description is derived mainly from Abbott; from a series of articles by Roy V. Simpson titled "People, Places & Plants" in *The Looking Glass* from 1981 through 1985; and from interviews with Simpson and others who lived in the Ouachitas early in this century.

5. The idea of wood as life-supporting, second only to food, comes from Michael Williams, "Predicting from Inventories: A Timely Issue," *Journal of Forest History* 28.2 (Apr. 1984): 92.

6. Nollie W. Hickman, in *Mississippi Harvest: Lumbering in the Longleaf Pine Belt 1840–1915* (University, MS: University of Mississippi, 1962) 5, states that longleaf pine in southern Mississippi averaged between ten and twelve thousand board feet per acre.

G. C. Morbeck, "Logging Shortleaf Pine in Arkansas," *The Ames Forester* 3 (1915): 92, says that shortleaf on the coastal plain near Fordyce, Arkansas, averaged seven to ten thousand feet per acre.

7. Charles T. Mohr, *Timber Pines of the Southern United States* (Washington: U.S. Div. of Forestry, 1896) 13.

8. McRae to Barney, 7 Mar. 1902, Series 1, Thomas C. McRae Papers, Special Collections, Mullins Library, University of Arkansas, Fayetteville.

9. Ray Allen Billington, *Westward Expansion* (New York: Macmillan, 1949) 700; Marion Clawson, *The Land System of the United States* (Lincoln: University of Nebraska Press, 1968) 57, 65–66.

10. *American Lumbermen: The Personal History and Public and Business Achievements of One Hundred Eminent Lumbermen of the United States* 3 vols. (Chicago: The American Lumberman, 1905–06) 3: 121–24. (Hereafter cited as *Lumbermen.*)

11. In Clark to McRae, 14 Apr. 1902, Series 1, McRae Papers, Clark says that he hopes to cut timber on Sections 1, 2, and 12 in Township 7 South, Range 25 West, near the lumber company's railroad out of Pike City. County tax records for 1902 show that land in those sections was owned by Clark's Detroit Timber and Lumber Company, and by Roy McDonald who was identified in the Clark-McRae correspondence as an agent for Clark. But tax records for 1903 show this land as tax-forfeited, as well as much land of other owners along the lumber company railroad. By that time, apparently, the timber had been cut.

12. U.S. to Santa Fe Pacific Railroad Co., 21 Dec. 1904, 68: 1–113, Deeds, Yell County, AR. The Santa Fe also acquired government land in adjoining Perry County on 23 Feb. 1904.

13. Duane Dale Fischer, "The John S. Owen Enterprises," diss., University of Wisconsin, 1964, 13, 393, indicates that Rust's mother was a Drummond.

14. Drummond operated in Perry County and the eastern end of Yell County, and Rust in the remainder of Yell County and in eastern Scott County. See the map at the end of this book for the overall extent of their landholding.

15. U.S. to Paul D. Rust, 15 Aug. 1906, 68: 114, Deeds, Yell County; various owners to Rust, 1904, Y: 116, 167–170, Deeds, Yell County.

16. Among abstracts of title for several small tracts that Rust acquired—now on file with the lands division of Weyerhaeuser Company at Hot Springs, Arkansas—most indicate that the land was patented for homesteads in the 1890s. Apparently, then, the patentees attempted for several years to farm their land before selling to Rust in 1904 or later.

17. F. McD. (Don) Dierks, Jr., *The Legacy of Peter Henry Dierks, 1824 to 1972* (Tacoma: privately published, 1972); "A Present Day Pioneer" [Herman Dierks], *American Lumberman* 24 May 1913: 1, 73; interviews with Fred M. Dierks, grandson of Herman Dierks; interviews with F. McD. (Don) Dierks, Jr., great-grandson of Hans Dierks. Except as later noted, all subsequent discussion of Dierks history will be based on information from these sources. (The Dierks surname is pronounced "Durks.")

18. Recollections of Hans Dierks in 1927, as reported in *The Dierks Industries Co-Operator* 10 May 1927.

19. Glen R. Durrell, a forester who knew Hall, says that he traveled in a lumber wagon on this trip.

20. James Boyd, "Fifty Years in the Southern Pine Industry," *Southern Lumberman* 15 Dec. 1931: 62; Arrell M. Gibson, *Oklahoma: A History of Five Centuries,* 2nd ed. (Norman: University of Oklahoma Press, 1981) 165.

21. "The Warrant for Use of a Royal Name," *American Lumberman* 9 Jan. 1904: 43–46; *Lumbermen* 3: 109–12.

22. *Lumbermen* 2: 357–60.

23. *Malvern Meteor* (AR) 21 Mar. 1913; outline of history of Malvern Lumber Co. written by Thomas J. (Jack) Strauss, grandson of Adalbert Strauss, and interview with Jack Strauss.

24. "Genesis and Personnel of the Fourche River Lumber Company, of Esau, Ark.," *American Lumberman* 21 Jan. 105: 45–46; *Lumbermen* 2: 125–28; Malvin U. Brand, Jr., "The Fourche River Lumber Company 1903–1921," *Pulaski County Historical Review* 23.1 (Mar. 1975): 1–4.

25. The foregoing description of lumber manufacturing is based on Hickman 161–62; Ralph Clement Bryant, *Lumber: Its Manufacture and Distribution* (New York: John Wiley & Sons, 1922) xviii–xxi, 5; Nelson Courtlandt Brown, *Lumber: Manufacture, Conditioning, Grading, Distribution, and Use* (New York: John Wiley & Sons, 1947) 36–40; and the author's interviews and visits to mills.

26. Ralph W. Andrews, *This Was Sawmilling* (Seattle: Superior, 1957) 159; interviews with George F. Morris, sawyer, and with Melvin E. McConnell and John L. Wiley, blocksetters.

27. Interview with Walter Rogers, saw filer.

28. Ruth Alice Allen, *East Texas Lumber Workers: An Economic and Social Picture 1870–1950* (Austin: University of Texas Press, 1961) 95.

29. Boyd 59–67.

30. William B. Greeley, *Forests and Men* (Garden City: Doubleday & Company, 1951) 41–47; Hickman 205.

31. Southern Pine Association (SPA), *Economic Conditions in Southern Pine Industry* (New Orleans: SPA, 1931) 77; James E. Fickle, *The New South and the "New Competition": Trade Association Development in the Southern Pine Industry* (Urbana: University of Illinois Press, 1980) 79; Hickman 172, 174, 200, 202.

32. Interview with Richard A. Grigsby, grandson of Garland Anthony.

33. William Blake Barton, "Early Days in Cove," *The Looking Glass* Nov. 1981: 22.

34. Joel A. Walker interview.

35. Hickman 203, 246–47, 295; Philip P. Wells, "Philip P. Wells in the Forest Service Law Office," *Forest History* 16:1 (Apr. 1972): 26.

36. Lance E. Davis, et al., *American Economic Growth: An Economist's History of the United States* (New York: Harper & Row, 1972) 447, 500; Society of American Foresters (SAF), *Problems and Progress of Forestry in the United States* (Washington: SAF, 1947) 23.

Chapter 2. Getting Started

1. Ralph Clement Bryant, *Logging: The Principles and General Methods of Operation in the United States,* 2nd ed. (New York: John Wiley & Sons, 1923) 301, describes the use of drag (Fresno) scrapers.

2. "C. L. Bardwell," *The Looking Glass* Jan. 1978: 12, provides background for the situation reconstructed here.

3. "With Caddo in Arkansas," reprinted from *Gulf Coast Lumberman* 1 Dec. 1937: n.p.; "Kansas City Lumbermen," *American Lumberman* 24 May 1913: 40. (Caddo is pronounced "CAD-doh.")

4. The foregoing descriptions of Rosborough's family and boyhood are based on Mary Rosborough Bair, comp., *The Rosborough Book* (N.p.: n.p., n.d.) 193–94; Mary Parrish Truesdell, comp., *The Genealogy and History of the Jacob Kimball Parish Family of Randolph, Vermont* (Kissimmee, FL: Cody Publications, 1975) 86; obituary of James Thomas Rosborough, *Daily Texarkanian* (Texarkana, AR-TX) 18 May 1918; Lucy Marion Reaves, "Glimpses of Yesterday," *Texarkana Gazette* (?) 1950 (?); college record of T. W. Rosborough, University of the South, 1886; and telephone interview with Dorothy Bemis Stewart, niece of T. W. Rosborough. The Rosborough name is pronounced "ROSE-burro."

5. The foregoing description of Rosborough's early career in lumbering is based mainly on "'You're a Goner If the Sawmill Bug Bites You!' says T. W. Rosborough," reprinted from *The Timberman* 45.4 (Feb. 1944): n. p.

6. Frank A. Reed, "The Bemis Family," typescript in the possession of Mr. and Mrs. J. R. Bemis, Prescott, AR, 1–6, 8–9; William M. Leshe, "The Prescott and Northwestern Railroad: A Geographical Analysis," M.A. thesis, University of Arkansas, 1977, 29, 33; Clifton E. Hull, *Shortline Railroads of Arkansas* (Norman: University of Oklahoma Press, 1969) 360, 367.

7. Paul B. Cole interview; Velma Oden Merritt interview.

8. Ozan Lumber Co. to Caddo River Lumber Co., 7 Dec. 1908, 35: 462, Deeds, Pike County, AR.

9. Caddo River Lumber Co. of Missouri, file 103, card index to defunct corporations, office of Secretary of State, state capitol, Little Rock, AR.

10. Nelson Courtlandt Brown, *Logging—Transportatiion: The Principles and Methods of Log Transportation in the United States and Canada* (New York: John Wiley & Sons, 1936) 203, states that $50,000 was needed as a minimum initial investment to build a logging railroad. Nollie W. Hickman, *Mississippi Harvest: Lumbering in the Longleaf Pine Belt 1840–1915* (University, MS: University of Mississippi, 1962) 160, says that in 1907 a double-band mill would have cost $325,000, so that Rosborough's single-band mill may have cost about $150,000.

11. Ozan to Caddo River, 22 May 1906, K: 606, Deeds, Pike County; various owners to Caddo River, 1906–7, Deeds, Pike County.

12. Ozan to Caddo River, 8 June 1906, 35: 496; 6 Oct. 1906, 76: 210; 3 Jan. 1907, 40: 114; 28 Mar. 1907, 35: 463, Deeds, Pike County.

13. Contract between Caddo River and Dierks, 19 May 1908, in archives of lands division, Weyerhaeuser Co., Hot Springs, AR.

14. Dierks to Caddo River, 18 June 1908, 36: 47, Deeds, Pike County.

15. Truesdell 86.

16. Some features of the Rosborough home may have been added after 1907 as time and funds became available. The house remained at Rosboro in 1984, little changed from the later years of Rosborough's residency.

17. Truesdell 104.

18. "The Heart of Arkansas' Shortleaf Pine Belt and Phases of Its Growth," *American Lumberman* 31 Dec. 1904: 36–37; Hull 319–20; Fred O. Henker, M.D., "Ferndale, Western Pulaski County," *Pulaski County Historical Review* 21.1 (Mar. 1973): 12.

19. Frederick Hauenstein, Sr., "Frederick Hauenstein," typescript, copy with author, 27.

20. "A. L. Clark Lumber Co.," *Glenwood Press* 10 Feb. 1916.

21. "A Pioneer in Southern Pine," *American Lumberman* 19 Apr. 1902: 1, 49; *American Lumbermen: The Personal History and Public and Business Achievements of One Hundred Eminent Lumbermen of the United States* 3 vols. (Chicago: The American Lumberman, 1905–06) 2: 321–24. (Hereafter cited as *Lumbermen.*)

22. *Lumbermen* 2: 325–28.

23. Two land and timber plat books of the Grayson-McLeod Lumber Co., in the care of the author, show that the company owned 103,383.42 acres in Clark and Pike counties around 1907, and that the company completed purchasing the mill and town site in 1907.

24. "Harry Hartley Tells of Early Days at Graysonia," *Southern Standard* (Arkadelphia, AR) 1 Nov. 1963; "Revolutionary Idea in Lumber Manufacture," *American Lumberman* 31 Oct. 1908: 43–46; "Raising the Efficiency of a Great Lumber Producing Plant," *American Lumberman* 19 Feb. 1910: 59–66.

25. "Memories of Graysonia," *The Clark County Historical Journal* 1.2 (Spring 1974):

38; undated article from *Southern Standard* (Arkadelphia, AR) written by the editor after his visit in April 1909, in possession of Janet Jackson Pearcy, daughter of Cavanaugh C. Jackson.

26. *American Lumberman* 19 Feb. 1910: 65.

27. Era Baxter McKeown interview.

28. William L. Hall, address, "Progress in Saving Wood Waste," typescript dated 3 June 1915, Office File of Assistant Forester W. L. Hall, 1910–1917, Division of Land Acquisition, U.S. Forest Service, Record Group 95, National Archives, Washington, D.C.

29. Arkansas Writers' Program, *Arkansas: A Guide to the State,* American Guide Series (New York: Hastings House, 1941) 69; James Boyd, "Fifty Years in the Southern Pine Industry," *Southern Lumberman* 15 Dec. 1931: 63; National Lumber Manufacturers Association (NLMA), *Lumber and Timber Information: Facts and Figures for Ready Reference in the Lumber Industry* (Washington, D.C.: NLMA, 1924) 3. Because of differences in methods of compilation, production figures from other sources may differ from those given here. In Oklahoma the peak year was 1916, when the Dierks mills were producing and the state's total output of pine lumber was nearly two hundred and ten million feet.

30. Fred H. Lang, "Two Decades of State Forestry in Arkansas," *Arkansas Historical Quarterly* 24.3 (Fall 1965): 209–210. Lang states that Hall also visited federal lands in the Ozarks of northern Arkansas, resulting in the creation of the Ozark National Forest by presidential proclamation on March 6, 1908.

31. Velma Oden Merritt interview; McKinley Williams interview.

32. Information about L. D. Williams and his wife is derived mainly from their daughter Jessie Williams Diamond; two sons, Vernon and Max A. Williams; a grandson, Charles E. Williams; and a housekeeper for the Williams family, Lillie Taft.

33. Joe F. Maxey interview.

34. Hess Maxey interview.

Chapter 3. Growing Up

1. J. Fred Jones interview; Felbert Vaught interview.

2. Jeff J. Barnett interview.

3. In later years Caddo River introduced one important change in building railroad grade: they used a power shovel and the team drivers moved dirt in four-wheeled dump wagons pulled by two big mules. When a driver with a load of dirt reached an area to be filled, he hit a lever to open the dump gates in the bottom and release the load. While returning to get another load, he wound up a ratchet to close the bottom.

4. Articles of Incorporation of Cooper Townsite Co., 31 Dec. 1910, 1: 205, Articles of Incorporation / Miscellaneous Records, Pike County, AR; plat of Cooper, 20 Jan. 1911, plat map book, Pike County.

5. The *Glenwood News Press* 1 July and 8 July 1921, describes one of these picnics. Caddo River's logging train brought more than six hundred people and the Missouri Pacific's local train was also loaded to capacity.

6. In 1920 a movie theater opened at Rosboro, and in the spring of 1921, Rosborough arranged to have the logging train bring people from the log camps once a month to Saturday night movies. Presumably they had to pay admission at the New Dixie Theater (children 17¢, adults 33¢) but the train ride was free. See *Glenwood News Press* 17 Sep. 1920, 22 Apr. 1921, and 20 May 1921.

7. Clint Thornton interview.

8. Frank Jones interview; Velma Oden Merritt interview; Alex Nichols interview; Clint Thornton interview. McKinley Williams, a black who worked at Rosboro, says in an interview: "One time they fired a fella . . . up in the woods. He said he would make trouble. He talked about giving the colored people some trouble. Rosborough was wor-

ried . . . He armed the colored people with .30-30 rifles. He kept those rifles in the office. . . ."

Apparently this incident occurred in the early 1920s. The Ku Klux Klan appeared in Arkansas in late 1921, and indirectly may have encouraged whites to threaten blacks at Rosboro. One writer, however, says that the Klan at that time was more interested in "law and order" among whites than in "the Negro problem." See Charles C. Alexander, *The Invisible Empire in the Southwest: The Ku Klux Klan in Texas, Louisiana, Oklahoma and Arkansas, 1920–1930* (Lexington: University of Kentucky Press, 1965) 18, 20.

9. Vernon Bardwell interview.

10. Nollie W. Hickman, *Mississippi Harvest: Lumbering in the Longleaf Pine Belt 1840–1915* (University, MS: University of Mississippi, 1962) 244.

11. Velma Oden Merritt interview.

12. John C. Howard, *The Negro in the Lumber Industry* (Philadelphia: University of Pennsylvania Press, 1970) 34.

13. Hickman 245.

14. *Glenwood Press* 10 Feb. 1916: 2.

15. Pike County Heritage Club, comp., *Early History of Pike County, Arkansas: The First One Hundred Years* (Murfreesboro, AR: Pike County Heritage Club, 1978) 213.

16. Teden H. Cole interview. Other interviewees say that Halcy may have come to Rosboro earlier (Frank Jones, Velma Oden Merritt, Clint Thornton); or later (McKinley Williams).

17. Clint Thornton interview.

18. "With Caddo in Arkansas," reprinted from *Gulf Coast Lumberman* 1 Dec. 1937: n.p.

19. Graham Lumber Co. to Caddo River Lumber Co., 1 July 1918, U: 246, Deeds, Montgomery County, AR.

20. Vernon Williams interview.

21. Mary Parrish Truesdell, comp., *The Genealogy and History of the Jacob Kimball Parish Family of Randolph, Vermont* (Kissimmee, FL: Cody Publications, 1975) 86.

22. Teden H. Cole interview.

23. Some white interviewees say that Halcy and Fred may not have been legally married, at least in their first years together. At that time a black couple in a mill town could obtain a "sawmill license" to marry; the mill manager would assign them a house in which they could live "sawmill married" as common-law partners (and, on request, the manager could grant a sawmill divorce). It appears that sawmill marriages were more common among blacks of lower status, and that Halcy and Fred were legally married at the outset. In any case, they remained together the rest of their lives.

24. Vernon Williams interview.

25. *Glenwood News Press* 4 Mar. 1921.

26. Jessie Williams Diamond interview; Sam Hickey, Jr., interview.

27. Grady D. Gaston interview; Macy Gaston interview; J. Fred Jones interview.

28. The exact time of completing the railroad and the building of Mauldin is debatable. Some would say the railroad was completed in 1921.

29. Clark is quoted in *American Lumberman* 24 Mar. 1923: 51.

30. A. L. Clark Lumber Co. to Caddo River Lumber Co., 3 April 1922, 43: 274, Deeds, Pike County.

31. Dee Climons Blackmon interview.

Chapter 4. Second Biggest

1. "Arkansas Land & Lumber Co.," *Malvern Meteor* 21 Mar. 1913, Industrial and Agricultural Prosperity Edition: sec. 2; H. H. Foster, letter to _____ Mattison, 2 Sep. 1912, in private collection, Malvern, AR.

2. H. H. Foster, letter to Walter Alexander, 23 Nov. 1914, in private collection, Malvern, AR.

3. James Hervey Bemis interview.

4. "Walter Edward Grayson," *American Lumberman* 8 Feb. 1913: 28.

5. Arkansas Land and Lumber Co. records in private collection, Malvern, AR.

6. Entries for 9 Dec. 1915 and 6 Feb. 1917, minute book of directors' meetings, Ozan-Graysonia Lumber Co. The book is in the possession of Mr. and Mrs. J. R. Bemis, Prescott, AR.

7. Entries for 9 Dec. 1915, 7 Feb. 1928, 2 Feb. 1932, and 6 Feb. 1934, minute book, Ozan-Graysonia.

8. Frederick Hauenstein, Sr., "Frederick Hauenstein," typescript, copy with author, 49.

9. A. J. Neimeyer Lumber Co. annual reports to stockholders, Q: 539–41; X: 94; and 27: 20, Incorporated Companies, Pulaski County, AR.

10. Malvin U. Brand, Jr., "The Fourche River Lumber Company 1903–1921," *Pulaski County Historical Review* 23.1 (Mar. 1975): 5.

11. Pine Belt Lumber Co. to Hans, Herman, and DeVere Dierks, 24 Mar. 1923, 78: 357, 418, Deeds, Pushmataha County, OK; Clay W. Beckner and A. A. McDonald, trustees for Pine Belt Lumber Co., to Herbert Dierks, 7 June 1927, 80: 234, Deeds, Pushmataha County.

12. Receiver, Fourche River Lumber Co., to Dierks Lumber and Coal Co., 4 Sept. 1923, 125: 24, Deeds, Garland County, AR.

13. Hauenstein 48.

14. Hauenstein 50.

15. Disciplinary record and academic transcript of T. W. Rosborough, Jr., Kemper Military School, Boonville, MO, 1923–25; Certificate of school work of Thomas Rosborough, Columbia Military Academy, Columbia, TN, 1921–23.

16. The home and most of the outbuildings remained at Glenwood in 1984, little changed from the years Rosborough lived there.

17. The description of the heading mill at Big Fork is based on information from Glen R. Durrell, Ray Paetzell, and G. W. Sisk.

18. William Blake Barton, "Early Days in Cove," *The Looking Glass* Jan. 1982: 25.

19. Hauenstein 30.

20. Interview with Fred M. Dierks, son of Fred H. Dierks; interview with Joe J. Angel, who was told about the origin of the Pine Valley project by DeVere Dierks.

21. *The Dierks Industries Co-Operator* 10 Nov. 1926: 3.

22. *Co-Operator* 10 Apr. 1927: 1, 2.

23. *Co-Operator* 10 May 1929: 7.

24. *Co-Operator* 10 Sept. 1929: 8.

25. The Wisconsin and Arkansas Lumber Company, or WALCO, opened a double-band mill at Malvern in 1902 with a railroad into the coastal plain south of Malvern; see "A Notable Northern-Southern Lumber Enterprise," *American Lumberman* 14 Mar. 1903: 43–47. Many of the investors in WALCO were also investors in the Arkansas Land and Lumber Company, and H. H. Foster was president in both companies. When WALCO bought Arkansas Land in 1921, one mill began to cut pine from the combined landholdings while the other cut hardwood.

26. James E. Fickle, *The New South and the "New Competition": Trade Association Development in the Southern Pine Industry* (Urbana: University of Illinois Press, 1980) 373. Betty Taylor, "Logging in the Ouachitas," *The Looking Glass* Nov. 1980: 10, mentions a small mill east of Hatfield, Arkansas, in the 1920s that was powered by an old airplane engine.

27. Ralph Clement Bryant, *Lumber: Its Manufacture and Distribution* (New York: John Wiley & Sons, 1922) 4; Nelson Courtlandt Brown, *Lumber: Manufacture, Conditioning,*

Grading, Distribution, and Use (New York: John Wiley & Sons, 1947) 207. Lloyd Lane, "The Joe Smith Sawmill," *The Looking Glass* 24 Apr. 1975, describes a portable mill near Mena, Arkansas, about 1920 that had sixteen employees: sawyer, log scaler, fireman, log tumbler, blocksetter, two slab offbearers, lumber trucker (using a two-wheel cart), three loggers, two lumber haulers, and three others. In small mills the number of employees varied with the mill's output, of course, and because workers switched from one task to another—or did not—as help was needed.

28. Fickle 63 says that by the mid-1930s more than ninety percent of over ten thousand sawmills in the South were small, portable mills. Brown, 247 states that at that time "probably 60% to 80% of the entire lumber production of the South [came] from small sawmills."

29. Inez Lane, "The Joe Smith Sawmill," *The Looking Glass* 8 May 1975: 14 describes a shack of similar construction at a mill near Mena, Arkansas, about 1920.

30. Era Baxter McKeown interview.

31. Information about Will and Sid Ingham is derived mainly from interviews with one of Will's sons, Gordon W. Ingham; one of the daughters of Will's associate Hal Shaffer, Martha Jane Shaffer Warren; Matt Turner (M. T.) Read; and Joel A. Walker.

32. Information about Hal Shaffer is derived from interviews with Gordon W. Ingham; Shaffer's daughters, Ione Shaffer Leith and Martha Jane Shaffer Warren; L. D. Williams' son Vernon Williams; and L. D.'s grandson Charles E. Williams.

33. Max A. Williams interview.

34. James Boyd in "Fifty Years in the Southern Pine Industry," *Southern Lumberman* 15 Dec. 1931: 45, says that Rust was secretary of the Gulf Lumber Co. at Fullerton, Louisiana, that operated from 1907 to 1927.

35. Frank H. Drummond to Yell Lumber Co., 30 Aug. 1913, P: 494, Deeds, Perry County, AR; Frank H. Drummond to Yell Lumber Co., 30 Aug. 1913, 44: 130–65, Deeds, Yell County, AR; Paul D. Rust and wife to Yell Lumber Co., 7 June 1915, 44: 165–69, Deeds, Yell County.

36. Rust purchased more than thirty-five separate parcels of land, as recorded in volumes 13, 14, 15, and 17, Deeds, Montgomery County, Arkansas. The locations of tracts that most effectively blocked Caddo River's railroads are shown on the map of Mauldin's railroad system in Chapter 5.

Duane Dale Fischer, in "The John S. Owen Enterprises," diss., University of Wisconsin, 1964, 397, footnote 72, writes about Rust's relationship with his cousins who ran the Rust-Owen Lumber Company in Wisconsin: "Paul D. Rust apparently had a highly suspicious nature. He mistrusted almost everything his . . . cousins tried to do. It took a good deal of tact to handle Paul Rust. . . ."

37. Yell Lumber Co. to Caddo River Lumber Co., 21 Mar. 1925, 23: 63, Deeds, Montgomery County.

38. Yell to Caddo River, 29 June 1926, 18: 282–88, Deeds, Montgomery County.

39. Yell Lumber Co. to Dierks Lumber and Coal Co., 24 Oct. 1925, 65: 213, Deeds, Montgomery County.

40. Dierks to Caddo River, 28 June 1926, 51: 1, Deeds, Scott County, AR.

41. *United States Statutes at Large, 45th Congress, 1877–1879* 20: 89; *United States Statutes at Large, 52nd Congress, 1891–1893* 27: 348.

42. William K. Wyant, *Westward in Eden: The Public Lands and the Conservation Movement* (Berkeley: University of California Press, 1982) 131–33; Everett Dick, *The Lure of the Land: A Social History of the Public Lands from the Articles of Confederation to the New Deal* (Lincoln: University of Nebraska Press, 1970) 137; U.S. Dept. of the Interior, General Land Office, *Regulations under the Timber and Stone Law*, Circular No. 851 (Washington, D.C.: Government Printing Office, 1926) 1, 3.

43. Several of the patents from the United States to members of the Williams family

are recorded in 11: 426; 14: 309; 14: 401; and 16: 67, Deeds, Montgomery County; and in 61: 484, Deeds, Yell County. Deeds from members of the Williams family to the Caddo River Lumber Co. are recorded in 12: 113; 13: 348; 15: 339; and 17: 483, Deeds, Montgomery County; in 48: 339–41, Deeds, Scott County; and in 63: 200, Deeds, Yell County.

Chapter 5. Mauldin

1. Joe F. Maxey interview.
2. John R. Gwathney interview.
3. Ruby McKay interview.
4. Ervin D. Black interview.
5. Jessie Williams Diamond interview.
6. Interview with John Merchant. In an interview, Manuel A. Norman says the incident took place at a logging camp of the A. L. Clark Lumber Company instead of at Mauldin, which suggests that the story was passed around from one camp to another.
7. Interview with Mrs. Carl Depriest, who recalls living at Mauldin from July 2, 1927, to April 11, 1928. Interview with Vernon Orbria Dollar, who says that it was Ed Depriest's suing of the company, rather than the death of Arthur Depriest, that caused Caddo River to fire the remaining male relatives. Interview with Daisy Maxey Scoggins, who recalls that her brother-in-law, Chester Yeargan, sued Caddo River after breaking his leg on the job, and that Yeargan and his brother were fired. Interviews with Creo A. Jones, J. Fred Jones, O. O. Stafford, Archie Dennis Taylor, and Alva White also provide details of the Depriest affair.
8. Interviews with Dixie Gaston, Ernest Jackson, J. Fred Jones, Robert B. Lyons, Leonard Maxey, and Delzie Fagan Williamson.
9. Lamar Smith interview.
10. Macy Gaston interview.
11. This is the most prevalent of several versions of how Sock City got its name. Whatever the reason, the name became commonly used and even appeared on maps. Local people who were embarrassed about the name eventually renamed the community Pencil Bluff.
12. Interview with confidential source.
13. Macy Gaston interview.
14. Interview with confidential source.
15. J. Fred Jones interview.
16. Interview with Roy Vergil Simpson, who was living at the Gaston home at the time and overheard the argument between Jack and his son.
17. The description of the time checker's activities is based mainly on interviews with Grady D. Gaston, and with John Merchant, who became a time checker after Gaston moved to another job.
18. William G. (Guy) Baker interview.

Chapter 6. An Awakening

1. National Lumber Manufacturers Association (NLMA), *Lumber and Timber Information: Facts and Figures for Ready Reference in the Lumber Industry* (Washington, D.C.: NLMA, 1924) 13.
2. Fred M. Dierks interview. A number of writers have also discussed the economic constraints of the cut-out-and-get-out era that prevented good forestry practices. See, for example, Nollie W. Hickman, *Mississippi Harvest: Lumbering in the Longleaf Pine Belt 1840–1915* (University, MS: University of Mississippi, 1962) 260–61; and James E.

Fickle, *The New South and the "New Competition": Trade Association Development in the South-ern Pine Industry* (Urbana: University of Illinois Press, 1980) 247–48. Harold K. Steen in *The U.S. Forest Service: A History* (Seattle: University of Washington Press, 1976) 190–92, considers how land taxes affected lumbering and forestry.

3. Fickle 201, 203.

4. Southern Pine Association (SPA), *Economic Conditions in Southern Pine Industry* (New Orleans: SPA, 1931) 57.

5. James Boyd, "Fifty Years in the Southern Pine Industry," *Southern Lumberman* 15 Dec. 1931: 19.

6. *The Dawn of a New Constructive Era: Proceedings of the Cut-Over Land Conference of the South* (New Orleans: Southern Cut-Over Land Association, 1917) 113. The Southern Cut-Over Land Association was organized under the auspices of the Southern Pine Association.

7. *The Dawn of a New Constructive Era* 48.

8. *The Dawn of a New Constructive Era* 44.

9. *Glenwood Press* 10 Feb. 1916: 3–4; Howard County Heritage Club, comp., *History of Howard County, Arkansas 1873–1973* (Nashville, AR: Howard County Heritage Club, 1973) 25. *The Dierks Industries Co-Operator* in the 1920s also carried news of the land disposal program.

10. "A Modern Lumber Operation: Arkansas and Oklahoma Soft Pine and Hard-woods," *American Lumberman* 25 Dec. 1920: 96.

11. "A Modern Lumber Operation" 75.

12. Betty Taylor, "Joe Hough: 65 Years in Broken Bow," *The Looking Glass* Mar. 1983: 11–12; Hickman 263–65.

13. DeVere V. Dierks, "Making Our Lumber Operations Permanent," *American Forests* Apr. 1928: 209–11.

14. Boyd 20.

15. *Bogalusa Daily News* (LA) 9 Apr. 1957: 6.

16. *The Dawn of a New Constructive Era* 32.

17. *Bogalusa Daily News* 9 Apr. 1957: 1, 8; Fickle 253.

18. "William L. Hall (1873–1960)," *Journal of Forestry* Nov. 1960: 904.

19. William L. Hall, "Arkansas' Romance Reforestation," *Nature Magazine* Oct. 1925: 235.

20. Hall, "Arkansas' Romance Reforestation" 236; Nelson Courtlandt Brown, *Lumber: Manufacture, Conditioning, Grading, Distribution, and Use* (New York: John Wiley & Sons, 1947) 250.

21. William L. Hall, "Industrial Forestry Moves Forward," *American Forests* Apr. 1927: 210–14.

22. Dierks, "Making Our Lumber Operations Permanent" 211.

23. Interview with Glen R. Durrell, who was with the Forest Service on the Ouachita National Forest in the 1920s.

24. *Co-Operator* 10 Aug. 1928: 3.

25. Glen R. Durrell, letter, *The Looking Glass* Sept. 1982: 18; "Mountain Men and Rolling Stores," *The Looking Glass* Aug. 1982: 19–20.

26. "Grazing Not Improved by Woods Burning," *Co-Operator* 10 Mar. 1929: 1; "What Causes Density of Underbrush?" *Co-Operator* 10 Jan. 1929: 1.

27. Glen R. Durrell, "A Woodsman's Return," *The Looking Glass* Mar. 1984: 8–9.

28. "Mountain Men and Rolling Stores" 18–19; Glen R. Durrell, letter, *The Looking Glass* Oct. 1982: 32.

29. The foregoing summary of Forest Service activities before the 1920s is based mainly on information in unsorted historical records at headquarters of the Ouachita National Forest at Hot Springs, Arkansas.

30. *United States Statutes at Large* 43: 653, Section 2.

31. Sharon M. W. Bass, *For the Trees: An Illustrated History of the Ozark-St. Francis National Forests 1908–1978* (Atlanta: U.S. Forest Service, Southern Region, 1981) 58–59, 60–63.

32. Thomas J. (Jack) Strauss interview; *Malvern Daily Record* (AR) 27 Oct. 1926; William L. Hall, "Is Pine Coming or Going in South Arkansas?" *Journal of Forestry* 43 (1945) 636.

33. Caddo River Lumber Co. to Dierks Lumber and Coal Co., 12 Dec. 1924, 47: 146, Deeds, Pike County, AR.

34. Durrell, "A Woodsman's Return" 9.

35. Dierks, "Making Our Lumber Operations Permanent" 211.

36. George Soule, *Prosperity Decade, from War to Depression: 1917–1929* (1947; New York: Harper, 1968) 146.

37. Society of American Foresters (SAF), *Problems and Progress of Forestry in the United States* (Washington: SAF, 1947) 24.

38. NLMA 5.

39. "Forest Industries in Arkansas," *The Looking Glass* Aug. 1976: 8.

40. Soule 287.

Chapter 7. Hard Times

1. Lester V. Chandler, *America's Greatest Depression, 1929–1941* (New York: Harper, 1970) 21, 36. Chandler says that "along with metal mining, lumber was the hardest hit industry in the United States."

2. James E. Fickle, *The New South and the "New Competition": Trade Association Development in the Southern Pine Industry* (Urbana: University of Illinois Press, 1980) 61–62.

3. *Southern Lumberman* 15 Dec. 1956: 153; James W. Leslie, "Some Economic Aspects of the Arkansas Lumber Industry Up to 1935," class paper, University of Arkansas, 1935, 34.

4. James W. Leslie, "The Arkansas Lumber Industry," MS thesis, University of Arkansas, 1938, 64.

5. Deeds recorded in Scott County show that from 1923 through 1928, Caddo River purchased about 8,300 acres of timberland from Forrester or from firms that he controlled, while selling about 2,000 acres of land to him. The land sold to Forrester probably lay beyond reach of Caddo River's projected mill.

6. George F. Morris interview.

7. Various sellers to Caddo River Lumber Co., 8 Nov. 1928 through 14 Feb. 1929, 52: 271, 272, 274, 311, and 314, Deeds, Scott County, AR.

8. Interviewees disagree on the opening date for the Forester mill, but the majority say it was around July 1, 1931. The Waldron, Arkansas, *Advance Reporter* on April 9, 1931, noted briefly that the "Forrester" mill "would be ready to begin operations in June or July of this year." But when the mill actually started up—Scott County's largest employer, getting underway in the depths of the depression—the *Advance Reporter* failed to note.

9. Official transcript, T. W. Rosborough, Jr., Agricultural and Mechanical College of Texas, 1925–26; Official transcript, T. W. Rosborough, Jr., Massachusetts Institute of Technology, 1926–32.

10. George F. Morris interview.

11. George F. Morris interview.

12. Glen Roberts interview.

13. Estey Campbell Read interview.

14. Harry Standerfer interview.

15. Floyd Kimble interview.

16. Mr. and Mrs. Philip Guyol of Arkadelphia, Arkansas, provide this explanation of the origin of the word *brozine* in "The Sawmill Commissary," *The Clark County Historical Journal* 1.2 (Spring 1974): 56.

17. James B. Allen, in *The Company Town in the American West* (Norman: University of Oklahoma Press, 1967) 135–37, indicates that the system of issuing scrip as advances against pay was basically the same everywhere that employers operated company stores. He adds that a longtime company store clerk at a mining town in Wyoming estimated that only two percent of the employees used up all their wages before they received them. Perhaps, then, not more than two or three percent were as deeply in debt in the sawmill towns of the Ouachitas.

18. G. C. Morbeck in "Logging Shortleaf Pine in Arkansas," *The Ames Forester* 3 (1915): 112, describes the finances of a company store operated by the Fordyce Lumber Company at their camp near Fordyce, Arkansas.

19. Ione Shaffer Leith telephone interview.

20. Martha Jane Shaffer Warren telephone interview.

21. Caddo River Lumber Co. to Fidelity National Bank and Trust Co., First Mortgage Deed of Trust, 1 July 1932, recorded in 22: 391, Real Estate Mortgages, Scott County, AR. This mortgage is also recorded in Montgomery, Pike, and Yell counties. The company mortgaged timberlands and mill sites totaling 77,137.80 acres; timber cutting rights on 2,867.27 acres; approximately 64.5 miles of railroad (which was probably all the trackage in use at that time); all three of the company's mills; other equipment, including four locomotives, four log loaders, forty-two flatcars, two power shovels, and 50.4 miles of railroad steel; and five hundred shares of capital stock of the Caddo & Choctaw Railroad Company.

22. Frank Jones interview.

23. "Thomas W. Rosborough Jr. Died After Auto Accident, Saturday," *Glenwood Herald* 15 Feb. 1934.

24. Interview with Gordon W. Ingham, son of W. F. Ingham. As a visitor in the Rosborough home, Ingham saw Rosborough counseling blacks and others.

25. Norma Armstrong Tackett interview.

26. Ted Gaston interview.

27. Hubert T. (Red) Crawford interview. Crawford says that the insurance agent showed him the check before taking it to Rosborough.

28. Vernon Williams interview. Era McKeown, Lester Williams, and others say that Rosborough liked to travel fast, to a fixed time schedule, and that he would tell Fred Wingfield to "speed it up." In doing this, Rosborough may have unwittingly influenced his son's driving habits.

29. John F. and Ida L. Kelly to T. W. Rosborough, 1 Feb. 1936, 186: 10, Deeds, Lane County, OR.

30. Jeff Carpenter interview. The story about Rosborough's hat is hearsay, but it appears to be in character.

31. Marlin Davis interview.

32. Marlin Davis interview.

33. Norma Armstrong Tackett interview.

34. "$500,000 Loss in Fire at Glenwood," *Arkansas Gazette* 24 June 1936; "Caddo River Lumber Co. Has $500,000 Fire," *Glenwood Herald* 25 June 1936.

Chapter 8. Winding Down

1. "Big Lumber Mill at Glenwood to Be Abandoned," *Arkansas Gazette* 22 Dec. 1937; "The Lumber Mill Here Closed Down," *Glenwood Herald* 30 Dec. 1937.

2. Teden H. Cole interview.

3. Entries for 7 Dec. and 21 Dec. 1936, minute book of directors' meetings of the Ozan-Graysonia Lumber Co., in the possession of Mr. and Mrs. J. R. Bemis, Prescott, AR; J. R. Bemis, letter to Ozan-Graysonia stockholders, 12 Dec. 1936, copy with author.

4. H. W. (Bill) McMillan interview; Ozan-Graysonia Lumber Co. to Dougald McMillan, Jr., 30 Dec. 1936, 166: 206, Deeds, Clark County, AR. The final sale was for 10,618.22 acres for $2,656.30 to be paid in four installments over a one-year period.

5. Act of June 11, 1906, *United States Statutes at Large* 34: 233; *United States Statutes at Large* 37: 287.

6. For a discussion of these public land controversies in a national context, see E. Louise Peffer, *The Closing of the Public Domain: Disposal and Reservation Policies 1900–1950* (Stanford University Press, 1951) 319–40.

7. Evidence of this activity is scattered through unsorted historical records at headquarters of the Ouachita National Forest at Hot Springs, Arkansas (cited hereafter as Ouachita NF historical records); and in the General Land Office Division "R" file for the Ouachita National Forest in Record Group 49 of the National Archives in Washington.

8. *Hearings Held Before the Committee on the Public Lands of the House of Representatives, May 18, 20, 21, 23, 24, 1910 on . . . H. R. 21894. . . .* (Washington, D.C.: Government Printing Office, 1910) 158–59.

9. Ouachita NF historical records.

10. William E. Wootten, "Extensive and Intensive Land Classification of the Arkansas National Forest," report submitted 19 Dec. 1917, 3. In Ouachita NF historical records.

11. Wootten 31.

12. Wootten 10.

13. W. B. Greeley, Acting Forester, letter, 11 May 1915, filed with the Wooten report, Ouachita NF historical records.

14. Glen Durrell, "Happy Golden Anniversary, Battiest C.C.C. Camp," *The Looking Glass* June 1983: 6–7.

15. The forest supervisor's annual statistical reports to the regional forester, Ouachita NF historical records, show that only 540.3 acres of shortleaf pine were planted in the four-year period from June 30, 1934, to June 30, 1938.

16. Act of 1 Mar. 1911, *United States Statutes at Large* 36: 961; Act of 7 June 1924, *United States Statutes at Large* 43: 653.

17. Buschow Lumber Co. to United States, 10 Dec. 1930, 178: 567, Deeds, Leflore County, OK; Buschow to U.S., 19 Dec. 1930, 178: 577, Deeds, Leflore County.

18. A. C. Shaw, forest supervisor, letter to O. C. Buschow, 6 June 1933, K-1 file, land acquisition records, Ouachita National Forest, Hot Springs, AR (cited hereafter as Ouachita NF land records).

19. K-6 files, Ouachita NF land records.

20. E. L. Demmon, address, "Oklahoma's Forest Resources," Oklahoma Farm Chemurgic Conference, Tulsa, 23 Nov. 1940.

21. In the Ouachita NF land records, Caddo River's land sales are assigned the number 219, and occur in a series in chronological order by date of taking option to purchase, from 219a through 219m. Deeds resulting from these sales are recorded in the counties—Montgomery, Scott, Yell—having the land. Where one sale involved land in more than one county, the deed is recorded in each county affected.

22. Caddo River to U.S., 2 July 1931, 77: 140, Deeds, Yell County.

23. 219b file, Ouachita NF land records.

24. Regional forester to forester (chief of the Forest Service), letter, 19 Apr. 1934, 219c,d file, Ouachita NF land records.

25. Forest supervisor to regional forester, letter, 28 Apr. 1934, 219c,d file, Ouachita NF land records.

26. Hal Shaffer to forest supervisor, letter, 3 May 1934, 219e file, Ouachita NF land records.

27. A. W. Hartman, forest supervisor, to regional forester, letter, 16 May 1935, 219e file, Ouachita NF land records.

28. A mortgage document, 25 May 1936, 25: 206, Mortgages, Montgomery County, indicates that principal and interest had been paid in full and that the bank was releasing the lien on Caddo River's mortgaged assets.

29. File 219k and file 219h, Ouachita NF land records. The sale of the Mauldin site was completed on January 7, 1938.

30. Paul B. Cole, son of Beuford Cole who was manager of the Rosboro mill, says that his father told him that Caddo River made a profit throughout the depression. Max A. Williams, son of L. D. Williams, also recalls that Caddo River made a small profit. The regional forester for the Forest Service, in a memorandum dated July 9, 1935 (in file 219e, Ouachita NF land records), says that he heard Caddo River's bankers in Kansas City say that "the company had a very high credit rating with them."

31. Nelson Courtlandt Brown, *Logging—Transportation: The Principles and Methods of Log Transportation in the United States and Canada* (New York: John Wiley & Sons, 1936) 10.

32. Brown, *Logging—Transportation* 192.

33. Samuel Lubell and Al Pollard, "Pine-Tree Bankers," *American Forests* Dec. 1939: 46.

34. James W. Leslie, "Some Economic Aspects of the Arkansas Lumber Industry Up to 1935," class paper, University of Arkansas, 1935, 13.

35. File 219c,d, Ouachita NF land records.

36. "Ouachita National Forest, Arkansas and Oklahoma, Facts and Figures, 1907–1947" (Hot Springs, AR: U.S. Forest Service, 1947) n. p.

37. "Sawmill at Rosboro Burned," *Glenwood Herald* 9 Mar. 1939.

38. Caddo River Lumber Co. to Ozan Lumber Co., 3 Apr. 1939, 58: 334, Deeds, Pike County. The lands in this sale were in Pike, Clark, and Hot Spring counties, outside the boundaries of the Ouachita National Forest.

39. *Glenwood Herald* 30 Mar. 1939; *Glenwood Herald* 23 Mar. 1939.

Chapter 9. Forester

1. Gladys Hamm interview.

2. Max Adams interview.

3. Mary Helen Edwards interview.

4. Norman Dean (Mutt) Turner interview. Roy V. Simpson in "People, Places & Plants," *The Looking Glass* June 1985: 16, says that in the rural Ouachitas of Arkansas about 1900, children made balls using yarn from discarded socks.

5. Vada Bowen Wilson interview.

6. Naomi Powell Phillips interview.

7. Entries for January 1934 and October 1934, in Quarterly Conference Record Book of Forester's Methodist Church, in possession of William R. Wilson, Jr.

8. Entry dated August 2, 1937, in Quarterly Conference Record Book of Forester's Methodist Church.

9. Frank Jones interview.

10. Gaylon Kitchens interview.

11. Lynn Barker interview.

12. Criminologists and sociologists who have researched black-on-black violence generally agree that its underlying causes include frustrations from living in a white-dominated society. Blacks in places like Forester could not travel freely, could not work at

many of the jobs, and dared not react directly to practical jokes and verbal abuse by some of the whites. But they could have their Barrel House and were free to drink and gamble; some say the Barrel House itself was intentionally allowed as compensation for the restrictions. Blacks were free to carry guns and knives and knew they would not suffer much for committing violence on other blacks. Investigations in this area include John Dollard, *Caste and Class in a Southern Town,* 3rd ed. (1937; Garden City, NY: Doubleday Anchor, 1957); John Dollard, et al., *Frustration and Aggression* (1939; Westport, CT: Greenwood Press, 1980); and Alvin F. Poussaint, M.D., *Why Blacks Kill Blacks* (White Plains, N.Y.: Emerson Books, Inc., 1972).

13. Henry Overby interview.

14. John R. Gwathney interview.

15. Frances Rodgers Dalton interview.

16. Alma Ruth Douglas Raines interview.

17. Gerlene Angel Wiley interview.

18. Harry Standerfer interview.

19. Louise Williams interview.

20. Bill C. Malone, "Country Music in the Depression Southwest," *The Depression in the Southwest,* ed. Donald W. Whisenhunt (Port Washington, NY: Kennikat, 1980) 73.

21. Malone 64.

22. Hubert T. (Red) Crawford interview.

23. Gerlene Angel Wiley interview.

24. *Forester Herald* 12 July through 21 Sept., and 12 Oct. and 19 Oct. 1940. These issues were provided the author by the one-time *Herald* editor, H. W. (Woody) Gann.

25. *Forester Herald* 19 July 1940: 1.

26. Cynthia Hastas Morris in "Arkansas's Reaction to the Men Who Said 'No' to World War II," *Arkansas Historical Quarterly* 43.2 (Summer 1984): 157–58, outlines the Witnesses' religious beliefs that caused them to become conscientious objectors, and states that during World War II "people looked on the Witnesses as a group of religious zealots who proclaimed their religion to be above patriotism to one's country."

27. "Lumber Plant At Glenwood Sold," *Arkansas Gazette* 28 Dec. 1937, states that the buyer intended to "scrap the Glenwood plant and sell the materials."

28. "$50,000 Loss In Mill Fire At Forrester," *Arkansas Gazette* 18 Oct. 1938 states that the fire was "of undetermined origin."

29. Rosboro Lumber Co. to RFC, Mortgage and Chattel Mortgage, 17 Aug. 1939, 101: 308, Mortgages, Lane County, OR.

30. Rosboro Lumber Co. to RFC, Mortgage and Chattel Mortgage, 17 Aug. 1940, 107: 129, Mortgages, Lane County, OR.

31. Anna Watts Rosborough, letter to William Park Watts, 10 Oct. 1942, copy with author.

32. Margaret Lay interview.

33. Daniel S. Bray, "Remember: 'Pearl Harbor.'" As a patriotic gesture during World War II, Bray had this poem printed on cards that he distributed to his friends. He also published this and several other poems of his as a little book.

Chapter 10. Last Years

1. From what they say themselves, blacks left Forester to seek better jobs rather than to escape any racial animosity. John C. Howard, in *The Negro in the Lumber Industry* (Philadelphia: University of Pennsylvania Press, 1970) 62, states that the number of blacks employed at skilled jobs doubled nationwide during World War II and that "the war gave many Negroes their first opportunity to demonstrate ability to perform basic factory operations of skilled, single-skilled, and semi-skilled types in a wide range of

industries and plants." T. Lynn Smith, in "The Redistribution of the Negro Population of the United States, 1910–1960," *Journal of Negro History* 51.3 (July 1966): 166–67, says that the exodus of Negroes during the war was not only to northern cities, but also to communities on the West Coast where "an insatiable demand for labor" had developed.

2. James E. Fickle, *The New South and the "New Competition"; Trade Association Development in the Southern Pine Industry* (Urbana: University of Illinois Press, 1980) 306–07; Harold K. Steen, *The U.S. Forest Service: A History* (Seattle: University of Washington Press, 1976) 253. Ficke 354–61 also describes the continuing manpower shortages throughout the southern pine industry during the war.

3. *The Dierks Industries Co-Operator* Aug. 1945.

4. Letha Jameson interview. Mrs. Jameson's rescue of the man from the saw is described also in the *Co-Operator* Feb. 1949.

5. "T. W. Rosboro, of Texarkana, Springfield, Eugene," editorial, *Eugene (OR) Register-Guard* 7 May 1952.

6. Jeff Carpenter interview.

7. Loyd Sanders interview.

8. Clinton (Barber) Moore interview. Lenard Cockburn recalls a similar incident at Forester in which a "snake" laid around a black's neck was a length of rubber hose having a snake's head of carved wood.

9. Colvin Irons interview.

10. Joe J. Angel interview.

11. James Davis interview.

12. Frank Jones interview; Charley Nichols interview.

13. Joe J. Angel interview; Colvin Irons interview.

14. Floyd Kimble interview.

15. Colvin Irons interview.

16. Floyd Kimble interview; L. J. Thompson interview.

17. Frank Jones interview; L. J. Thompson interview.

18. Ronald L. Mendell, in *Who's Who in Basketball* (New Rochelle, NY: Arlington House, 1973) 223–24, says that Tatum was born at El Dorado, and gives his height and arm measurements. L. J. Thompson says that Tatum had ties to the mill at Glenwood and "was just really another sawmill boy."

19. James B. Allen, in *The Company Town in the American West* (Norman: University of Oklahoma Press, 1967) 105, notes that the residents of many company towns in the West developed loyalty to their communities, and lumber towns in general seemed to have some degree of community pride. Former residents of Graysonia and Rosboro, as well as Forester, say their towns were good places to live.

20. *The Dierks Industries Co-Operator* Sept. 1948; *Co-Operator* Oct. 1948.

21. William R. Wilson, Jr. interview.

22. Earl Herrin interview.

23. Herman R. Lantz, in *People of Coal Town* (New York: Columbia University Press, 1958) 236–37, says that, in a coal mining town whose social workings he studied, people left the churches controlled by the upper classes and formed their own because of differences in socioeconomic class rather than in basic religious beliefs. At Forester the division may have been caused more by differences in at least the form of religious observance.

24. Fickle 329; James W. Leslie, "The Arkansas Lumber Industry," M.S. thesis, University of Arkansas, 1938, 117–18.

25. Corliss C. Curry, in "A History of the Timber Industry in Ashley, Bradley and Drew Counties, Arkansas," MA thesis, University of Arkansas, 1953, 58, describes the organization of the Bradley County Employees Association in 1937; as does Vernon H. Jensen in *Lumber and Labor* (New York: Farrar, 1945) 192–94. The *Glenwood Herald* 24

June 1937 states that the Federated Employees Association which had been organized at Glenwood and Rosboro (and undoubtedly Forester also) had accepted the bylaws of the Bradley County Employees Association. "In organizing these units," the *Herald* added, "the lumber industry of the South will settle all disputes among themselves."

26. Thomas D. Clark, in *The Emerging South,* 2nd ed. (1961; New York: Oxford University Press, 1968) 18–19, says that lumbering "brought weekly pay days to the rural South without disrupting the established social pattern." Ruth Alice Allen, in *East Texas Lumber Workers: An Economic and Social Picture 1870–1950* (Austin: University of Texas Press, 1961) 185, 192, 194–95, further describes this environment that made it difficult for organized labor to gain headway; so also does I. F. Eldredge in *The 4 Forests and the Future of the South* (Washington, D.C.: Charles Lathrop Pack Forestry Foundation, 1947) 43–44.

27. Allen, *East Texas Lumber Workers* 136.

28. Allen, *East Texas Lumber Workers* 93.

29. Allen, *East Texas Lumber Workers* 17.

30. Allen, *East Texas Lumber Workers* 95, 140, 193.

31. Leslie, "The Arkansas Lumber Industry" 103.

32. Fickle 314.

33. Nollie W. Hickman, *Mississippi Harvest: Lumbering in the Longleaf Pine Belt 1840–1915* (University, MS: University of Mississippi, 1962) 247–48.

34. Fickle, in *The New South and the "New Competition"* 378, paints an even darker picture: "There was little that was enlightened, or progressive, in the southern pine industry's attitudes toward labor, black or white. Laborers were generally regarded as a commodity to be bought as cheaply and utilized as thoroughly as possible. At best, physical conditions in the woods and mill towns were generally poor, working conditions bad, wages low, and the attitudes of employers paternalistic. Organized labor was anathema."

Lance E. Davis and others, in *American Economic Growth: An Economist's History of the United States* (New York: Harper & Row, 1972) 226, see the 1930s as "a great divide in the history of the American labor movement." The Wagner Act allowed workers to organize unions, and industrial unions recruited many new members among semiskilled and unskilled workers. Also, as war approached, an increasing demand for labor made it safer and more renumerative for workers to organize.

35. Fickle 315–21.

36. Henry Overby interview.

37. Era Baxter McKeown interview.

38. William Roy Wilson, Jr. interview.

39. Arnold Ingle interview.

40. *Co-Operator* Feb. 1952.

41. The closing of the mill was announced to newspapers on August 26, 1952. For newspaper articles relating to the closing, see *Arkansas Gazette* 27 Aug. and 9 Nov. 1952; and *Southwest American* (Fort Smith, AR) 27 Aug. and 28 Aug. 1952.

42. *Co-Operator* Oct. 1952.

43. *Co-Operator* Sept. 1952.

44. Interviews with Letha Jameson, Leonard (Whit) Maxey, and Louise Cockburn Maxey.

45. This statement by Fred M. Dierks is in agreement with one in the *Co-Operator* in August 1953: "The [Forester] plant was sold to the Dierks interests in 1945 at a time when it was virtually cut-out. However the Dierks Company was able to keep it in operation by purchasing government timber and hauling logs from its own timber-lands which were more properly tributary to its other mills. . . ." And in September 1952 the *Co-Operator* stated: "The Company has been operating the plant for many months at a

loss, and after careful study, reluctantly came to the conclusion that it could no longer continue to absorb this loss."

46. *Co-Operator* Dec. 1952; *Co-Operator* Mar. 1953; *Co-Operator* Apr. 1953.

Epilogue

1. Paul Burka, in "King of the Forest," *Texas Monthly* Aug. 1982: 198, 201, 204 writes perceptively about the financial dilemmas in perpetuating another family-owned timber firm, Temple Industries, in east Texas. Still another case with similarities to Dierks is described by George Walter Balogh in "Crossett, Arkansas: The History of a Forest Industry, a Community, and Change," MA thesis, University of Central Arkansas, 1981, 41–46, 50–54, 73–74, dealing with the sale of the family-held Crossett Company. Balogh's thesis is condensed as "Crossett: The Community, the Company, and Change," *Arkansas Historical Quarterly* 44.2 (Summer 1985): 156–174.

2. "Dierks Is Sold for Cash, Stock of $317 Million," *Arkansas Gazette* 19 Sept. 1969: 1B.

3. As a rural growth area during the 1970s, the Ouachitas were again involved in a broader migration, gaining people as were other "scenic" areas in California, Colorado, the upper Great Lakes, and the southern Appalachians, says Peter A. Morrison in "Americans' Endless Migration: A Discussion of Trends," *Sierra Club Bulletin* Apr. 1976: 20.

4. Information about land and timber prices comes principally from staff of the lands and minerals division, Ouachita National Forest.

5. In a letter to the author on March 21, 1985, Lee Robinette of Weyerhaeuser Company at Hot Springs, Arkansas, says: "Actually, current manufacturing capacity is well below tree-growing *capacity*. As the pine plantations come on, Weyerhaeuser will be facing the same kind of expansion needs Dierks Forests faced 30–40 years before."

6. John Naisbitt, in *Megatrends: Ten New Directions Transforming Our Lives* (New York: Warner, 1982) 14–15, emphasizes the transition of Americans from farmer to laborer to clerk. Naisbitt notes that "60 percent of us work with information" and "only 13 percent of our labor force is engaged in manufacturing operations today. . . ."

7. Don Swiger interview.

8. *The Dierks Industries Co-Operator* 10 Nov. 1930.

9. Max A. Williams interview.

10. *Co-Operator* Aug. 1952.

11. *Co-Operator* 10 Nov. 1926.

12. U.S. Department of Agriculture, Forest Service, Bulletin 106, *Wood-Using Industries and National Forests of Arkansas* (Washington, D.C.: Government Printing Office, 1912) 8.

13. "Arkansas Group's Promotion Profitable," *Southern Lumberman* 15 Dec. 1957: 136; Robert H. Brooks Company, *Arkansas Soft Pine Handbook*, 9th ed. (1925; Little Rock: Arkansas Soft Pine Bureau, 1940) 64.

14. *Arkansas Soft Pine Handbook* 5, 7.

15. Alex Nichols interview.

16. Roger D. Kinkle, comp., *The Complete Encyclopedia of Popular Music and Jazz 1900–1950*, 3 vols. (New Rochelle, NY: Arlington House, 1974) 2: 1206–07.

17. Nollie W. Hickman, *Mississippi Harvest: Lumbering in the Longleaf Pine Belt 1840–1915* (University, MS: University of Mississippi, 1962) 139–52; George Brown Tindall, *The Emergence of the New South, 1913–1945* (Baton Rouge: Louisiana State University Press, 1967) 329.

18. Richard L. Strout, in "Depression II: It Probably Won't Happen," *Christian Science Monitor* 5 Oct. 1979: 15, writes that the "final cause" of the Great Depression was "lack of purchasing power, the maldistribution of income. The steelworkers on 12-hour shifts,

the farmers working from dawn to dark, didn't have income enough to buy the goods they produced. . . ." Strout was a journalist and observer of the national scene during the 1920s and 1930s.

Foldout map, "The Big-Sawmill Era in the Ouachitas"

The map shows every major logging railroad in the Ouachitas, but its scale is too small to include most of their spurs and extensions, whose locations, in any case, are often in doubt.

Nor is it possible to show several minor, short-lived railroads whose exact locations have been lost in time. For example, the Ouachita Falls Lumber Company reportedly built a logging line in the 1880s from the west bank of the Ouachita River near Malvern, Arkansas. That may have been the first logging railroad in the Ouachitas, but the lumber company went out of business around 1890 and the railroad disappeared. Similarly, little is known of the narrow guage Perla, Magnet & Pacific Railroad that the Malvern Lumber Company operated in the 1890s, except that the tracks went some miles northwest into the Ouachitas from the company's mill at Perla. (In 1904 the Malvern Lumber Company organized another railroad, the Perla Northern, that is shown on the map.)

Farther west, the map shows the short logging line that ran northwest from a mill at Pike City, Arkansas, for a few years after 1900, until the mill burned. But still farther west, the map leaves out a little one-engine railroad known to have carried logs to a small sawmill west of Moyers, Oklahoma. (By 1910 this last operation had moved and expanded to become the Walker-Hopkins Lumber Company's mill at Moyers and the Walker Logging Company's railroad to the north.)

In addition to railroads having steam locomotives, there were wood-rail tram lines using mule cars. The Black Springs Lumber Company built trams around 1920 to bring logs to their small mills in the countryside near Norman, Arkansas. The Buschow Lumber Company used a tram about 1915 to haul green lumber from a small mill in the woods to the KCS Railroad at Page, Oklahoma. Probably other wood-railed tram lines existed as well, but all were laid on the ground with little grading at all, and evidence of them has disappeared.

Logging railroads were found on maps of the U.S. Geological Survey, the U.S. Forest Service, Weyerhaeuser Company, and International Paper Company. Walt Stinson of Malvern, Arkansas, provided information about railroads in his county, and Ed Crane of Bonnerdale, Arkansas, shared data on logging railroads in other areas. Aerial photographs made in 1934 and 1940 for the Forest Service showed many railroad grades in and near the Ouachita National Forest, including the Caddo River Lumber Company's trackage for Mauldin and Forester. Locations on maps and photos were verified by using land tax records to plot lumber company ownership on county and topographic maps (wherever a company had continuous holdings, they probably built a railroad); by questioning old-timers; and by spot checking to find railroad grades on the ground.

On the map, the railroads indicate each company's general area of operations, and the opening and closing dates for sawmills suggest each company's place in time during the big-mill era of cutting Ouachitas pine. Many of the mills' dates are unverified, and therefore are followed by question marks. Nor are the dates for a mill necessarily the key to a company's longevity. The Malvern Lumber Company's single-band mill burned in 1918 but the company continued on a reduced scale, holding cutover lands and practicing timber conservation so that eventually Malvern was equalled only by Dierks for length of operation in the Ouachita Mountains. Both of these companies existed in the Ouachitas from 1900 to the late 1960s.

Bibliography

The principal documentary sources for forestry, lumbering, and the Ouachitas are listed here. Other documents are cited in the preceding Notes.

Books

Abbott, Shirley. *Womenfolks: Growing Up Down South*. New Haven, CT: Ticknor & Fields, 1983. Autobiography, but largely the lives and folkways of Scotch-Irish hill people of the South who settled in the Ouachitas. Highly readable.

Allen, Ruth Alice. *East Texas Lumber Workers: An Economic and Social Picture, 1870–1950*. Austin: University of Texas Press, 1961. Includes statistics worth noting.

American Lumbermen: The Personal History and Public and Business Achievements of One Hundred Eminent Lumbermen of the United States. 3 vols. Chicago: The American Lumberman, 1905–06. Biographical sketches, including several of mill owners in the Ouachitas suggesting what lumber entrepreneurship was like during its heyday around 1900.

Brown, Nelson Courtlandt. *Logging—Transportation: The Principles and Methods of Log Transportation in the United States and Canada*. New York: John Wiley & Sons, 1936. This and the logging book by Bryant are textbooks that describe logging as it was in the 1930s and earlier.

————. *Lumber: Manufacture, Conditioning, Grading, Distribution, and Use*. New York: John Wiley & Sons, 1947. This and the lumber book by Bryant are textbooks that describe sawmilling as it was in the 1940s and earlier.

Bryant, Ralph Clement. *Logging: The Principles and General Methods of Operation in the United States*. 2nd ed. New York: John Wiley & Sons, 1923.

————. *Lumber: Its Manufacture and Distribution*. New York: John Wiley & Sons, 1922.

Dierks, F. McD. (Don), Jr. *The Legacy of Peter Henry Dierks, 1824 to 1972*. Tacoma, WA: Privately Printed, 1972. Well researched family genealogy with a summary of the Dierks lumber enterprises.

Fickle, James E. *The New South and the "New Competition": Trade Association Devel-*

opment in the Southern Pine Industry. Urbana: University of Illinois Press for Forest History Society, 1980. Encompasses an economic history of the southern pine industry since the late nineteenth century.

Greeley, William B. *Forests and Men.* Garden City, NY: Doubleday & Co., 1951. An account of forest conservation in the United States up to 1950.

Hickman, Nollie W. *Mississippi Harvest: Lumbering in the Longleaf Pine Belt 1840–1915.* University, MS: University of Mississippi, 1962. A regional study of an industry having many similarities to lumbering in the Ouachitas.

Hull, Clifton E. *Shortline Railroads of Arkansas.* Norman: University of Oklahoma Press, 1969. Several of the railroads described are Ouachitas logging lines.

Jones, Creo A. *Memoirs of an Ozark Hill Boy.* Mount Ida, AR: Privately Printed, [1975?]. Life on a homestead and at Mauldin, and conditions in the Ouachitas during the 1930s depression.

Maxwell, Robert S., and Robert D. Baker. *Sawdust Empire: The Texas Lumber Industry, 1830–1940.* College Station: Texas A&M University Press, 1983. Describes the cut-out-and-get-out era in east Texas, and later efforts at timber conservation.

Rafferty, Milton D. *The Ozarks, Land and Life.* Norman: University of Oklahoma Press, 1980. A chapter on the development and geography of lumbering in the Ozarks (north of the Ouachitas) is the only overview of the industry in that region yet in print.

Theses

Balogh, George Walter. "Crossett, Arkansas: The History of a Forest Industry, a Community, and Change." MA thesis, University of Central Arkansas, 1981. Explains how a family-owned company became part of a national timber corporation.

Curry, Corliss Colby. "A History of the Timber Industry in Ashley, Bradley and Drew Counties, Arkansas." MA thesis, University of Arkansas, 1953. Describes lumbering and forestry on the coastal plain in southeastern Arkansas.

Leslie, James W. "The Arkansas Lumber Industry." MS thesis, University of Arkansas, 1938. An economic history having statistical information.

Periodicals

American Lumberman. Among many lumber trade journals from the early 1900s, this one published in Chicago contains the most news about the Ouachitas, including illustrated features on several major companies. The largest, most complete concentration of trade magazine files, including *American Lumberman,* is in the Library of Congress, Washington, D.C., and in the National Agricultural Library at nearby Beltsville, Maryland. Unfortunately, the magazines are not indexed. A list of the more important feature articles in *American Lumberman* from 1899 to 1913, plus a few from later years, is found in Ronald J. Fahl, comp., *North American Forest and Conservation History: A Bibliography* (Santa Barbara, CA: A.B.C.–Clio Press, 1977) 14–24.

Clark County Historical Journal. Vol. 1, no. 2 (Spring 1974) is devoted to lumbering in Clark County, in and around Arkadelphia, Arkansas.

Dierks Industries Co-Operator. An employees' monthly newsletter having details of the Dierks companies' history and working environment from 1925 to 1969.

Journal of Forest History (formerly *Forest History*). Published quarterly by the Forest History Society (North Carolina) since 1958, it contains much useful context material on lumbering and forestry in the South and elsewhere.

The Looking Glass. Since 1975 this monthly has frequently carried history about rural people, and occasionally about lumber operations, existing in the Ouachitas around Hatfield, Arkansas, where the magazine is published.

Texas Monthly. A lengthy and perceptive article by Paul Burka, "King of the Forest," Aug. 1982: 114+, is the story of a family-owned lumber firm in east Texas from 1893 to the 1980s, resembling in many ways the histories of companies in the Ouachitas.

Archival Materials

Arkansas History Commission, One Capitol Mall, Little Rock, AR 72201. Photographs, maps, microfilmed newspapers; also the Forest History Archives, established in 1983 to gather and preserve historical documents and photographs relating to lumbering and forestry in Arkansas.

County courthouses. Recorded deeds, mortgages, corporation records, tax records, plat maps, and other data to 1900 and earlier. Especially useful for historical research relating to land transactions.

Forest Heritage Center, P. O. Box 157, Broken Bow, OK 74728. A lumber and forestry museum at Beavers Bend State Park, well worth visiting; it also preserves documents and historic photographs, primarily from southeastern Oklahoma.

Forest History Society, 701 Vickers Av., Durham, NC 27701. A collection of documents and photographs includes some material relevant to the Ouachitas.

Mullins Library, University of Arkansas, Fayetteville, AR 72701. Special Collections include the Thomas C. McRae papers, detailing McRae's dealings in timberland shortly after 1900; the Bert Hiltebrand photographs that include sawmills around Mena, Arkansas, early in the century; and other Arkansas related materials.

Torreyson Library, University of Central Arkansas, Conway, AR 72032. The Office of Oral History at UCA has deposited transcripts of tape recorded oral history interviews, including a number on which *Sawmill* is based, with the Torreyson Library.

U.S. Forest Service, Ouachita National Forest, P. O. Box 1270, Hot Springs, AR 71902. With the Lands and Minerals division are aerial photographs made in 1934 and land acquisition records from the 1930s. The Public Affairs office has historic photographs and other records from 1910 through the 1930s.

Interviewees

Nearly four hundred men and women contributed recollections that form the basis for much of this book. A few talked only about rural life in the Ouachitas during the early decades of this century. Others, including relatives, spoke primarily about lumberman T. W. Rosborough. Most of the interviewees, however, focused on their own lives in the Ouachitas lumber industry. All of the informants had lived in the region, or had been involved with lumbering through employment, family, or business connections during the period covered in this history.

Of the 389 individuals providing firsthand knowledge in communications with the author between 1979 and 1985, 356 granted oral history interviews in personal meetings or by telephone, and 33 replied to questions by mail. The group included 247 men (17 black) and 142 women (6 black). Three had witnessed the building of the first mill at Rosboro in 1907; two hundred had participated in life at Forester between 1929 and 1953.

Fred Hauenstein, an informant born in 1880, was 104 years old when he typed some of his remembrances in a letter to the author. Other informants fell into the following birth date categories:

1890–1899	38
1900–1909	130
1910–1919	125
1920–1929	73
1930–1939	21
1941	1

Index

Page numbers in italics refer to photographs, photo captions, or sidebars.
M *refers to foldout map at end of book.*

The Big-Sawmill Era
in the Ouachita Mountains

Researched and designed by Kenneth L. Smith
Drawn by Richard W. Stauffacher
1986

Fort
Smith

Poteau

KCS

STL-SF

CRI&P

Willburton

McAlester

Heavener
Petros

LATIMER

BUSCHOW

Stapp

SCOTT

PITTSBURG

Talihina

PINE VALLEY

Page

KANSAS CITY SOUTHERN

Pine Valley

(DIERKS)

ST. LOUIS

SAN FRANCISCO

Kiamichi

LE FLORE

Mena

Stringtown

WALKER
LOGGING
CO.

PUSHMATAHA

McCURTAIN

POLK

Hatfield

Cove

Vandervoort

Atoka

ATOKA

Moyers

PINE BELT

CHOCTAW

(DIERKS)

KCS

Antlers

CHOCTAW

STL-SF

Hugo

Fort Towson

Wright
City

OKLAHOMA

Broken
Bow

AND

EASTERN

De Queen

DE QUEEN

Durant

ST. LOUIS

SAN FRANCISCO

RED

RIVER

Idabel

SEVIER

MISSOURI — KANSAS — TEXAS

TEXAS

(A & O)

OKLAHOMA

ARKANSAS

TEXAS

Geologic boundary of
the Ouachita Mountains,
Arkansas and Oklahoma

LEGEND

Major Mills

■ Single band saw
■ Two band saws

Railroads

—+— Trunk lines and branch lines
—+— Short lines and logging trackage
owned by lumber interests

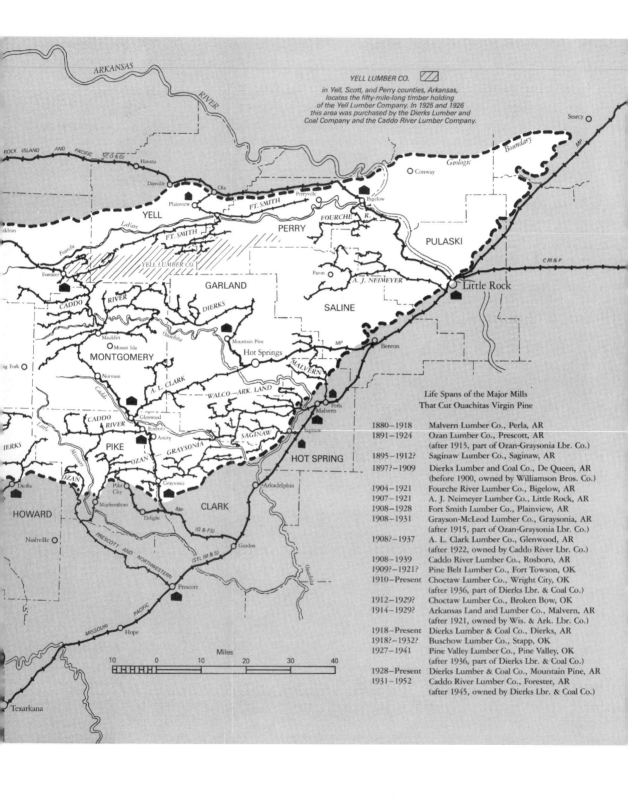

YELL LUMBER CO.

in Yell, Scott, and Perry counties, Arkansas,
locates the fifty-mile-long timber holding
of the Yell Lumber Company. In 1925 and 1926
this area was purchased by the Dierks Lumber and
Coal Company and the Caddo River Lumber Company.

Life Spans of the Major Mills
That Cut Ouachitas Virgin Pine

1880–1918	Malvern Lumber Co., Perla, AR
1891–1924	Ozan Lumber Co., Prescott, AR
	(after 1915, part of Ozan-Graysonia Lbr. Co.)
1895–1912?	Saginaw Lumber Co., Saginaw, AR
1897?–1909	Dierks Lumber and Coal Co., De Queen, AR
	(before 1900, owned by Williamson Bros. Co.)
1904–1921	Fourche River Lumber Co., Bigelow, AR
1907–1921	A. J. Neimeyer Lumber Co., Little Rock, AR
1908–1928	Fort Smith Lumber Co., Plainview, AR
1908–1931	Grayson-McLeod Lumber Co., Graysonia, AR
	(after 1915, part of Ozan-Graysonia Lbr. Co.)
1908?–1937	A. L. Clark Lumber Co., Glenwood, AR
	(after 1922, owned by Caddo River Lbr. Co.)
1908–1939	Caddo River Lumber Co., Rosboro, AR
1909?–1921?	Pine Belt Lumber Co., Fort Towson, OK
1910–Present	Choctaw Lumber Co., Wright City, OK
	(after 1936, part of Dierks Lbr. & Coal Co.)
1912–1929?	Choctaw Lumber Co., Broken Bow, OK
1914–1929?	Arkansas Land and Lumber Co., Malvern, AR
	(after 1921, owned by Wis. & Ark. Lbr. Co.)
1918–Present	Dierks Lumber & Coal Co., Dierks, AR
1918?–1932?	Buschow Lumber Co., Stapp, OK
1927–1941	Pine Valley Lumber Co., Pine Valley, OK
	(after 1936, part of Dierks Lbr. & Coal Co.)
1928–Present	Dierks Lumber & Coal Co., Mountain Pine, AR
1931–1952	Caddo River Lumber Co., Forester, AR
	(after 1945, owned by Dierks Lbr. & Coal Co.)